W-Hollow
Kitchen Adventure

*Glennis Stuart Liles
& Helen Shultz*

The Jesse Stuart Foundation
Ashland, Kentucky
1999

Dedication

To the memory of Mary Belle Johnson, Helen's mother and Glennis' cousin, who was an excellent cook. She grew and dried enough herbs each summer to supply the whole family.

W-Hollow Kitchen Adventure

Copyright © 1999 The Jesse Stuart Foundation

All rights reserved. No part of this book may be reproduced or utilized in any form or by any means, electronic or mechanical, including photocopying, recording or by any information storage or retrieval system, without permission in writing from the publisher.

Library of Congress Cataloging-in-Publication Data

Liles, Glennis Stuart, 1929-
   W-Hollow kitchen adventure / Glennis Stuart Liles & Helen Shultz.
      p.   cm.
   ISBN 0-945084-77-3
   1. Cookery (Herbs) 2. Cookery (Hot peppers) I. Shultz, Helen,
   1929-   . II. Title.
   TX819.H4L54   1999
   641.6'57--dc21
   99-27716
   CIP

Design by
BRETT NANCE

Published by:
The Jesse Stuart Foundation
P.O. Box 391 • Ashland, KY 41114
(606) 329-5232 or 5233

Preface

The *W-Hollow Kitchen Adventure* is the result of more than five years of work by a great Appalachian family. This book was compiled by Jesse Stuart's sister, Glennis Stuart Liles, and her cousin, Helen Shultz. But it is really a family project that involves Glennis' husband, Herbert (Whitey) Liles; Orville Shultz, Helen's husband; the late Mary Belle Johnson, Helen's mother; and a wide variety of cousins, neighbors, and interested friends.

Glennis had already authored two very successful cookbooks when she and Helen approached me about this project. The book that you have in your hands, a product of Glennis and Helen's hard work, is a monument to the cooperative strength and spirit of the Stuarts and their extended family.

Glennis Stuart Liles

Helen's mother, the late Mary Belle Johnson, played a major role in this project by developing and encouraging Glennis' and Helen's interest in herbs. Mary Belle, like many early twentieth century Appalachian women, had an in-depth knowledge of herb use—for culinary purposes, medicinal reasons, and ornamental uses.

Once, when she "wearied of Glennis always being out of sage and asking for more," she collected and dried enough sage to fill a ten-pound container. It took her hours and hours to pick the leaves from the stems and fill that container.

Helen remembers her saying: "This time I'm giving Glennis enough sage to furnish all of W-Hollow." Although the sage is long-since gone, Glennis still has the container, a cardboard barrell which originally contained "soap powders."

Several years ago, circumstances pushed this book forward. Whitey had retired from Ashland Oil, Inc, in February 1993. That winter, he kept busy making baskets and doing odd jobs around the house. But when spring arrived, he grew restless. Glennis knew that Helen's husband Orville needed help in his greenhouse, so she "volunteered" Whitey to transplant plants one day a week. That worked out well, because Orville and Whitey were good friends who both liked to plant and grow flowers and vegetables.

Before long, Whitey had talked Glennis into going with him to the Shultz home in nearby Lucasville, Ohio. Helen cooked a big meal at noon, and out of these work-and-visit sessions, Glennis and Helen started experimenting with herbs and hot peppers. They took them from seed to the table and became more and more enthusiastic about their work in the greenhouse. Eventually Glennis and Whitey recruited their neighbors, Debbie Thomas and Ora Jean Hill, to go with them and help in the greenhouse. With Debbie and Ora Jean's help, they could set out over 200 flats in a day (72 plants per flat). By contrast, Orville said his hired help had never set out more than 12 flats per person per day.

For the past two years Glennis and Helen experimented with salsas, vinegars, stuffed hot peppers, and hot sauces. They even experimented with using herbs and hot sauce in sweets. The hottest sauce they make is the "Hobbies Breath." It's the one they pass when someone says: "They don't make anything too hot for me." (see page 55)

Most of the recipes in this book are original from Glennis and Helen. Others are from friends and family. When Glennis and Helen tried recipes, they needed tasters. At first they used their families. Then they branched out to friends, Glennis' Sunday School class at the Greenup Christian Church, and, eventually, neighbors that she called "The Little Sandy Tasters." "Maybe they just wanted to make me feel good," Glennis remembered, "but whenever they said, 'This is a keeper,' that recipe went into the book!"

Helen Shultz

The authors grew up in a tradition of food being a part of hospitality. Family activities centered around home cooked meals. Visitors were invited to "sit down and make yourself at home." If visitors came at mealtime they were also invited to eat with the family. There was always plenty of food to share. Helen remembers her mother, Mary Belle, when they lived at Oldtown, Kentucky, saying that her father would go out to the road in front of the house and invite total strangers who were passing by to come in and join the family at the table. She said they seldom sat down at the table without a non-family member present. "Some people," she reflects, may have "deliberately timed their passing to coincide with mealtimes."

On Sunday, the Stuarts gather at mealtime. These gatherings almost always include close friends who are considered a part of the extended family. In these homes "take-out" is the food parcels which are sent home with family and friends.

The Stuarts have annual fish fries or chicken barbecues where as many as forty people are invited. In addition, the Hylton family reunion is held at Glennis and Whitey's home in W-Hollow during the Labor Day Weekend. Several generations meet and renew family ties and reminisce about times past.

So the book in your hands has a unique history. Glennis and Helen worked on it for more than five years, combining cooking, herb gardening, and family fun into the *W-Hollow Kitchen Adventure*. It was time well spent!

James M. Gifford
Executive Director
Jesse Stuart Foundation

Authors' Introduction

Once you've tasted the difference a sprinkling of chives or some chopped jalepeno peppers can make in a simple egg dish or the wonderful warmth some ground fennel seed gives to apple pie, then you're in on the secret! Cooking with herbs and hot peppers can be a real kitchen adventure. As you experiment and become familiar with the different tastes and flavors of herbs and hot peppers you realize that a pinch of this…a dash of that and you've added a new dimension to your cooking. The emphasis today on healthy eating habits and a lowered intake of fat and salt can make foods seem very dull; adding herbs and hot peppers increase the flavor so much that the absence of fats and salt is not a problem.

HERBS

Herbs bring out the best in foods, enhancing the flavor and appearance. The best way to learn about cooking with herbs is to try them. Start with a single herb to learn its characteristic taste and the amount needed for the flavor you want in your recipe, adjusting the amount used to suit your individual taste. It is much better to err on the side of too little than too much as you can always add more but with too much you end up with an inedible recipe. Initial enthusiasm may lead you to be too liberal and this can result in disaster.

There is a wide variety of fresh and dried herbs available in supermarkets, but for people who garden it is much more enjoyable to grow your own. All herbs need is warmth, a moderately rich soil and sunshine. A few plants will supply enough for the average household. The majority of them are very attractive plants. They do well in vegetable gardens, flower beds and some of them can even be grown in containers. The only insects to frequent them are bees and butterflies and herbs are not prone to diseases. The advantage of growing your own is you are able to have them when you need them. Use a sharp pair of scissors and snip just what you need. At the end of summer you can pot up a few of them and keep them over in a sunny window for fresh herbs all winter long.

To dry your own herbs, cut them just after the sun dries the dew and spread on screens, paper or tie them in bunches and hang in a dry, dark place until they are brittle. When they are dry, strip the leaves and place in jars and seal tightly. Be sure to label them as some of them look very much alike when dried. Baby food jars make wonderful containers since the lids have a sealer inside them.

Although a rack of herbs looks very attractive over the stove, this is the very worst place you can have them. They should be kept in a cool place out of direct sunlight to preserve their flavor and appearance.

Some herbs have a stronger flavor than others and a smaller amount will be needed. It is practically impossible to give exact amounts of herbs to use as the strength of the herb varies and there is also the matter of individual tastes. In order to become familiar with the basic flavor of a herb you haven't used before, try this method: mix 1/2 teaspoon of the herb in 1 tablespoon of butter or cream cheese, let stand for about 15 minutes then spread on a piece of bread and sample.

There is always the question of the difference between herbs and spices. One source defines the difference as herbs are grown in the temperate zone and can be gathered and used fresh. Spices are the leaves, stems, roots, seeds, flowers and barks of aromatic plants which can only be grown in the tropics and are used in the dry stage. This makes as much sense as any other explanation.

HERB GUIDELINES

BEEF — Garlic and Regular Chives, Marjoram, Oregano, Savory, Thyme

BREADS — Lemon Basil, Coriander, Dill, Marjoram, Oregano, Thyme

CHEESE — Basil, Garlic and Regular Chives, Chervil, Dill, Fennel, Thyme

EGGS — Basil, Chervil, Garlic and Regular Chives, Oregano, Parsley

FISH — Anise & Lemon Basil, Ground Coriander Seed

FRUIT — Anise, Cinnamon and Lemon Basil, Ground Coriander Seed

LAMB — Lemon Basil, Garlic Chives, Marjoram, Oregano, Thyme, Rosemary (make little slits in the lamb and insert herbs before cooking)

PORK — Coriander/Cilantro, Garlic Chives, Sage, Savory, Thyme

POULTRY — Scented Basils, Regular and Garlic Chives, Oregano, Sage, Savory, Thyme

SALADS — Basil, Garlic, Chives, Cilantro, Dill, Marjoram, Parsley, Savory (all can also be made into herb vinegars for extra flavor)

SOUPS — Basil, Garlic, Chives, Dill, Marjoram, Parsley, Savory, Thyme

VEGETABLES — Basil, Chervil, Regular and Garlic

CHILI PEPPERS

Cloves, Dill, Marjoram, Parsley, Savory, Thyme

Mention the word chili and you get one of two reactions: 1. the hotter the better, and 2. I DON'T like them. The first group swoon with pleasure while breaking out in a sweat and the other group will not try them or if they do they break out in tears. The cause of this is a substance called capsaicin which is contained primarily in the seeds and ribs of the chili. This substance is extremely powerful; it can be detected by the human toungue which sends a signal to the brain which in turn causes the brain to release a substance called endomorphins that is a natural painkiller, which in excess causes euphoria. Each bite sends another message to the brain and the cycle continues. A man by the name of Scoville developed a test to judge the heat of chilies and chilies are measured in heat units called the Scoville unit with the mild green pepper considered to be zero in heat units and the Scotch Bonnet over 350,000 heat units.

Hot peppers or chilies are technically not peppers at all. They are a member of the plant family which includes eggplant and tomatoes. They got their name from explorers in the 15th century whose experience with the bite of the black pepper mistakenly thought this plant was a relative of the black pepper spice. The pungency of the chili pepper caught on in the new world for its ability to spice up food at a much lower price than the very expensive black pepper which at that time was one of the most expensive spices in the world. It also helped offset the taste of foods which were tainted because of the lack of refrigeration. Their diversity is remarkable, both in variety and flavor. They range from searingly hot to sweet and some have a fruity flavor. They are very prone to cross with other varieties so there are thousands of varieties or names for them.

The most commonly used fresh chilies are hot bananas, jalapenos, and serranos. Most supermarkets have these in their produce section year round. Chilies are also available canned, dried, frozen, pickled and ground. Fresh chilies are the most flavorful and are richer in Vitamin C and A.

The best way to have fresh peppers of the kind you want is to grow them. They require the same care that eggplant or tomatoes do.

When adding hot peppers to food keep in mind that the heat of fresh chilies can vary in intensity, so tasting during the addition to recipes is the only reliable way to predict how hot the dish will be. Generally the dried flakes or ground chilies are consistent in their fiery flavor so start with the amount recommended and adjust according to an individual taste. Tasting for seasoning is tricky at first since a small sample doesn't deliver the same impact of a full serving and judging the overall flavor becomes reliable only with considerable experience. The irony is that while gaining this experience the chances are good that the cook will develop an increased tolerance to the spiciness and will overdo, which makes the dish too hot for others.

In working with chilies, remember that the oils that are hot to your taste can also make your eyes water and your skin smart. Wearing gloves is a wise precaution; be careful not to touch your face or eyes after you have touched the chilies or they will feel like they're on fire for several hours.

In addition to traditional uses for chilies in salsas, chile con carne and relishes, chilies will add flavor to a lot of your favorite recipes. Any kind of soup will benefit from a judicious use of chilies and scrambled eggs take on a completely different taste. Chilies liven up otherwise bland foods such as rice, beans and potatoes. Some studies have shown that while chilies may give some people heartburn they do not cause any visible to the stomach lining--at least in normally healthy people.

Finally, remember that the majority of heat in a chili is in the seeds and ribs so you can adjust the spiciness by the amount of these you remove. Also, if you do happen to set your mouth on fire with a bite, don't try to put out the fire with water or a cold liquid as this just spreads the heat around. The best remedy is milk, yogurt or ice cream. The fat in these products eases the pain.

SOME OF OUR FAVORITE CHILI PEPPERS

HOT BANANA — used fresh in salads, salsa and salsas, good for pickling but do not dry well. They can be frozen for cooked recipes. Just wash and dry them and bag in plastic bags or chop and freeze.

NEW MEXICO CHILI — a variety used in Chili Rellenos and the main ingredient in commercial chili powder. When green they are roasted and peeled. After they turn red and ripen they can be strung up to dry for winter use or in decorative ristras.

CAYENNE — good fresh & dried. When dried and ground they are sold as cayenne or hot red pepper.

HABANERO/SCOTCH BONNET — this chili is incendiary, making a sauce that really lights a fire.

JALEPENO — used both fresh and in cooking. It is widely available in stores. It is good in salsas, sauces, south-western dishes and jalepeno poppers. It also makes a good pickled pepper.

POBLANO/ANCHO — the dried form is called "ancho" and is used widely in southwest cooking. The fresh ones are best roasted and peeled because of its tough skin.

SERRANO — a very fiery chili, used fresh in salads and salsas. It is good with beans, soups, sauces and stews.

TABASCO — made famous by the McILhenny family who use it in their Tabasco sauce. It is used mainly in cooking.

HOW TO ROAST & PEEL FRESH CHILIES

Chilies are roasted to enhance their flavor and make peeling easier. Three methods which work well are:

Oven Method: Preheat broiler. Cut small slit in chili to prevent bursting. Arrange on baking sheet & broil 4 inches from heat until blistered and charred on all sides, about 6 minutes, turning every few minutes.

Electric Stove: Set heatproof rack on burner. Cut small slit in pepper to avoid bursting. Arrange chilies in center of rack so all will be in contact with heat. Turn heat to medium-high and roast chilies until blistered and charred on all sides, about 4 minutes, turning often.

Gas Stove: Cut small slit in chili to avoid bursting. Spear with a fork and hold each chili over flame until thoroughly charred on all sides.

Note: When handling chilies, wear gloves and do not touch your face. When using a food processor or blender to chop chilies, DON'T look down the feed tube as even the fumes are irritating.

After you have roasted the chilies, place them in a paper bag and seal tightly or in a bowl and seal with plastic wrap. After about 10 to 15 minutes, use a paring knife to strip the skin off, pull or cut the stem off and squeeze to remove the seeds.

PRESERVING CHILIES

FREEZING: Freezing chilies is very easy. Just wash them and prepare them as you want them for cooking, pop them in a plastic bag, put them in the freezer and you're done. Blanching is not necessary. They will be softer than fresh ones, but will have the same flavor.

DRYING: Drying is the oldest method to preserve chilies. The object is to remove enough moisture to prevent spoiling. This can be done using several methods:

Oven Drying — Heat oven to 200. Place chilies on a sheet pan, place in oven, turn frequently until dry, it usually takes about 6-8 hours. They will dry faster if cut in pieces with the seeds and membranes removed.

Food Dehydrator — Cut in half or in small pieces and follow manufacturer's directions, usually between 8 to 24 hours depending on the type of chili.

Microwave Oven — Coarsley chop the chilies and microwave a minute or two on low power or until most of the moisture is removed.

When using any of the above drying methods, allow to cool completely before placing in containers. After storing in containers you should check them the first few days to see if moisture is forming on the sides of the container. If this happens they need to be dried some more. At this point they can also be stored in the freezer.

AIR-DRYING: For this method you can pull up the entire plant when the chilies are ripe and hang them in a warm, dry place until they become dry and then remove them from the plant. OR — Pick the ripe chilies and thread them on string using a large needle, hang them up and pick the dry chilies off as you need them. OR — Spread the peppers out on newspapers or a screen in a warm dry place until they are dry and brittle.

CHILI HOTNESS SCALE

HOTTEST

- Habanero
- Tabasco
- Thai Dragon
- Bulgarian Carrot
- Cayenne
- Serrano
- Jalepeno
- Ancho
- New Mexico
- Hot Banana

MILDEST

MEASUREMENTS

How many times have you had to stop in the middle of preparing a recipe to decide a measurement? If you have you're in good company because equivalent measurements can stymy the most experienced cooks. The following guide may help.

Butter/Margarine

1/2 stick = 1/4 cup or 4 tablespoons
1 stick = 1/2 cup or 8 tablespoons
2 sticks = 1 cup or 1/2 lb
4 sticks = 2 cup or 1 lb

Everyday Measures

1 1/2 teaspoon = 1/2 tablespoon
3 tsp = 1 tablespoon
2 tablespoon = 1 fluid oz.
4 tablespoon = 1/4 cup
5 tablespoons + 1 teaspoon = 1/3 cup
8 tablespoons = 1/2 cup
10 tablespoons + 2 teaspoons = 2/3 cup
12 tablespoons = 3/4 cup
16 tablespoons = 1 cup

Cups

1 cup = 8 oz.
2 cup = 1 lb.
4 cup = 1 qt. or 32 oz.
1/2 pint = 1 cup
1 pint = 2 cup
2 pints = 4 cup or 1 quart
1 cup uncooked rice = 4 cup cooked
1/2 lb. shortening = 1 cup
1 cup cottage or cream cheese = 8 oz.
2 cup cottage or cream cheese = 1 lb.

Grated or Shredded Cheese

1/4 cup or 1 oz. ungrated = 4 tablespoon
2 oz. ungrated = 1/2 cup
1/4 lb. cheese ungrated = 1 cup grated
* exception to this is store bought Parmesan or Romano 3 oz. = 1 cup

EASY SUBSTITUTIONS

Out of baking powder? A recipe calls for cake or self-rising flour and you have only all purpose flour. No cream cheese or buttermilk. Here is a list of alternatives to use in a pinch.

CHEESE

Cream Cheese — cottage cheese blended with butter or milk

Ricotta Cheese — cottage cheese

1 cup sifted all purpose flour — 1 cup less 2 tablespoons unsifted all purpose flour

EASY SUBSTITUTIONS CONTINUED

1 cup sifted cake flour — 1 cup less 2 tablespoons all purpose flour

1 cup sifted self-rising flour — 1 cup sifted all purpose flour plus 1 1/2 teaspoon baking powder and a pinch of salt

MILK/CREAM

1 cup buttermilk — 1 cup plain yogurt or 1 tablespoon lemon juice or vinegar and enough milk to make 1 cup; let stand 5 minutes

1 cup heavy cream or 1/2 & 1/2 — 7/8 cup whole milk plus 1 1/2 tablespoon butter, well mixed

1 cup sour cream — 1 cup yogurt

1 package active dry yeast — 1/2 cake compressed yeast

1 tablespoon lemon juice — 1/2 tablespoon vinegar

1 cup butter — 1 cup margarine and 7/8 cup vegetable oil

1 tablespoon cornstarch — 2 tablespoon all purpose flour

1 cup confectioner's sugar — 1/2 cup plus 1 tablespoon granulated sugar

1 oz. unsweetened chocolate — 3 tablespoon unsweetened cocoa powder plus 1 tablespoon butter or margarine

1 (41/2 oz. can) green chilies — about 6 fresh ones

HELPFUL HINTS

• There will probably be times when you're left with a tag end of cheese, a small bit of herb, some pieces of sweet or hot peppers—don't waste them, sprinkle in soup, over bread, toss in stew pot, add to cooked vegetables or add flavor to sauces.
• When cooking grains the eventual volume will be the same as the amount of liquid you put in.
• Even those who do not drink alcoholic beverages can use wine in cooking. During the cooking process the alcohol evaporates leaving the aroma and flavor that only wine can give. Wine also acts as a tenderizing agent when used on meats and poultry because of its acidic quality.
• Soak dried beans in water overnight or covered with water and brought to a boil and let stand for an hour or two. Discard the soaking water and add fresh water to cover, bring to a boil, lower heat to simmer and cook until tender. With this method of cooking, the substance in the bean which causes the embarassing problem called "GAS" is eliminated.
• Tomatillos are a pale green fruit with a distinctive lemon flavor. They have a husk covering them which must be removed before using. The tomatillo tones down the fire in hot chilies.
• When using pecans, the flavor is greatly improved if they are toasted first. Place in a single layer on a baking sheet and put in a 325 oven for about 20 minutes, stirring once or twice.
• To ripen still-firm or slightly green tomatoes, place them stem up on the kitchen counter top out of direct sunlight. They should be fully ripe in a day or two. Tomatoes can be refrigerated so they will keep longer, but should be served at room temperature for the best flavor.
• A vanilla bean or lemon verbena leaf stored in a closed container with sugar will flavor the sugar.
• One way to preserve fresh herbs is in vinegar or oil. When you need a sprig, remove and rinse it in cold water and you have a fresh tasting herb. The vinegar or oil can then be used for flavoring.
• Bouquet garni is a fancy name for a combination of herbs either tied with string or in a cheese cloth bag for easy removal from the cooking pot. The classic combination of herbs used are 2 sprigs thyme, 5 sprigs parsley and 1 bay leaf. It is usually added at the start of the cooking process for maximum flavor. The alternative is to use a stainless tea ball which has a hook so you can attach it to the rim of the pot for easy removal.

Contents

Beverages *15*

Appetizers *27*

Salsas, sauces, and marinades *49*

Soups and stews *63*

Lunch and One Dish meals *81*

Salads *95*

Eggs and cheese *115*

Vegetables *121*

Pasta and Rice *139*

Entrees *153*

Poultry *167*

Fish and Seafood *175*

Breads *181*

Condiments *195*

Sweet Endings *203*

Canning and Preserving *215*

Acknowledgements *224*

Above: Martha Hilton Stuart, Glennis' mother, and Mary Hilton Johnson, Helen's grandmother..

Left: Mary Belle Johnson, Helen's mother, and Jesse Stuart.

Above: James Stuart, Mary Belle Johnson, and Nathan Johnson at Plum Grove Cemetery.

Right: Nathan Hylton, who was Mary and Martha's father, Glennis' grandfather, Helen's great grandfather.

Beverages

HERBAL TEAS

1 teaspoon dried herb for each cupful or 3 teaspoon fresh crushed herb for each cupful. Have water boiling and pour over the herb. Let stand 5 minutes, then strain out the leaves.

There are a lot of combinations you can use. A good mixture for a soothing tea is a few sprigs of lemon verbena, some lemon balm, flavored mint and borage leaves all mixed together.

APRICOT MINT COOLER

6 fresh mint sprigs, chopped
1 1/3 cup boiling water
3 tablespoon sugar
1 (12 oz. can) apricot nectar
1/2 cup lemon juice
1/4 cup lime juice

Combine chopped mint, boiling water and sugar in a large bowl; stir until sugar dissolves. Cover and let stand one hour; strain and discard mint leaves. Combine with the apricot nectar, lemon and lime juice; chill. Makes about 5 cups.

ALASKAN COOLER

1 (13 1/2 oz.) can grapefruit sections
1 can chilled grapefruit juice
1 lime, sliced
Mint leaves

Freeze unopened can grapefruit sections until solid. Cut both ends from can; push frozen grapefruit out of can. Cut lengthwise into quarters; place each quarter into a tall glass. Fill glasses with grapefruit juice; garnish with lime slices and mint leaves. If desired orange juice, limeade or iced tea may be substituted for grapefruit juice. Makes 4 servings.

BLOODY MARY MIX

1 quart V-8 juice
2 tablespoon worchestershire sauce
1 tablespoon lemon juice
1/4 teaspoon sugar
1/4 teaspoon pepper
1/4 teaspoon hot pepper sauce
1/8 teaspoon garlic powder

In a pitcher thoroughly combine all ingredients. Chill. Serve over ice. Garnish with celery stalks and lemon wedges.

RED-HOT BLOODY MARY
(For nonalcoholic leave out vodka)

3 cup tomato juice
6 oz. (3/4 cup) peppered or plain vodka
3 tablespoon mild or peppered horseradish
3 tablespoon lemon juice
2 tablespoon worcestershire sauce
1/2 teaspoon hot red-pepper sauce
1/2 teaspoon black pepper
Ice cubes
6 small celery stalks

In 2 quart pitcher combine tomato juice, vodka, horseradish, lemon juice, worcestershire sauce, red-pepper sauce and black pepper. Fill 6 glasses with ice cubes. Divide tomato mixture between glasses. Garnish each glass with a celery stalk.

BLOODY MARY WITH HOT-SPIKED ICE CUBES
(For nonacoholic leave out vodka)

4 cup tomato juice
6 tablespoon fresh lemon juice
3 tablespoon fresh lime juice
2 teaspoon hot sauce
3/4 cup vodka
4 teaspoon worchestershire sauce
1 teaspoon garlic
1 teaspoon dried oregano
4 green onions, trimmed

Combine 1 cup tomato juice, 2 tablespoon lemon juice, 1 tablespoon lime juice and 1 teaspoon hot sauce. Pour into ice cube tray; freeze overnight. Combine vodka, worchestershire sauce, garlic salt, oregano and remaining 3 cups tomato juice, 4 tablespoon lemon juice, 2 tablespoon lime juice, and 1 teaspoon hot sauce in pitcher. Divide ice cubes among 4 tall glasses. Pour tomato juice mixture over cubes. Garnish each glass with 1 green onion.

CANTALOUPE COOLER

1 medium cantaloupe
1 tablespoon lime juice
4 sprigs fresh mint

Peel and seed cantaloupe. Cut into 4 inch chunks. Put about 1/2 in blender or food processor. Add 1/3 cup water and puree until smooth. Pour into pitcher. Repeat with remaining melon. Stir in lime juice. Cover and refrigerate at least 1 hour. Serve in stemmed glasses with a sprig of mint.

LEMON BALM PUNCH

1/4 cup sugar
1/4 cup boiling water
1/2 cup fresh lemon balm leaves, finely chopped
1/2 cup fresh mint leaves, finely chopped
1/2 cup lemon juice
4 quarts ginger ale, chilled
orange slices, optional
Fresh lemon balm leaves, optional

Combine sugar and water; stir until sugar dissolves. Combine sugar mixture, chopped lemon balm leaves, mint leaves and lemon juice in a bowl; cover and let stand overnight. When ready to serve strain liquid in punch bowl or pitcher; pour in ginger ale, stirring gently. Garnish with floating orange slices and additional lemon balm leaves, if desired. Delicious.

Note: Lemon Balm is a hardy perennial with a lemony mint flavor. Use the fresh leaves in salads, fruit cups and iced or hot teas. The leaves can be chopped and used as a substitute for lemon in recipes.

EASY MINT TEA

1 quart boiling water
10 regular size, mint flavored tea bags
2 cup sugar
1 1/2 cup lemon juice
3 quarts water
2 cup pineapple juice
1 (33.8 oz.) bottle ginger ale

Pour boiling water over the bags; cover and steep 5 minutes. Remove tea bags. Add sugar and lemon juice; stir until sugar is dissolved. Stir in 3 quarts water, pineapple juice and ginger ale. Serve over ice. Makes about 1 1/2 gallons.

FROSTED MINT TEA

3 quarts boiling water
24 regular tea bags
1/4 cup mint jelly
1/4 cup sugar
Lemon juice
Sugar
3 quarts lemon-lime carbonated beverage or ginger ale, chilled
Lemon or lime slices, optional
Fresh mint sprigs, optional

Pour boiling water over tea bags; cover and let stand 5 minutes. Remove tea bags; add mint jelly and 1/4 cup sugar; stir until dissolved. Chill. Dip rims of glasses in lemon juice and then in sugar; freeze glasses. To serve, combine tea and carbonated beverage; pour over ice in glasses. Garnish each glass with lemon and mint. Makes 6 quarts.

ORANGE MINT COFFEE

6 sprigs fresh mint
6 orange slices
10 cup fresh brewed coffee
Sweetened whipped cream or 2 1/2 cup vanilla ice cream

For hot coffee: Place 1 sprig mint and 1 orange slice in each of 6 cups. Pour fresh brewed coffee in each cup. Serve with a dollop of sweetened whipped cream in each cup. Cups can be refilled with coffee.

For iced coffee: Place sprigs of mint and orange slices into heat proof pitcher; add fresh brewed coffee. Let cool one hour. Cover and refrigerate until chilled. Into each glass place a scoop of vanilla ice cream; pour chilled coffee over ice cream.

Note: There are several varieties of mint. The most commonly used are peppermint, spearmint, and apple mint. Spearmint is best for most recipes. The chopped fresh leaves are excellent sprinkled over buttered new potatoes, tomatoes and in some egg dishes. Spearmint is also the mint used in juleps. A tea of peppermint, spearmint or apple mint will relieve indigestion and is a relaxing drink at bedtime to aid in sleeping.

FRUITED MINT TEA

3 cup boiling water
4 regular-size tea bags
12 fresh mint sprigs
1 cup sugar
1/4 cup lemon juice
1 cup orange juice
5 cup water
Fresh mint sprigs and orange slices, optional

Pour boiling water over tea bags and 12 mint sprigs; cover and steep 5 minutes. Remove tea bags and mint, squeezing gently. Stir in sugar and next three ingredients. Serve over ice. Garnish with mint sprigs and orange slices, if desired. Makes 2 1/2 quarts.

KENTUCKY SPARKLER

2 1/2 cup lemon juice
2/3 cup fresh mint leaves
2 cup sugar
1 cup water
3 quarts ginger ale
Sprigs of mint

Pour lemon juice over mint leaves. Add sugar and water; bring to a boil. Remove from heat; cool and strain. Add ginger ale. Pour over ice. Garnish each glass with a sprig of mint.

LEMON-MINT TEA

2 cup water
6 regular tea bags
3 lemons, cut in 1/2 inch thick slices
1 cup mint leaves, crushed
2 (46 oz.) cans pineapple juice
4 cup water
1 cup sugar
1 1/2 teaspoon vanilla extract
1 1/2 teaspoon almond extract

Bring water to a boil and pour over tea bags. Add lemons and mint; cover and let stand 20 minutes. Strain. Combine tea mixture and remaining ingredients; stir well. Serve over ice. Makes about 3 quarts.

MINTED APPLE COOLER

1/4 cup + 2 tablespoon chopped fresh mint
1 cup sugar
1 1/2 cup water
1 cup orange juice
1/2 cup lemon juice
4 cup apple juice
Fresh mint sprigs, optional

Combine chopped fresh mint, sugar and water in saucepan; bring to a boil and simmer 5 minutes. Cool and strain syrup mixture into a large pitcher; discard mint. Add remaining juices. Stir well. Serve over ice. Garnish with mint sprigs, if desired. Makes about 7 cups.

MINTED HOT-COCOA MIX

3 sticks hard peppermint candy
1 cup powdered non-dairy coffee creamer
1 cup sifted powdered sugar
1/4 cup cocoa

Place candy in a heavy-duty zip-top plastic bag; crush candy with a mallet. Combine candy with remaining ingredients. Store in airtight container. To serve, combine 1/4 cup cocoa mix with 3/4 cup boiling water; stir well. Makes 2 1/4 cups of mix.

MINT JULEP I

Put a few sprigs of mint into a tumbler. Add a tablespoon of sugar and fill the glass 1/3 full of bourbon. Stir to dissolve sugar. Then fill the tumbler with shaved ice, stick several sprigs of mint in the tumbler and stir until glass frost over on the outside. It is improved by shaking a little rum over the top of the crushed ice before serving.

MINT JULEP II

1/4 cup sugar
1/4 cup water
36 - 48 whole mint leaves
12 oz. good bourbon
Shaved ice
Sprigs of mint, for garnish

Heat water and sugar until sugar dissolves. Cool. Mix sugar syrup, mint leaves and bourbon. Bruise mint by pressing it against sides of bowl. Fill 6 chilled glasses or silver mugs with shaved ice. To each add 2 - 3 tablespoons bourbon mixture. Stir well and add more ice to fill mug. Add about 2 more tablespoons bourbon mixture to mug and more ice if necessary. Garnish each mug with fresh sprigs of mint. Makes 6 servings.

MINT TEA I

Boil 2 cups sugar, 1/2 cup water & grated rind of 1 orange about 5 minutes to make a syrup. Remove from heat & add crushed mint leaves from several sprigs of mint & let cool. Make 6 glasses of strong tea, add the juice of 6 oranges. Half fill glasses with ice, add tea & sweeten with more sugar if needed.

MINT TEA II

2 teaspoon leaves
1/4 cup chopped mint
3 3/4 cup boiling water
sugar to taste

Warm the teapot and put in the tea and chopped mint. Pour on the water as soon as it comes to a boil and let steep for 5 minutes. Strain into tea cups, adding sugar to taste.

Note: For an added touch, serve with lemon slice & a mint sprig. Also good served over ice as a cold drink.

ICED MINT TEA

2 quart size tea bags
1 cup fresh mint leaves
Juice of 2 lemons
1 cup sugar
1 quart boiling water
1 quart water
Lemon slices
Fresh mint sprigs

Combine first 4 ingredients. Pour boiling water over mixture; cover and let stand 5 minutes. Remove and discard tea bags and mint leaves. Transfer tea to a 2 quart pitcher, and add 1 quart water and lemon slices. Serve over ice. Garnish with mint sprigs. Makes 2 quarts.

MINTED LIME MIST

2 cup warm water
1/2 cup fresh lime juice
1/4 teaspoon mint extract
4 drops green food coloring
1 1/2 teaspoon non-caloric liquid sweetener or 12 tablets crushed
1 pint lime non-caloric lime carbonated beverage

Combine warm water, lime juice, mint extract, green food coloring and sweetener; mix well. Chill for several hours; add carbonated beverage. Fill glasses with ice; pour lime mist over ice. Garnish each glass with a maraschino cherry, wedge of lime and fresh mint. Makes 6 servings.

MINTED TEA

1 3/4 cup sugar
2 cup water
8 regular size tea bags
8 sprigs fresh mint
1 quart boiling water
2 quarts cold water
2 cup orange juice
3/4 cup lemon juice
Fresh mint sprigs (optional)

Combine sugar and 2 cups water in a saucepan; stir well. Bring to a boil; boil 5 minutes. Remove from heat. Add tea bags and 8 sprigs fresh mint to 1 quart boiling water; cover and let stand 10 minutes. Remove tea bags and mint. Combine sugar water, tea mixture, 2 quarts cold water, orange juice, and lemon juice; stir well. Serve over ice. Garnish with mint sprigs, if desired. Makes about 1 gallon.

MIXED MINT TEA

1 part crushed spearmint
1 part crushed peppermint
1 part lemon balm

If using dried leaves, measure 1 or 2 teaspoon per cup plus 1 teaspoon for the pot. If using fresh herbs, measure 1 tablespoon per cup. Pour boiling water over herbs. Cover and let steep for 5 - 10 minutes. Herb teas are light in color, so strength must be judged by taste, not appearance. If tea is too weak, add more herbs. Do not steep too long.

ORANGE-MINT PUNCH

2 cup sugar
2 1/2 cup water
1/4 cup dried mint leaves
1 (12 oz.) can frozen orange juice concentrate, thawed and undiluted
1/3 cup lemon juice
6 cup cold water

Combine sugar and 2 1/2 cups water in a saucepan; bring to a boil and boil 10 minutes. Stir in mint leaves; cover and steep 1 hour. Strain. Stir in remaining ingredients. Serve over crushed ice. Makes about 2 1/2 quarts.

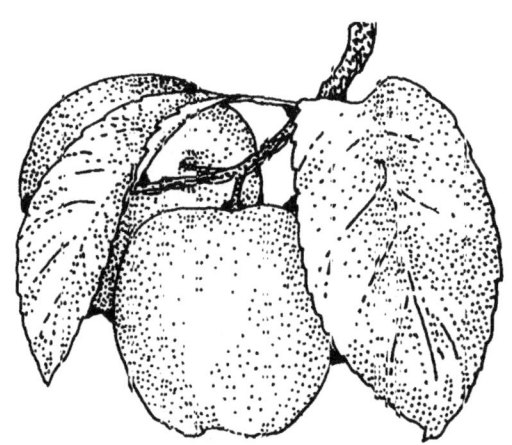

PINEAPPLE-MINT PUNCH

2 cup boiling water
4 regular-size tea bags
1 cup sugar
2 cup orange juice
3/4 cup lemon juice
2 Tablespoon lime juice
2 cup mint leaves
2 (33.8 oz.) bottles sparkling water, chilled
1 (67.6 oz.) bottle ginger ale, chilled
1 (15 1/4 oz.) can chunk pineapple, undrained

Pour boiling water over tea bags; cover. Let stand 10 minutes; discard bags. Add sugar and next 4 ingredients. Stir until sugar dissolves. Chill. Strain mint from tea mixture; discard mint. To serve combine tea mixture, sparkling water, ginger ale and pineapple. Stir well. Garnish with mint sprigs, if desired. Makes about 1 1/2 gallon.

ROSEMARY FRUIT PUNCH

1 (46 oz) can pineapple juice
5 sprigs fresh rosemary (1 tablespoon dried)
1/2 cup sugar
Pinch salt
1 1/2 cup lemon juice
2 cup water
1 quart ginger ale

Heat 1 cup pineapple juice until boiling; add rosemary and let steep 5 - 8 minutes. Dissolve sugar and salt in hot juice, then strain into a pitcher containing the remaining pineapple juice, lemon juice and water. Chill, and before serving, add ginger ale. Garnish with lemon slices and mint leaves if desired.

ROSE GERANIUM TEA

3 cup water
1 tea bag
3 rose geranium leaves
3 whole cloves
1/2 stick cinnamon

Put water on to boil. Rinse teapot with hot water to warm it; place tea bag, geranium leaves, cloves and the cinnamon stick in tea pot and pour the boiling water over as soon as it comes to a boil. Cover and let stand for 5 minutes. Strain and serve.

Note: The leaves of the scented geraniums do not resemble the regular garden variety of geranium nor do they have the large brightly colored blooms, their beauty is in the wonderful fragrance and flavor of their leaves. Their fragrance mimics the perfume of spices, fruits and flowers. A few which are useful in culinary dishes are ginger, lemon, rose, peach and orange. Use the leaves in teas, punches, jams or jellies and cakes.

SANGRITA

1 cup freshly squeezed orange juice
2 tablespoon grenadine syrup
1/2 cup canned tomato juice
1/2 cup fresh lime juice
4 to 6 dashes Tabasco, to taste

Mix all ingredients in a pitcher. Cover and refrigerate at least 1 hour. Serve in small glasses. Keeps a week covered in refrigerator.

SPICED TEA BASE

1 lemon, sliced
4 whole cloves
cinnamon stick
1/2 cup sugar
1 quart fresh orange juice
Ice cubes
Lemon wedge
Fresh mint sprigs

Simmer sliced lemon, cloves, cinnamon stick, sugar and orange juice for 15 minutes. Do not allow to boil. Strain juice and discard other ingredients. Refrigerate until well chilled. To serve use one half of this mixture to one half cool brewed tea. Garnish with lemon wedge and fresh mint sprigs. Always allow tea to cool before adding to juice base, or tea will discolor. Keep refrigerated.

STRAWBERRY-MINT COOLER

4 cup tonic water, divided
1 cup strawberry jam
1 cup chopped fresh mint
1/2 cup lemon juice

Combine 2 cups tonic water, jam and mint in a saucepan; bring to a boil. Boil 3 minutes. Let stand one hour; strain. Combine remaining two cups tonic water, strained jam mixture and lemon juice. Serve over ice. Makes 5 cups.

TOMATO JUICE WITH BASIL

2 pounds tomatoes
2 tablespoon fresh chopped basil
2 tablespoon lemon juice

Cut tomatoes into quarters. Put them through juice extractor or fine sieve. Stir the chopped basil and lemon juice into the tomato juice and chill 2 hours before serving.

TOMATO JUICE COCKTAIL I

1 (46 oz.) can tomato juice
1/4 cup lemon juice
1 teaspoon salt
1 teaspoon worcestershire sauce
Few drops hot sauce or to taste

Combine all ingredients. On a cold winter night, heat and serve in punch cups. To serve chilled, brush rim of each glass with slightly beaten egg white and dip into salt.

TOMATO JUICE COCKTAIL II

1 sprig parsley, chopped
1 teaspoon worcestershire sauce
1 teaspoon salt
2 cup tomato juice
1 tablespoon lemon juice

Add seasonings to tomato juice. Cover and refrigerate several hours or overnight. Strain, add lemon juice before serving. Makes 4 servings.

HOT TOMATO PUNCH

3 (46 oz.) cans tomato juice
3 (10 1/2 oz.) cans beef broth
1 teaspoon horseradish
Hot sauce to taste
3 teaspoon Worcestershire sauce
lemons
whole cloves

Combine and heat all ingredients except lemons and cloves. Cut 1 lemon in thirds; stick with cloves; add to hot punch and simmer for a few minutes. Serve with a thin slice of lemon in each cup.

VEGETABLE COCKTAIL

2 cup tomato juice
1 cup carrot juice
1 teaspoon grated onion
1 teaspoon grated celery
1 teaspoon grated green pepper
Dash hot sauce

Mix all ingredients together. Serve cold. Makes 6 servings.

Orville and Helen Shultz's greenhouse.

Orville Shultz and his prize tomatoes.

Lincoln Memorial University Reunion in W-Hollow. Glennis Liles, Maxine Tracy, Charles Gannon, Pinky Love, and Mary Gannon.

Whitey Liles and Orville Shultz making a herb garden at the Hylton house in W-Hollow, 1985.

Orville and Helen Shultz

Carole Abdon, Glennis' niece, Betty Stuart, James' wife, and Mary Belle Johnson, Glennis' cousin and Helen's mother.

Glennis Liles and Mary Belle Johnson.

Lincoln Memorial University Reunion.

Glennis at Helen's home. "All the cookbooks in the background," said Helen, "proves I'm a good cook."

Boys at a Hylton Reunion

Appetizers, Party Foods, & Sandwiches

ARTICHOKE-PARMESAN STRUDEL

1 medium onion, finely chopped
2 cloves garlic, minced
1/4 cup butter or margarine
3 (6 oz.) jars marinated artichoke hearts, drained and chopped
1 (8 oz.) pkg. cream cheese, softened
1 cup cottage cheese
1 1/4 cup parmesan cheese
3 eggs, beaten
1/2 cup cracker crumbs
1 teaspoon garlic salt
1 teaspoon dried whole marjoram
1 teaspoon fresh minced parsley
3/4 teaspoon dried whole tarragon
15 (18 1/2 x 12 in.) phyllo pastry sheets thawed and divided
1 cup butter or margarine

Saute onion in 1/2 cup butter until tender. Add artichoke hearts and next 9 ingredients; cook over medium heat until cheese melts, stirring often. Set aside. Place 1 phyllo sheet on a flat surface (keep remaining phyllo covered with a damp towel) brush with melted butter. Layer 4 phyllo sheets on first phyllo sheet, brushing each with melted butter. Spread 1/3 artichoke mixture crosswise, one inch from narrow end of phyllo. Starting at narrow end, carefully roll up jellyroll fashion. Tuck ends under, carefully place on baking sheet (lightly greased). Repeat procedure with remaining phyllo and artichoke mixture. Bake at 350 degrees for 30 minutes or until lightly browned. Cut into 1 inch slices and serve warm. Makes 30 appetizer servings.

HOT ARTICHOKE DIP

1/4 cup mayonnaise
1/2 cup sour cream
1 can (14 oz.) artichoke hearts, drained and chopped
1/3 cup grated Parmesan cheese
1/8 teaspoon hot pepper sauce

Stir all ingredients until well mixed. Spoon into ovenproof dish. Bake at 350 degrees for 30 minutes or until bubbly. Makes 2 cups.

AVOCADO DIP

4 ripe avocados
3 garlic cloves
1/2 teaspoon red pepper flakes
1/2 cup lemon juice
1 cup olive oil
1/2 teaspoon salt

Peel and pit avocados (save one pit). Chop the pulp coarsely then puree in blender or food processor for 30 seconds. Add remaining ingredients and process another 30 seconds. Spoon into bowl and place pit in the center of the mixture. Cover with plastic wrap and refrigerate for several hours. The avocado pit prevents the mixture from darkening.

BACON HORSERADISH DIP

1 cup mayonnaise
1 cup sour cream
1/2 cup real bacon bits
1/4 cup prepared horseradish

Stir all ingredients together until well mixed. Cover, Chill. Makes 2 cups.

LOW FAT BARBECUE DIP

1 cup nonfat sour cream
1/2 cup hickory smoke-flavored barbecue sauce
1/2 cup chopped red onion
1/2 cup chopped green onion
1/2 cup chopped tomato
1 tablespoon horseradish
Hot pepper sauce to taste

Mix all ingredients, chill. Serve with baked potato, chips or pretzels.

BEAN DIP

1 (16 oz.) can white kidney beans, drained and rinsed
1 clove garlic, sliced
1 tablespoon olive oil
2 teaspoon fresh lemon juice
1 teaspoon, or to taste, hot pepper sauce
1/4 teaspoon salt
1/2 teaspoon cumin
1 teaspoon coriander

Combine all ingredients and process in food processor or blender until smooth. Refrigerate until ready to use. Serve with fresh vegetables or tortilla chips. Makes 1 1/2 cups.

HOT CHEDDAR BEAN DIP

1/2 cup mayonnaise
1 can (16 oz.) pinto beans, drained and mashed
1 cup shredded cheddar cheese
1 (4 oz.) can chopped green chilies
1/4 teaspoon hot pepper sauce

Stir all ingredients until well mixed. Spoon into ovenproof dish. Bake at 350 degrees for 30 minutes or until bubbly. Makes 2 1/2 cups.

CARAWAY DIP

8 oz cream cheese
3 tablespoon light cream
1/2 cup finely chopped celery
2 tablespoon caraway seeds
1 teaspoon grated onion
Few drops of hot pepper sauce

Blend cream cheese and cream until smooth. Stir in remaining ingredients. Chill and serve with vegetable sticks or crackers.

CHICKEN CHIVE DIP

1 cup cream style cottage cheese
1 (5 oz.) can chicken spread
2 tablespoon light cream
1 teaspoon cider vinegar
2 teaspoon finely snipped chives

Combine cottage cheese, chicken, cream and vinegar and beat until smooth. Stir in chives and chill. Before serving sprinkle with more chives. Good served with thin cucumber slices or carrot sticks.

CHILI CON QUESO I
(Tortilla Chip Dip)

1 tablespoon vegetable oil
1 large onion, chopped
1 clove garlic, minced
1 tablespoon all-purpose flour
1 tablespoon chili powder or to taste
1 (10 oz.) can tomatoes and green chilies or 1 (16 oz.) can whole tomatoes mixed with 1/4 cup diced green chilies
1 lb American Cheese, cut in 1 inch cubes
2 jalapeno peppers (or to taste) seeded and chopped

Heat onion in oil, add garlic and saute until onion is translucent, about 5 minutes. Stir in flour and chili powder and cook, stirring constantly for 1 minute. Add tomatoes and chilies and cook until thickened, about 5 or 6 minutes. Reduce heat to low and gradually add cheese, stirring constantly until cheese is melted. Taste and adjust seasonings. Serve hot. Makes about 4 cups.

CHILE CON QUESO II

1 large onion, finely chopped
1 tablespoon bacon drippings
2 (10oz.) cans tomatoes w/ green chilies, undrained
1 (4 oz.) can chopped green chilies, undrained
1 teaspoon salt
1/8 teaspoon pepper
4 cup (16 oz.) shredded process cheddar cheese

Saute onion in bacon drippings until tender. Drain tomatoes with chilies, reserving juice; coarsely chop tomatoes. Add tomatoes with chilies, chopped green chilies, salt and pepper to onion; cover and simmer for 15 minutes. Add cheese and stir constantly until cheese melts. Thin mixture to desired consistency with tomato liquid, one tablespoon at a time. Serve with tortilla chips. Makes 4 cups.

JALAPENO PEPPER APPETIZERS

10 fresh jalapeno peppers
4 oz. cream cheese, softened
10 bacon strips, halved

Cut peppers in half lenthwise; remove seeds and membrane. Stuff each half with 2 teaspoons of cream cheese. Wrap with bacon strips and secure with toothpick. Place on broiler rack that has been coated with non-stick cooking spray. Bake at 350 degrees for 20-25 minutes, or until the bacon is crisp. Remove toothpicks and serve immediately.

(Submitted by Alan Smith. Alan's wife, Joann, says he is an excellent cook!"

HOT CRAB AND CHEESE DIP

1 (8 oz.) pkg cream cheese
2 tablespoon milk
6 oz. can crabmeat
pinch of salt
1 teaspoon grated onion
1 tablespoon horseradish
1 tablespoon worcestershire
tabasco to taste
slivered almonds
1 teaspoon lemon juice

Cream the cheese with milk. Mix in other ingredients except almonds. Pour into buttered casserole and sprinkle with almonds. Bake 1/2 hour at 375 degrees. Serve with snack crackers.

HOT CRAB DIP

1 pkg (3 oz.) cream cheese, softened
1/2 cup mayonnaise
1 cup (6 oz.) crabmeat, drained
1/4 cup minced onion
1 tablespoon lemon juice
1/8 teaspoon hot pepper sauce

Beat cream cheese until smooth. Stir in other ingredients. Spoon into ovenproof dish. Bake at 350 degrees for 30 minutes or until bubbly. Makes 1 cup.

CUCUMBER DILL DIP

1 pkg. (8 oz.) cream cheese
1 cup mayonnaise
2 med. cucumbers, peeled, seeded and chopped
2 tablespoon sliced green onion
1 tablespoon lemon juice
2 teaspoon snipped fresh dill or 1/2 teaspoon dried dill weed
1/2 teaspoon hot pepper sauce

Beat cream cheese until smooth. Stir in remaining ingredients until well mixed. Cover and chill. Makes 2 1/2 cups.

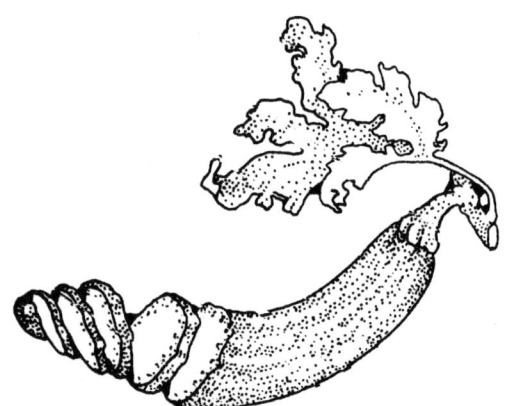

HORSERADISH DIP

1 (16 oz.) carton sour cream
1 tablespoon minced green onions
1 clove garlic, crushed
1 tablespoon paprika
1 1/2 teaspoon dried horseradish
1 teaspoon salt
1 teaspoon dried whole tarragon, crushed
1/2 teaspoon pepper
1/4 teaspoon garlic salt

Combine all ingredients, stir well. Chill at least three hours. Serve with an assortment of fresh vegetables. Makes 2 cups.

Note: Horseradish is a perennial herb and only the roots are used as the leaves have no flavor. Dig the horseradish, cut off the tops with some of the pulp left on and replant this for future horseradish roots. It is not an attractive plant so put it in an out-of-the-way place in your garden. Scraping the roots under water helps prevent eyes burning. It is very pungent and if possible prepare it outdoors. A food-processor is an ideal tool to use. After grinding it can be stored in vinegar in a tightly closed container in your refrigerator.

DILL DIP

1 cup sour cream
1 cup mayonnaise
1 tablespoon dried minced onion
1 tablespoon minced parsley
1 tablespoon minced dill leaves
1 tablespoon beau monde (seasoned salt)

Mix all ingredients and chill. Serve with assorted fresh vegetables.

GUACAMOLE DIP

1/2 cup mayonnaise
1 large avocado, peeled and mashed
1 small tomato, chopped
1/4 cup minced onion
1/4 cup drained chopped green chilies
1 tablespoon lemon juice
1/2 teaspoon salt

Stir all ingredients until well mixed. Cover, chill. Makes 2 cups.

GREEN ONION DIP

1 cup mayonnaise
1 cup sour cream
1/2 cup sliced green onions
1/3 cup parsley sprigs
1 teaspoon Dijon mustard
1 clove garlic, crushed

Process all ingredients in blender until almost smooth. Cover and chill. Makes 2 cups.

PEPPER CHEESE DIP

2 cup shredded Monterey Jack cheese
2 cup shredded American cheese
6 green onions, sliced
2/3 cup chopped red bell pepper
2 tablespoon diced jalapeno

Lightly spray saucepan with cooking spray. Melt cheese over low heat 5 to 10 minutes. Stir in other ingredients. Serve with tortilla chips.

SHOE PEG CORN DIP

1 (15 oz.) can shoe peg corn, drained
1 large tomato, peeled, seeded and chopped
1/2 med. sweet green pepper, chopped
1/2 med. sweet red pepper, chopped
12 pitted ripe olives, sliced
1/2 cup chopped red onion
2 green onions, chopped
1 jalapeno pepper, chopped
2 tablespoon sour cream
1 1/2 tablespoon chopped cilantro leaves
1/4 cup lime juice
1/4 teaspoon salt
1/4 teaspoon pepper

Combine all ingredients several hours or a day or two ahead of serving. Cover tightly and refrigerate. Serve with crackers or chips.

PESTO DIP

1 cup mayonnaise
1 cup sour cream
1 pkg. (10 oz.) frozen chopped spinach, thawed and well drained
1/3 cup grated Parmesan cheese
1/4 cup walnut pieces
1 teaspoon dried basil
1/4 teaspoon salt
1 clove garlic, crushed

Blend all ingredients in blender until almost smooth; cover and chill. Makes 2 cups.

SHRIMP DIP

1 cup mayonnaise
1 cup sour cream
1/3 cup finely chopped green pepper
1/4 cup chili sauce
1 tablespoon prepared horseradish
1/4 teaspoon salt
1/8 teaspoon pepper
2 cup finely chopped cooked shrimp

Stir all ingredients together until well mixed. Chill. Makes 3 cups.

SPINACH ARTICHOKE DIP

2 boxes frozen creamed spinach
1 can canned chopped artichoke hearts
1 bunch shallots, chopped
4 oz. cream cheese
8 oz. mixed Italian cheese
1 cup grated parmesan cheese
Hot sauce to taste

Thaw creamed spinach and mix in bowl with the rest of the ingredients. Spoon into casserole dish and bake 350 degrees for 20-30 minutes. Serve hot with salsa and sour cream.

TARRAGON VEGETABLE DIP

1 cup mayonnaise
2 teaspoon chopped onion
1 teaspoon dried tarragon
1 teaspoon chopped fresh parsley
1/2 teaspoon salt
1/2 teaspoon pepper
1 teaspoon horseradish (optional)

Mix all ingredients and store in refrigerator until ready to serve with your favorite vegetables.

SPINACH VEGETABLE DIP

2 (10 oz.) pkgs. frozen spinach, chopped
1/4 cup butter or margarine
2 tablespoon all purpose flour
2 tablespoon chopped onion
1/4 cup evaporated milk
1 (6 oz.) roll jalapeno cheese, sliced
1 tablespoon prepared horseradish
1 teaspoon worcestershire sauce
3/4 teaspoon celery salt
1/2 teaspoon salt
1/2 teaspoon pepper
1/2 cup soft bread crumbs

Cook spinach according to package directions. Drain well, reserving 1/2 cup liquid and set aside. Melt butter, add flour, stirring until smooth. Cook 1 minute, stirring constantly. Add chopped onion and cook 1 minute. Gradually stir in milk and 1/2 cup spinach liquid. Cook, stirring constantly until thickened. Stir in jalapeno cheese, worcestershire sauce, celery salt, salt and pepper. Cook stirring constantly until cheese melts. Stir in spinach. Pour in baking dish and top with bread crumbs; bake 20 minutes. Serve with fresh vegetables. Makes 3 cups.

TUNA HERB DIP

1 can tuna
1 (3 oz.) pkg. cream cheese
1/4 cup sherry
2 tablespoon minced parsley
2 tablespoon minced chives or 1 teaspoon dried
1 teaspoon minced tarragon or 1/4 teaspoon dried
salt
sour cream

Combine all ingredients, using enough sour cream to make of dunking consistency. If desired add 1 or 2 tablespoon of chopped capers or nuts. Makes 1 cup.

TARRAGON DIP

1 cup mayonnaise
2 teaspoon chopped onion
1 teaspoon dried tarragon
1 teaspoon chopped fresh parsley
1/2 teaspoon salt
1/2 teaspoon pepper
1 teaspoon horseradish

Mix all ingredients and store in refrigerator. Serve with fresh vegetables.

CHEESIES

2 cup Swiss cheese, grated
1/2 cup Parmesan cheese, grated
1/2 cup butter at room temperature
3/4 cup sifted flour
3/4 teaspoon salt
1/8 teaspoon cayenne pepper
1/8 tesaspoon nutmeg
1 egg
1 teaspoon water
Paprika

Knead together 1 1/2 cups Swiss cheese and next 6 ingredients. Form into a ball and chill 15 minutes. Break off tablespoonful and form into a ball. Flatten into a circle on ungreased cookie sheet leaving space between each. Brush with mixture of egg and water. Sprinkle with a little of the remaining Swiss cheese.

Bake in 425 degree oven about 10 minutes or until puffed and lightly brown. Cool on wire rack. Sprinkle with paprika and store in air tight container.

MARINATED MOZZARELLA CHEESE

1 lb. mozzarella cheese, cut in 1 inch cubes
2 cup olive oil
1/2 teaspoon thyme leaves
1 teaspoon oregano flakes
1 1/2 teaspoon dried parsley flakes
3 cloves garlic, minced
1/4 teaspoon paprika
1 1/2 teaspoon dried bell pepper flakes

Combine all ingredients in a one quart glass jar. Cover and shake to blend. To marinate, allow to sit at room temperature 5 days, shaking jar daily. Store at room temperature.

GUACAMOLE AND VEGETABLE APPETIZER

Vegetables such as: jicama strips, cucumber, carrot & celery sticks, radishes or whatever you choose.

1 medium tomato
1/2 small onion
1 small clove garlic
2 medium avocados
2 tablespoon lemon juice
1 1/4 teaspoon salt
1 (4 oz.) can chopped mild green chilies, drained
Fresh coriander leaves for garnish

Peel and dice tomato. Finely chop onion and garlicup Cut each avocado in half lengthwise; remove seed and peel. Mash avocado with lemon juice; stir in salt, tomato, onion, garlic, chilies; spoon into bowl and garnish with fresh coriander leaves. Serve with vegetables. makes about 2 cups.

HAMBURGER FOLD OVERS

2 cup butter, softened
2 pkgs cream cheese, softened
1 teaspoon salt
4 cup all purpose flour
1 lb ground beef
3/4 cup finely chopped onion
3 cloves garlic, crushed
1 1/4 tablespoon finely chopped olives
2 (4 oz.) cans hot chilies, chopped and undrained
1/4 cup raisins, chopped
1/4 teaspoon salt
2 egg yolks, beaten
1/4 cup milk

Combine butter, cream cheese and 1 teaspoon salt. Beat with electric mixer until smooth. Add flour, 1 cup at a time, kneading until well blended. Shape pastry into an 8 x 6 inch rectangle; chill several hours or overnight. Combine ground beef, onions and garlic; cook until meat is brown and onion is tender. Stir in chilies, olives, raisins and 1/4 teaspoon salt. Cook until liquid has evaporated; let cool. Take pastry from refrigerator and let stand at room temperature for 30 minutes.

Divide pastry in half; roll half of pastry to 1/4 inch thickness. Cut into 24 (3 inch) circles. Place about 2 teaspoon hamburger mixture on each circle. Fold circles in half, making sure edges are even. Press edges firmly, using a fork dipped in flour. Repeat with other half of pastry and meat mixture. Place pastries on lightly greased baking sheets. Combine egg yolk and milk. Brush top of pastries. Bake at 375 degrees for 12 to 15 minutes or until pastries are golden brown. Makes 4 dozen.

BRAUNSWEIGER BALL

1 lb. braunsweiger, broke into chunks
1 (8 oz.) pkg. cream cheese, softened
2 tablespoon milk
1 tablespoon grated onion
1 teaspoon chili powder
1/4 teaspoon garlic salt
1 tablespoon milk
Few dashes of hot pepper sauce

In a small bowl beat braunsweiger, 1/2 of cream cheese, 2 tablespoon milk, onion, chili powder and garlic salt until smooth. Chill slightly.

Shape braunsweiger mixture into a ball; place on serving plate. Beat together the remaining cream cheese, 1 tablespoon milk and hot pepper sauce. Spread over braunsweiger mixture, refrigerate until firm. Sprinkle with snipped parsley. Serve with crackers.

CHEESE BALL

2 pkg cream cheese softened (8 oz.)
4 cup (16 oz.) sharp shredded cheddar cheese
1 or 2 large cloves of garlic, crushed
1/2 teaspoon hot sauce or 1/4 teaspoon ground red pepper
1 jar chopped pimento, undrained
1/3 c chopped pimento-stuffed olives
1 teaspoon Worcestershire sauce
1/2 cup finely chopped walnuts or pecans
Paprika

Combine first 7 ingredients and mix well. Stir in walnuts. Shape into 2 cheese balls, and sprinkle with paprika. Refrigerate. Makes 3 3/4 cups.

BLUE CHEESE - OLIVE BALL

1 (8 oz.) pkg cream cheese, softened
3 tablespoon butter or margarine, softened
1 tablespoon brandy
1 (4 oz.) pkg blue cheese, crumbled
1 tablespoon fresh or frozen chopped chives
1/2 c finely chopped ripe olives
1 c chopped pecans

Combine first three ingredients; beat until smooth. Add blue cheese and mix well. Stir in chives and olives. Shape into a ball, and roll in pecans. Refrigerate several hours or overnight. Makes 1 cheese ball.

CHILI PORCUPINE BALLS

1 lb ground beef
1/2 c uncooked rice
1 small onion, chopped
1 teaspoon salt
1/4 teaspoon black pepper
2 tablespoon butter or margarine
2 (8 oz.) cans tomato sauce
1 cup water
1 teaspoon chili powder
1/2 teaspoon ground cumin

Mix first 5 ingredients. Shape into 16-20 balls. Brown lightly on all sides in butter. Add remaining ingredients, bring to a boil, cover and simmer about 45 minutes.

HOT CHEESE BALL

1/2 lb grated Parmesan cheese
1/2 lb cream cheese, softened
2 eggs
1/2 teaspoon salt
1 Jalepeno pepper, diced finely
1 cup fresh white bread crumbs
Salad oil for deep frying

Combine cheeses, eggs, salt and jalepeno and beat until smooth. Form into 1 inch balls. Roll each ball in bread crumbs. Refrigerate until firm. Heat oil to 350 degrees and fry until golden brown. Drain on paper towels. Serve warm.

CHEESE STRAWS

1 c grated sharp cheese
3 tablespoon butter, softened
4 1/2 tablespoon milk
1/2 teaspoon salt
1/2 teaspoon cayenne pepper
1 1/2 c fine soft bread crumbs
3/4 c flour

Mix the cheese and butter. Add the remaining ingredients, mix and knead until smooth. Roll out on lightly floured surface to 3/8 inch thickness and cut into strips 6 inches long by 1/2 inches wide. Place on greased baking sheet. Bake at 400 degrees about 12 minutes or until lightly browned.

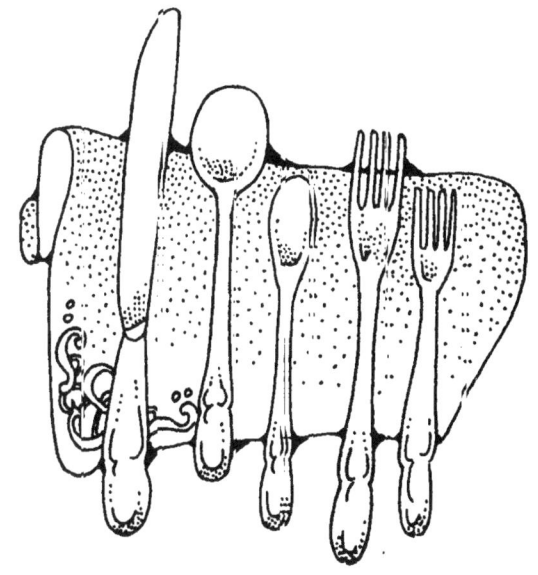

ZIPPY CHEESE BALL

2 oz. roasted & peeled green chilies (1/2 of 4oz. can)
1 lb sharp cheddar cheese
1 jar pimento, drained
1 tablespoon water
2 packets green onion dip mix
1/2 c mayonnaise
1/4 c softened butter

Rinse seeds from chilies and grind chilies, cheddar cheese and pimentos. Blend water with green onion dip mix. Add with butter and mayonnaise to cheese mixture. Beat with electric mixer until blended. Lightly butter a small bowl. Pack mixture into bowl, cover and refrigerate. Unmold about 1/2 hour before serving. Serve with assorted crackers. Makes about 3 cups.

BARBECUED SAUSAGE BALLS

1 lb pork sausage
1 slightly beaten egg
1/3 c dry bread crumbs
1/2 teaspoon sage
1/2 c catsup
2 tablespoon brown sugar
1 tablespoon vinegar
1 tablespoon soy sauce

Mix sausage, egg, bread crumbs and sage. Shape into 1 inch balls (about 2 dozen). Brown in an ungreased skillet slowly about 15 minutes. Pour off excess fat. Combine remaining ingredients and pour over sausage balls. Cover and simmer 30 minutes, stirring to coat balls occasionally.

ELIZABETH'S HOT WINGS

For Wings:
2 1/2 lb Chicken wings, disjointed, with tips removed
Flour, mixed with salt and pepper
Oil for frying
1/2 cup hot sauce (Preferably Tabasco)
1 stick butter (no substitute)

For dip:
1 8 oz. container sour cream
1/2 cup plain yogurt
1/4 lb. bleu cheese (preferably imported)
pepper
1/2 teaspoon hot sauce

For chicken:
Dredge wings lightly in flour, salt, pepper mixture. Fry wings on high until golden brown. Meanwhile, melt butter in small skillet and add Tabasco.

Drain wings thoroughly on paper towel. When oil is absorbed, spread them one layer deep on a baking pan. Pour Tabasco and butter mixture over and toss wings to coat. Bake at 425 for about 10 minutes until sizzling hot. Serve with bleu cheese dip.

For dipping sauce:
Crumble cheese. Combine all ingredients, and chill for at least one hour to develop flavor.

> *Note:* This was submitted by Elizabeth Reffett, who learned young to cook with herbs and hot peppers from her mother and dad, Gary and Katrina.

MEAT BALLS, STROGANOFF STYLE

1 1/2 lb ground beef
1 egg
1 1/2 teaspoon salt
1/4 teaspoon pepper
1/4 c dry, fine bread crumbs
1/3 c milk
1 teaspoon grated lemon rind
1/4 c chopped onions
1 tablespoon butter or margarine
1 (6 oz.) can sliced mushrooms
2 tablespoon flour
1 teaspoon hot pepper sauce
2 c beef broth
1 tablespoon dried parsley
1/2 c sour cream

Mix first 7 ingredients and 1/2 onion. Shape into balls and brown with butter. Set aside. Brown mushroom in drippings. Add remaining onion and blend in flour and hot sauce. Add remaining ingredients except sour cream and bring to a boil. Add meat balls, cover and simmer 15-20 minutes. Remove meat balls to a hot serving dish. Stir sour cream into liquid in skillet mixing well then pour over meat balls. Serve over hot buttered noodles.

LAMB MEATBALLS

2 tablespoon butter
5 shallots, minced
2 lbs ground lamb
1 c fresh breadcrumbs
1/4 c chopped fresh parsley
1 egg, lightly beaten
2 tablespoon finely grated lemon peel
1/2 teaspoon ground marjoram
salt and pepper to taste
1 tablespoon butter
1 tablespoon olive oil

Melt 2 tablespoon butter in skillet and saute shallots until softened. Place in a large bowl and add lamb, breadcrumbs, parsley, egg, lemon peel, marjoram, salt and pepper and blend well. Form into balls about the size of chestnuts. Heat remaining butter with oil, add meatballs in batches and saute on all sides until browned and cooked as desired. Drain on paper towels. Reheat in low oven before serving. Makes about 45 meatballs.

STUFFED CHEESE

1 (2 lb) round cheddar cheese
1 (16 oz.) can refried beans
1 (4 oz.) can chopped green chilies; drained
2 cloves garlic, minced
1/4 teaspoon dried whole oregano
1/4 teaspoon ground coriander
1/4 to 1 teaspoon hot sauce
5 (8 inch) corn tortillas
2 tablespoon vegetable oil

Hollow out cheese round, leaving a shell about 1/2 inch thick. Set shell aside. Shred cheese and set aside. Combine refried beans and next 6 ingredients. Cook until thoroughly heated, set aside. Fry tortillas, one at a time in hot oil 3 to 5 seconds or just until they are softened. Drain. Line a pie plate with tortillas. Place cheese shell on top; fill cheese shell with refried bean mixture. Top with shredded cheese. Bake at 350 degrees for 30 minutes or until cheese melts and bean mixture is heated. Serve immediately with tortilla chips. Makes 16 appetizer servings.

SUMMER TOMATO SPREAD

Serve on toasted bread with chicken, fish or beef patties.

2 cloves garlic, finely chopped
3 ripe red tomatoes, seeded, coarsely chopped and drained
1/4 c chopped fresh basil
1/4 c chopped fresh Italian parsley
1/3 c olive oil
1/2 teaspoon each salt and pepper
8 thick slices crusty or Italian or French bread

Combine all ingredients except bread. Grill bread slices on both sides over BBQ grill until crispy and marked with grill marks (or toast bread well). Top with tomato mixture and serve immediately. Makes 8 servings.

CHEESE FILLED TORTILLAS

16 (8 inch) flour tortillas
2 c (8 oz.) shredded mild cheddar cheese
1 onion, thinly sliced
1 jalapeno pepper, seeded and minced

Lay one tortilla on hot, lightly greased griddle, top with 1/4 c cheese, one onion slice and 1/2 teaspoon jalapeno pepper. Place another tortilla on top. Cook one minute, turn over and cook until cheese melts. Remove from heat, cut in 8 wedges. Repeat procedure with remaining ingredients. Makes about 5 dozen wedges.

BEEF AND CHEESE SPREAD

1/2 lb extra sharp cheddar, shredded
1 (8 oz.) pkg cream cheese, softened
1 (3 oz.) pkg dried beef, chopped
1/4 c beer
1 teaspoon Worchesterstire sauce
1 teaspoon hot pepper sauce

In blender or food processor, blend all ingredients until well mixed and smooth. Spoon into a small covered casserole or individual 1 cup containers. Refrigerate.

BACON AND CHEESE SPECIAL

1/3 c sour cream
2 tablespoon catsup
1/8 teaspoon oregano leaves, crushed
4 bread slices; toasted
8 tomato slices
8 bacon slices, crisply cooked
4 mozzarella cheese slices

Combine sour cream, catsup and oregano, chill. For each sandwich, spread one slice of toast with butter. Top with tomato slices, sour cream mixture, bacon and cheese. Broil until cheese begins to melt. Makes 4 servings. Serve open faced.

CHEDDAR CHEESE SPREAD

2 c (8 oz.) shredded cheddar cheese
2 hard-cooked eggs, mashed
3/4 c mayonnaise
8 pimento-stuffed olives, chopped
1 teaspoon chopped fresh parsley
1 teaspoon worchestershire sauce
3/4 teaspoon grated onion
1/2 teaspoon salt
1/4 teaspoon paprika

Combine all ingredients; stir well. Pack into container. Store in refrigerator. Serve with crackers. Makes 2 1/4 cups. Good to make ahead.

BRANDIED CHEDDAR CHEESE SPREAD

4 c (1 lb) shredded cheddar cheese
2 tablespoon butter
1 teaspoon sugar
cayenne pepper to suit taste
1/2 c brandy

Have cheese and butter at room temperature. Add sugar, cayenne and 1/4 cup brandy, mixing until creamy. Store in refrigerator. Serve with crackers. Makes about 2 cups.

SALMON SPREAD

1 (8 oz.) pkg cream cheese, softened
1/3 c plain yogurt
2 tablespoon dry sherry or milk
1/2 teaspoon dried dill weed or 1 teaspoon fresh
1/4 teaspoon lemon pepper seasoning
16 oz. can salmon; drained and flaked
3 tablespoon finely shredded carrot

Combine all ingredients except salmon and carrot in small bowl. Beat until smooth. Stir in carrot and salmon. Cover and chill at least 3 hours. Good served with party crackers or party rye.

HERBED CHEESE SPREAD

1 (8 oz.) pkg cream cheese
1 stick butter
2 tablespoon cream
1 clove garlic, crushed
1/2 teaspoon caraway seed
1/4 teaspoon basil leaves
1/2 teaspoon dill weed

Beat all ingredients on high speed until smooth. Refrigerate. Serve on crackers or bread at room temperature. Will keep several days in refrigerator.

SAVORY APPETIZER PASTRIES

1/2 lb ground beef
1 small onion, chopped fine
1 hard cooked egg, chopped fine
1 tablespoon dill weed, minced (can substitute parsley)
1/2 teaspoon salt
1/8 teaspoon pepper

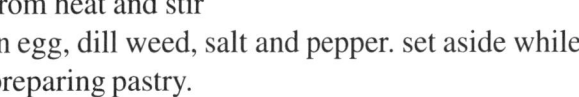

Cook and stir beef and onion until beef is light brown; drain well. Remove from heat and stir in egg, dill weed, salt and pepper. set aside while preparing pastry.

SOUR CREAM PASTRY

3/4 c margarine or butter, softened
2 c flour
1 teaspoon salt
1/2 c sour cream

Prepare pastry and divide into fourths. Roll each fourth into 12 inch circles. Cut into 3 inch circles. Place a rounded teaspoonful filling off center of each circle. Fold pastry over, moisten edges with water and crimp edges. Place on ungreased cookie sheet. Repeat with remaining pastry. Brush with egg wash made of 1 egg yolk and 1 tablespoon water. Bake at 400 degrees for 15-20 minutes until golden brown.

PIZZA POPCORN

4 tablespoon butter
1 clove garlic, minced
1/4 teaspoon leaf oregano, crumbled
1/4 teaspoon leaf basil, crumbled
8 cups freshly popped corn
1/2 teaspoon onion salt
2 tablespoon grated parmesan

Melt butter in small saucepan, stir in garlic, oregano and basil. Heat 1-2 minutes to release herb flavors. Pour over popcorn in large bowl; sprinkle with onion salt and cheese; toss until well coated.

PIZZA SANDWICH
(Microwave)

2 med. tomatoes, chopped
1/4 c chopped onion
1 tablespoon chopped green chili peppers
1/4 teaspoon garlic powder
1/4 teaspoon ground cumin
1/4 teaspoon oregano leaves
1/4 teaspoon basil leaves
2 slices firm bread toasted
2 tablespoon shredded mozzarella cheese
dash salt and cayenne pepper

Combine tomatoes, onion and chili peppers. Microwave 5-6 minutes or until tomatoes are tender, stirring after half the time. Drain; stir in seasonings. Arrange toasted bread in bottom of baking dish. Place half of tomato mixture on each slice. Top with 1 tablespoon cheese. Microwave at high 1-2 minutes, or until cheese melts. Rotate sandwiches once during cooking. Makes 2 servings.

HOT CHICKEN WINGS

4 lbs chicken wings
3/4 c teriyaki marinade and sauce
2 teaspoon dried crushed red pepper
1 teaspoon hot pepper sauce

Cut off and discard wing tips. Combine teriyaki sauce, red pepper and pepper sauce. Pour over chicken in large plastic storage bag. Close bag and turn several times to coat wings. Refrigerate 8 hours or overnight. Grill wings until tender, about 20-25 minutes. Turn frequently.

STUFFED MUSHROOMS

1 lb large fresh mushrooms
1 (8 oz.) pkg cream cheese
1 sm onion, minced fine
jalapeno peppers, minced fine to taste
1 c shredded monterey jack cheese
1 c shredded cheddar cheese
4 teaspoon butter

Wash and stem mushrooms (save stems for other dishes). Mix cream cheese, onion, and peppers. Stuff mushroom caps and place in baking dish. Scatter butter on top. Cover with shredded cheese and bake at 350 degrees for 25-30 minutes.

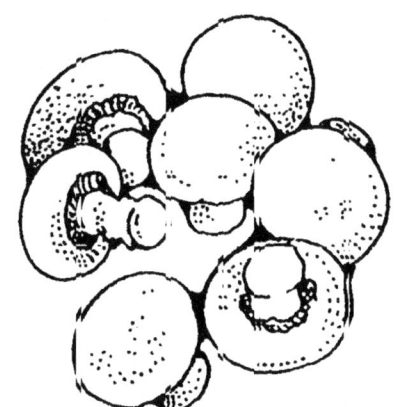

SPICY CORN CAKE

2 large or 3 med Italian frying peppers
1 lb chorizos (spanish sausages) finely chopped
oil, if necessary
1 large onion, finely chopped
1 clove garlic, minced
1 jalapeno pepper, seeded, deveined and minced
3 tablespoon soft butter
3 eggs
2 teaspoon honey
1 c sour cream
1 1/2 c fresh corn kernels, about 4 ears
1 (7 oz.) can green chili salsa
1 1/4 c yellow cornmeal
1/2 c all-purpose flour
1 teaspoon baking powder
1 teaspoon salt
1 c milk
Dash tabasco or hot pepper sauce
8 oz. grated Monterey Jack cheese

Roast peppers under broiler. Turn several times until skin is charred and blistered. Place in a paper bag to cool. Rub skins off with paper towels. Seed, mince and set aside. Saute sausage until browned and transfer to paper towels with slotted spoon. Pour off all except 2 tablespoon fat from skillet or add oil to make 2 tablespoon fat. Add onion and saute 2 minutes, add garlic and jalapeno pepper and cook 8 minutes longer. Remove from heat and set aside. Beat eggs; add honey, sour cream, reserved Italian peppers, onion, garlic, jalapeno pepper mix, corn kernels and green chili salsa. Spoon 1/3 of the batter over the bottom of a well greased casserole dish. Sprinkle the top with half the sausage (about 1 cup). Add another third of the batter, and sprinkle remaining sausage. Spoon remaining batter over the top and bake in 350 degree preheated oven and bake until golden, about 45-50 minutes. Let stand 8-10 minutes before serving. Makes 6-8 servings. Good eaten as a brunch, lunch or dinner adjunct. Perfect with eggs.

CRAB STUFFED MUSHROOMS

40 medium fresh mushrooms
2 c soft bread crumbs
1 1/2 c (8 oz.) flaked crabmeat
1/3 c grated parmesan
1/3 c finely chopped red bell pepper
1/4 c finely chopped green onions
1/2 teaspoon dried thyme
1/4 teaspoon black pepper
2 egg whites, lightly beaten
1/4 c sour cream

Remove stems from mushrooms. Mix the rest of the ingredients thoroughly. Fill caps with the mixture. Coat a shallow pan with cooking spray (Pam). Bake at 400 degrees for 20 minutes.

Note: You can finely chop the mushroom stems and use them in the stuffing.

CRAB DEVILS

1 pkg crabmeat, drained (or imitation)
3/4 c mayonnaise
1/2 c Parmesan cheese
1/2 teaspoon worcestershire sauce
hot sauce to taste
onion powder to taste
pimento strips and parsley for garnish
onion crackers

Combine crab meat, mayonnaise, cheese, worcestershire sauce, hot sauce, and onion powder and mix well. Spread on onion crackers. Sprinkle with extra parmesan cheese and broil until lightly browned and bubbly. Cool slightly and garnish with pimento and parsley, if desired.

MUSHROOM TARTS

24 slices white bread
1/4 cup butter or margarine, melted
1/4 cup minced green onion
1/2 lb fresh mushroom, finely chopped
2 tablespoon all purpose flour
1 cup whipping cream
1 tablespoon + 1 1/2 teaspoon minced fresh chives
1 tablespoon minced fresh parsley
1/2 teaspoon salt
1/2 teaspoon lemon juice
1/8 teaspoon ground red pepper
Grated parmesan cheese

Cut a 3-inch circle from each slice of bread, using a 3-inch biscuit cutter. Brush minature muffin pans with 1/4 cup melted butter. Gently fit bread rounds into muffin pans, forming cups. Brush bread with remaining melted butter. Bake at 400 degrees for 10 minutes. cool in pan. Saute onions in 1/4 cup margarine. Stir in mushrooms. Remove from heat and stir in flour. Gradually add whipping cream. Bring to a boil on medium heat; cook until thickened. Remove from heat, add chives and next four ingredients. Spoon mixture into toast cups. Sprinkle cheese on top. Bake at 350 degrees for 10 minutes. Serve immediately. Makes 2 dozen.

TURKEY SAUSAGE STUFFED HOT PEPPERS

1 lb ground turkey, seasoned with country sausage mix (store) or 1 lb ready made turkey sausage
2 cup grated Monterey Jack cheese, divided
2 tablespoon chili powder
1/4 cup diced onion
1 cup flour
4 eggs, beaten
12 hot banana peppers
1 (16 oz.) jar salsa

Combine sausage, 1 cup cheese, chili powder and onion; mix well. Make a slit in each pepper from end to end, remove veins and seeds. Fill peppers with sausage mixture and press slit together. Dip peppers in egg, then in flour and egg again. Place on baking sheet and bake in preheated 400 degree oven for about 25 minutes or until sausage is done. Transfer peppers to a baking dish and top with salsa, then sprinkle with remaining cup of cheese. Return to oven for 5 minutes or until ceese melts. Serves 6.

Note: This recipe was introduced to us by Ruth and Clarence Payne, very good cooks who like to experiment with food. These peppers make a delicious snack or can be used as a main dish.

STUFFED JALAPENO PEPPERS

1 (8 oz.) pkg cream cheese, softened
1/4 c mayonnaise
2 hard cooked eggs, finely chopped
1 tablespoon finely chopped onion
1/4 teaspoon garlic salt
2 (7 oz.) cans pickled jalapeno peppers, drained

Combine the first five ingredients; stir well. Cut peppers in half lengthwise; remove seeds and veins. Stuff peppers with cheese mixture. Cover and chill. Makes about 2 1/2 dozen.

STUFFED HOT BANANA PEPPERS

8 large hot banana peppers
1 lb ground beef
2 c cooked rice
1/2 teaspoon accent
Seasoned salt and pepper to taste
Sauce for peppers

Split peppers; wash and remove seeds and membrane. Parboil about 5 minutes. Cook beef until it loses its red color. Drain off fat. Mix beef, rice and seasonings. Add 1/4 cup sauce. Pack peppers with the mixture. Put in large shallow baking dish. Pour about 3/4 of remaining sauce around peppers. Cover, bake at 350 degrees for 45 minutes. Serve with remaining sauce.

Sauce for Peppers—Cook 1 chopped onion and 1/2 cup diced celery in 2 tablespoon butter for 5 minutes. Add 1 can (15 1/2 oz.) spaghetti sauce, 1 cup water, 1 bay leaf, 2 whole cloves and salt and pepper. Simmer 15 minutes. This recipe will work for sweet peppers too.

SAUSAGE STUFFED BANANA PEPPERS

1 lb pork sausage
2 c Monterey Jack cheese
2 tablespoon chili powder
1/4 c yellow onion, diced
12 banana peppers
1 c flour
4 eggs, beaten
2 c prepared salsa

Preheat oven to 400 degrees. In mixing bowl, combine sausage, 1 cup cheese, chili powder and onion. Mix well and set aside. Wearing rubber gloves, make a small cut lengthwise from stem of pepper to the tip, making sure not to cut all the way through. Pull out the core of the pepper and rinse out all seeds. When finished, fill peppers with equal amounts of the sausage mixture and mash closed. Dip peppers in egg, then in flour, then in egg again. Place on greased baking sheet and bake approximately 20 minutes until peppers are soft and sausage is done. Drain and place peppers in 13 X 9" baking dish, top with salsa and remaining 1 cup cheese. Return to oven and bake uncovered 5 minutes longer.

SEAFOOD SPREAD

This seafood appetizer is a real crowd pleaser.

1 (8 oz.) pkg cream cheese, softened
1 tablespoon finely chopped onion
1 tablespoon lemon juice
1 teaspoon worcestershire sauce
3/4 lb cooked crab, shrimp or imitation crab, patted dry and chopped
1 (12 oz.) jar seafood cocktail sauce
1/4 c chopped fresh parsley

In bowl combine cream cheese, onion, lemon juice and worcestershire sauce. Spread on bottom of 7 inch glass dish. Top with seafood. Spoon seafood sauce over seafood. Sprinkle with parsley. Cover and refrigerate 2 hours. Serve on crackers or sliced vegetables. Makes about 30 appetizer servings.

TUNA PATE

1 (8 oz.) pkg cream cheese, softened
2 tablespoon chili sauce
2 tablespoon snipped parsley
1 teaspoon finely chopped onion
1/2 teaspoon hot pepper sauce
2 (6 1/2 oz) cans tuna, drained

Blend all ingredients well and pack into a 4 cup mold. Chill at least 3 hours. Unmold and serve with snack crackers.

STUFFED JALAPENOS

1/3 lb cooked, peeled and deveined shrimp
1 (3 oz.) pkg cream cheese, softened
1 tablespoon grated onion
1 teaspoon worcestershire sauce
1/8 teaspoon garlic powder
Dash of salt and pepper
1/4 lb jalapeno peppers

Beat cream cheese until fluffy. Chop shrimp and add with other ingredients (except peppers) to the cream cheese. Chill. Remove stem ends from peppers and cut in half lengthwise (wear rubber gloves). Remove seeds and stuff with cream cheese mixture.

SPICED CHEESE-STUFFED JALAPENO

1 lb cream cheese, room temperature
4 oz. shredded Gruyere cheese
1/4 c butter, room temperature
1 tablespoon dijon mustard
2-3 teaspoon paprika
3 slices spicy Italian salami, chopped
6 green onions, minced
Jalapeno peppers, stemmed, halved (lengthwise), deveined and seeded

Combine cream cheese, Gruyere, butter, mustard and paprika in food processor and mix until smooth. Add salami and onions, mixing until well blended. Season with salt and pepper to taste, if desired. Stuff jalapenos. Makes 8-10 servings. Can be made a day ahead and refrigerated.

TUNA AND CHILI FONDUE

1 can tuna
1/2 c minced celery
2 tablespoon minced onion
1/4 c minced canned green chilies
1/4 c mayonnaise
1/4 teaspoon salt
1 teaspoon chili powder
12 slices bread
2 c grated cheddar cheese
3 eggs, beaten
1 c milk
1/4 c cream
1/4 teaspoon salt
Hot sauce to suit your taste

Combine first 7 ingredients. Spread on half the bread and make sandwiches. Cut each in quarters, and arrange in layers in square baking dish, putting cheese between layers and on top. Combine remaining ingredients and pour over all. Bake in slow oven 300 degrees for 50 minutes or until set. Serves 6.

HOT SPINACH HORS D' OEUVRES

2 (10 oz.) pkg chopped frozen spinach
2 c pepperidge farm herb stuffing
1 large onion, chopped
4 eggs
1/2 c shredded parmesan cheese
3/4 c butter, softened
1 tsp thyme
1 clove garlic, minced
salt and pepper

Cook spinach and drain, squeezing out liquid. Mix all ingredients. Chill about 2 hours. Roll into balls about 1 inch in diameter. Cook at 300 degrees for 30 minutes until golden brown.

SALMON MOUSSE

1 envelope unflavored gelatin
1/4 c cold water
1/2 c whipping cream
1 (8 oz.) pkg cream cheese
1 c sour cream
1 teaspoon lemon juice
1 teaspoon worcestershire sauce
1/8 teaspoon garlic salt
1/8 teaspoon hot sauce
1/2 c grated onion
3 tablespoon chopped fresh chives
2 tablespoon chopped fresh parsley
1 or 2 tablespoon prepared horseradish
1 lb smoked salmon, chopped
shredded lettuce
sliced pimento stuffed olives
shredded carrot

Soften gelatin in water. Place whipping cream in saucepan over low heat until thoroughly heated. Add gelatin mixture and stir until gelatin dissolves. Stir in sour cream, lemon juice, worcestershire sauce, garlic salt and hot sauce. Stir in gelatin mixture, onion, chives, parsley and horseradish. Spoon into greased mold (fish shaped if you have one.) Gently stir in salmon. Cover and chill until firm. Unmold mousse on platter covered with shredded lettuce. Garnish with olives and carrots. Serve with crackers. Makes 5 cups.

ZUCCHINI APPETIZERS

3 c thinly sliced zucchini (about 4 medium)
1 c Bisquick
1/2 c chopped onion
1/2 c grated parmesan
2 tablespoon snipped parsley
1/2 teaspoon salt
1/2 teaspoon seasoned salt
1/2 teaspoon dried marjoram or oregano
Dash of pepper
1 clove garlic, chopped
1/2 c vegetable oil
4 beaten eggs

Mix all ingredients. Spread in greased oblong pan. Bake at 350 degrees until golden. Cut in squares.

ZUCCHINI PIAZZA

1 large cookie sheet with sides, sprayed with cooking spray

Several small, 6"-7" zucchini
3 large eggs
1/2 cup milk
1/4 cup freshly grated parmesan
4 tablespoon finely minced fresh basil
1 tablespoon finely minced fresh fennel, or 1 teaspoon crushed fennel seeds
1 teaspoon garlic bits
1/2 teaspoon salt
1/2 teaspoon pepper
1/2 cup shredded hot pepper cheese

Slice zucchini across into 1/2" thick rounds. Lay slices to cover cookie sheet. Combine eggs, parmesan, basil, fennel, garlic bits, salt and pepper, and milk in food processor. Process for about 30 seconds until well blended, but not pureed. Pour over zucchini on cookie sheet. Sprinkle evenly with 1/2 cup hot pepper cheese. Bake at 350 degrees about 20-30 minutes, until puffed and golden brown. Slice in squares to serve.

> *Note:* This was submitted by Katrina Reffett. When Katrina cooks she dashes out the back door several times to get fresh herbs from her extensive herb garden.

Ron Arrick carving the roast.

Orville Shultz, Helen's Husband, barbecuing chicken at a Hylton Family Reunion in W-Hollow, 1997.

Whitey Liles cooking sweet corn at Hylton Family Reunion.

Orville Shultz making noodles.

Hylton Reunion: Stacy Nelson, Carol Abdon, Lori Grizzle, Whitey Liles, and Debbie Thomas.

Hylton Reunion: Glennis Stuart Liles, Helen Shultz, Mary and Charles Gannon.

Five First Cousins at a Hylton Reunion. Glennis Stuart Liles, Bob Hilton, Grace Hilton Carter, Fred Hilton, and Mary Nelson.

Salsas, Sauces, & Marinades

Marinades for tenderizing and adding flavor to meats.

SHANGHAI MARINADE

1/4 c soy sauce
1/4 c oil
1/4 c white wine
1 teaspoon sugar
1 garlic clove, minced
2 good dashes hot sauce
1-2 inch strip fresh orange or lemon peel

Combine all ingredients and pour over steak. Let marinate from 1-8 hours, or longer, depending on thickness of meat. Makes 3/4 cup.

PICKLED PEPPERS

4 large green bell peppers, cut into 3/4 inch strips
4 large red bell peppers, cut into 3/4 inch strips
4 large yellow bell peppers, cut into 3/4 inch strips
3 cloves garlic, quartered
12 whole black peppercorns
1 1/4 c white wine vinegar
1/3 c olive oil
1 teaspoon dried oregano, crushed
1 teaspoon dried rosemary, crushed
1 tablespoon sugar
1/2 teaspoon salt
1/2 teaspoon ground cumin
1 3/4 c water

In saucepan cover vegetables with boiling water. Boil 5 minutes and drain. Pack into 2 one quart jars that have tight fitting lids. Divide garlic and peppercorns evenly between jars. Combine remaining ingredients in small bowl and beat with fork until well mixed. Pour mixture over peppers. Apply lids and refrigerate at least 1 day before using.

Note: These will keep for several weeks in refrigerator if kept tightly covered.

SPANISH SHERRY MARINADE

1/2 c dry Spanish sherry
1/4 c olive oil
1 small onion, minced
1 bay leaf
1/4 teaspoon thyme
1/8 teaspoon pepper

Combine all ingredients, pour over meat and marinate 1-8 hours depending on the thickness of meat. Makes 3/4 cup.

AVOCADO SALSA

4 large tomatoes, seeded and chopped
1 c chopped green onions
2 or 3 jalapeno peppers, seeded and minced
3 tablespoon chopped fresh cilantro
salt to taste
1 teaspoon pepper
2 avocados
1/4 c lemon juice

Combine tomato, onions, jalapeno pepper, lemon juice, cilantro, salt and pepper; stir gently. Cover and chill at least six hours. Just before serving peel and chop avocado, and add to tomato mixture. Serve with chips. Makes 6 cups.

ANDY RUSSELLS' HOT SAUCE

2 pounds finely chopped Habanero peppers
3 cups distilled white vinegar
2 teaspoon salt

In a medium, nonreactive saucepan, combine the hot peppers and vinegar and heat to just below boiling. Add the salt and simmer about 5 minutes. Process the mixture in a blender or food processor. Pour into a glass container and allow to mellow about 3 weeks. Strain and bottle.

> *Note:* This is Andy Russell's basic recipe. He says the addition of a little rum after cooking makes a tastier sauce. Andy grows many varities of hot peppers to use in hot sauces for himself and many friends. He freezes surplus peppers to use in making batches of sauce all winter long.

GARY'S SALSA

1/3 cup cilantro
3 cloves garlic
1 large onion, chopped
1 jalapeno pepper, chopped
1 red or green pepper
4 cups ripe tomatoes, chopped
1 tablespoon tomato paste
salt and pepper to taste
juice of 1/2 lime

Using a food processor, chop cilantro, garlic and jalapeno pepper until finely diced. Remove to mixing bowl. Dice onion until coarsely diced in processor, then place in mixing bowl with above. Process red or green pepper until coarsely chopped, again place in bowl. Process tomato and paste (do not over process), and again place in bowl. Stir all ingredients, add salt and pepper to taste, add lime juice and serve with tortilla chips. The brave substitute 1/2 a habenaro pepper for the jalapeno.

BLACK AND WHITE BEAN SALSA

3 tablespoon corn oil
1 1/4 c fresh or frozen corn kernels
1 (16 oz.) can black beans, rinsed and drained
1 (15 oz.) can Great Northern beans, drained
1 c chopped bell pepper
3/4 c chopped red onion
2 tablespoon lime juice
3 large garlic cloves, pressed
1 large jalapeno, seeded and minced
1 tablespoon fresh oregano, minced
1 tablespoon chili powder
1 1/2 teaspoon cumin

Heat 1 tablespoon oil in heavy skillet. Add corn and saute until browned. Transfer to a large bowl. Add remaining oil and the rest of the ingredients. Season to taste with salt and pepper. This is also good as a filling for burritos.

Cumin—Throughout the world, cumin is second only to black pepper. Americans tend to use it mostly in chili, but its pungent flavor adds interest in any Mexican or Latin American recipe. Cumin is one of the ingredients in commercial chili powder. It is an annual herb which is very easy to grow, but is very hard to harvest. The seeds are the part used and they must be dry when picked. The problem with this is they shatter as soon as they become dry so you lose most of your crop. It is much easier to buy the ground cumin and it is just as good.

> *Note:* This is Gary Reffett's recipe. Gary was dating his wife, Katrina, before he learned that all vegetables are not hot. His mother, Mildred, added a hot pepper to every pot.

CARROT-HABANERO SALSA

1/2 Habanero chile, seeded, finely chopped
1 clove garlic, finely chopped
4 green onion, finely chopped
1/2 c raw carrot, finely chopped
1 large tomato, seeded, diced, drained
2 tablespoon fresh cilantro, chopped
1 tablespoon lime juice
pinch of salt

Combine all ingredients, salsa mixture should be coarse. If using a food processor, process chile and garlic, then add other ingredients and mix briefly. Do not over process. If you like fiery foods, use the whole habanero.

SALSA

5 lbs peeled, chopped tomatoes
2 c chopped onion
1 1/2 c seeded, chopped jalapeno peppers
2/3 c lemon juice
3 tablespoon fresh cilantro
2 1/2 teaspoon salt

Combine all ingredients and bring to a boil. Cook, uncovered, 30 minutes. Put in jars, seal, process in boiling water bath 15 minutes.

GREEN CHILE SALSA

6 tomatillos, husks discarded and fruit quartered
5 green Anaheim or poblano chilies, roasted and peeled, stemmed and seeded
2 unpeeled garlic cloves, roasted with the chilies and peeled
1/2 avocado, peeled
1 c Mexican cream, recipe follows
1/4 c loosely packed cilantro leaves
1/2 to 1 teaspoon salt (to taste)

Place tomatillos in skillet and cook over low heat until softened, 3-4 minutes. Transfer to processor. Add chilies, garlic and avocado and mix until smooth. Add cream, cilantro and salt and puree until smooth. Serve warm or cold. Can be prepared ahead and refrigerated. Makes 2-2 1/2 cups.

Mexican Cream

1 c sour cream
1/2 c whipping cream
1 teaspoon fresh lime juice

Blend all ingredients. Set aside at room temperature 2 hours to thicken. Refrigerate.

FRESH TOMATO SAUCE
(no cooking)

4 large tomatoes
1 red onion, very finely chopped
2 jalapeno chilies, stemmed, seeded, chopped
2 small cloves garlic, finely chopped
1 c fresh mint leaves, finely chopped
2 tablespoon olive oil
2 tablespoon red wine vinegar
1 teaspoon salt
pepper to taste
8 oz. spaghetti or linguini
1/2 c grated parmesan cheese

Combine vegetables and mint leaves. Mix oil and vinegar and pour over vegetables. Salt and pepper to taste. Let stand at room temperature 30 minutes to an hour. Cook spaghetti or linguine according to package directions. Drain well and toss with sauce. Pass the grated cheese when served. Makes 4 servings.

GUACAMOLE WITH HOMEMADE SALSA

4 medium avocados, peeled and coarsely chopped
1 medium tomato, seeded and coarsely chopped
1 green onion, finely chopped
1/2 c homemade salsa
Fresh cilantro sprigs

Combine avocado, tomato, green onions, 1/2 cup Homemade Salsa. Toss and garnish with cilantro sprigs. Serve with tortilla chips.

Homemade Salsa

2 jalapeno peppers, seeded and chopped
6 guero (hot yellow) peppers, seeded and chopped
2 large tomatoes, seeded and chopped
8 cloves garlic, minced
1 can (14.5 oz.) canned tomatoes, undrained & chopped
1/4 c + 2 tablespoon vegetable oil
1/2 teaspoon salt
1 tablespoon chopped fresh cilantro
1 teaspoon dried whole oregano
1/2 teaspoon pepper

Combine all ingredients and mix well. Serve as a condiment over fried eggs, cold meats, poultry or hamburgers, or as a dip with tortilla chips. Makes 4 cups.

FRESH GARDEN SALSA

3 large tomatoes, seeded and chopped
1 small green bell pepper, seeded and chopped
3 cloves garlic, finely chopped
1/2 c sliced green onion
2 tablespoon chopped fresh cilantro
1 tablespoon finely chopped jalapeno
2-3 tablespoon lime juice
1/2 teaspoon salt

Mix all ingredients in a glass or plastic bowl. Cover and refrigerate for a few minutes to blend the flavors. Serve as a dip with tortilla chips and crackers or as a sauce for vegetables, fish, chicken or Mexican dishes.

Note: Cilantro/coriander is an annual herb grown for both its seed and foliage. The seeds are used whole in vegetables such as cauliflower and celery. Ground, it is one of the main ingredients in curry powder. Ground coriander has a hint of orange flavor. The green leaves resemble parsley in appearance but have an entirely different taste. Some people cannot abide the taste and smell so use sparingly until you are sure your family will like it. Cilantro is one of the main ingredients in southwestern cooking and is a must for salsas. Another name for cilantro is Chinese parsley.

RED PEPPER SALSA
(Rubber gloves when handling chilies)

1 1/2 tablespoon chopped fresh oregano or 1/2 teaspoon dried
2 tablespoon olive oil
3/4 c roasted red peppers, cut into 1/2 inch strips (about 2 medium sweet peppers)
2 very ripe tomatoes, skinned, seeded and coarsely chopped (about 1 cup)

1/3 c chopped red onion
2 cloves garlic, finely minced
2 tablespoon red wine vinegar
3-4 fresh red or green hot chilies, seeded and minced
Salt and pepper to taste

Soak oregano in olive oil for 10 minutes. Add oregano and olive oil to all other ingredients in food processor. Process, using off-on switch until mixture is thoroughly combined, but still chunky. Add seasoning and adjust to taste. Chill well. Makes 2 cups.

TANGY SALSA I

2 (8 oz.) cans tomato sauce
1/2 c chopped cilantro
3 jalapeno peppers, stemmed and minced
1/4 medium onion, diced
2 tomatoes, diced
1 celery stalk, diced
1 tablespoon olive oil
2 cloves garlic, minced
1 dried small hot chili pepper, crushed
1/2 teaspoon salt
1/8 teaspoon pepper
3/4 c water (about)

Combine all ingredients except water. Add water until desired consistency is reached. Chill until ready to use.

TANGY SALSA II

2 1/2 c diced tomatoes, drained
1 small red onion, chopped
1 tablespoon olive oil
2 cloves garlic, minced
1 Serrano chile, seeded and chopped
2 Jalapeno chilies, seeded and chopped
1 Anaheim chile, seeded and chopped

1/2 teaspoon cumin
1 tablespoon dry oregano leaves
1 tablespoon red wine vinegar
2 tablespoon chopped fresh basil
1/4 c fresh cilantro
salt to taste

Combine tomatoes and onions in a bowl. Heat oil and add garlic, chilies, and oregano. Stir and cook 4-5 minutes. Combine with tomatoes and the remaining ingredients. Let stand a few hours to blend. Pour off excess liquid before serving. Makes 3 cups.

APPLESAUCE WITH HORSERADISH CREAM

1 (2 lb. 4 oz.) jar of applesauce
1-2 tablespoon horseradish
3/4 c heavy cream

Cream ingredients together. Cover and chill. Use horseradish to taste. Delicious with pork or sausage dish.

APPLESAUCE WITH SAGE

2 cooking apples, peeled and sliced
1/2 teaspoon sugar
1 teaspoon chopped sage
Dash black pepper
Enough water to cover apples

Cook the apples in water until soft. Add sugar, sprinkling of pepper and sage. Cover and let stand 5-7 minutes before serving. Excellent accompaniment to roast pork.

BAR-B-QUE SAUCE

1/2 gallon dark vinegar
1/2 bottle Tabasco sauce
1/2 stick butter
1/2 box black pepper
1 1/2 teaspoon red pepper

Mix well. Heat to boiling; allow to cool. Apply to meat before and during cooking.

BASIC "BBQ" SAUCE

1 tablespoon butter
1 onion, finely chopped
3/4 c catsup
3 tablespoon worchestersire sauce
2 tablespoon A-1 steak sauce
1 tablespoon cider vinegar
3 tablespoon brown sugar
1/4 c water
Hot pepper sauce

Cook onion in melted butter 5 minutes. Stir in remaining ingredients and simmer, uncovered 20 minutes. Brush on shrimp or other seafood, beef, pork or poultry and grill. Makes about 1 1/3 cups.

DILL SAUCE

1 envelope Hollandaise sauce mix
1/4 c mayonnaise
1/4 c sour cream
1 teaspoon dill weed
1 teaspoon Worchestersire sauce
1/8 teaspoon salt

Prepare Hollandaise according to package directions. Mix in other ingredients and refrigerate until ready to use. Serve with vegetables.

MINT SAUCE

2 tablespoon fresh chopped mint leaves
1/2 tablespoon sugar
1 tablespoon water
juice of 2 lemons, warmed

Mix together and let stand at least 1 hour before serving.

PIRI-PIRI SAUCE

6 small hot dried peppers
1 bay leaf, crushed
small piece of lemon rind
1 cup olive oil

Place ingredients in an airtight jar and seal. If sealed-tightly will keep for 1 month. Or in a warm place 24 hours, use at this time as the oil may allow harmful organisms to grow in the oil.

RED HOT PEPPER SAUCE
(Use rubber gloves when preparing peppers)

24 long hot peppers (Hot banana peppers make a mild sauce)
12 tomatoes
4 c vinegar
1 c sugar
1 tablespoon salt
2 tablespoon mixed spices

Wash and drain vegetables. Remove seed from peppers. Core tomatoes, chop vegetables. Add 2 cup vinegar. Boil until vegetables are soft. Press through sieve; add sugar, salt and spices (tied in a bag). Boil until thick. Add remaining vinegar. Boil 15 minutes more or until as thick as wanted. Pour boiling hot into jars. Seal.

RED CHILE SAUCE

24 dried, hot red chilies
2 cloves garlic
3 c water
2 teaspoon salt

Wash chilies, remove seeds and veins. If you grow your own peppers you might want to remove this before drying. Bake at 250 degrees for 10-15 minutes, turning often with tongs. Let cool. Rinse chilies with cold water, drain. Place chilies and garlic in food processor or electric blender. Process until finely chopped. Add water and salt, process until pureed. Store in refrigerator. Serve with beef, chicken, or eggs. Makes 3 1/4 cups.

FRESH HOT SAUCE

4 jalapeno peppers, seeded
4 poblano chilies, seeded
6 medium tomatoes, peeled, coarsely chopped
3 large cloves garlic, chopped
1 teaspoon salt
1/4 teaspoon pepper (ground)
1/4 teaspoon honey
1/2 c chopped green onions
1/4 c chopped fresh cilantro

Combine peppers, chilies, half the tomatoes, garlic, salt, pepper and honey in container of electric blender and process until finely chopped. Place in container and add remaining tomatoes, green onions and cilantro. Cover and chill. Serve as a dip with tortilla chips or as an accompaniment to scrambled eggs or beef. Makes 7 cups.

HOBBIE'S BREATH HOT SAUCE

Note: This sauce is dangerously hot and should be first tasted on a toothpick. Add to a pot of chili or soup one drop at a time; then taste before adding more. We recommend you definitely wear heavy rubber gloves and cook sauce outside if possible, to prevent coughing and choking.

2 lbs habanero peppers *(red is hotter than orange)*, chopped fine
3 c vinegar
2 teaspoon salt

Bring to just below boiling. Simmer 5 minutes. Store in glass jars for 2-3 weeks. Run through juicer to remove seeds and skins. For 2 gallons pepper juice add:

1 tablespoon lemon juice
1/2 teaspoon garlic powder and 1/2 teaspoon garlic juice
14 drops rum extract
8 tablespoon honey
1/2 c spiced rum

Mix. Bring to a boil and bottle.

CHUNKY GREEN & RED TOMATO SAUCE

3 tablespoon olive oil
4 cloves garlic, minced
2 large onion, chopped
6 medium green tomatoes, coarsely chopped
6 medium red tomatoes, coarsely chopped
1 carrot, finely grated
1/2 c chicken stock
1 c tomato puree
1/3 c dry red wine
1/4 c parsley, chopped
1 tablespoon fresh oregano, chopped
2 teaspoon fresh thyme, chopped
4 small sage leaves, minced
1 small chile, minced
salt and pepper to taste

In heavy saucepan heat olive oil. Add onions and garlic and saute slowly until onions are soft and golden. Add green tomatoes and saute 3 minutes, stirring frequently. Add remaining ingredients. Stir together, bring to a boil, then cover and simmer for 30-40 minutes. Uncover and stir well.

SHRIMP COCKTAIL SAUCE

1 c ketchup
4 teaspoon lemon juice
3 teaspoon horseradish
hot pepper sauce to taste *(3 drops +)*

Combine all ingredients. Mix well. Cover, refrigerate 2-3 hours to blend flavors. May store up to 2 weeks in refrigerator. Serve with chilled shrimp.

> *Note:* For steak sauces and flavorings, just add a few tablespoons per serving. Double the amount of herbs if you're using fresh rather than dried.

BEARNAISE WITH TOMATO & HERBS

1 c bearnaise sauce *(use your favorite recipe)*
1 c peeled, seeded and chopped tomatoes
1 teaspoon tarragon
1 teaspoon chervil
1/4 teaspoon thyme

Mix all ingredients together. Makes 2 cups.

DELICIOUS SAUCE

1/4 c water
2 tablespoon oil
2 tablespoon vinegar
2 tablespoon sugar
1 1/2 tablespoon soy sauce
1 1/2 tablespoon catsup
1/2-1 teaspoon hot red pepper flakes
1 tablespoon water
1 tablespoon bourbon
1 1/2 teaspoon cornstarch

Combine first 7 ingredients in small pan and bring to a boil. Mix remaining water and bourbon; add to pan and boil 2 minutes; stirring constantly. Serve hot. Makes about 1/4 cup.

HORSERADISH SAUCE

1/2 c whipping cream
2 tablespoon creamy horseradish
1 teaspoon lemon juice
pinch of sugar (optional)

Whip cream. Add remaining ingredients and mix well. Chill 2 hours before serving.

HOT SAUCE

50 cascabella chilies or 40 Thai Dragon chilies or 20 Bulgarian chilies or 20 Jalapenos
3 to 3 1/2 c distilled vinegar
3 cloves garlic
1 1/2 teaspoon sea salt
1 tablespoon sugar
1/2 fresh lemon
1 quart glass canning jar
Options:
1/2 ripe mango or papaya or 3 ripe figs or 1/2 c blended whiskey *(Jack Daniels is a good choice)*.

Cut stems off chilies and put chilies in a quart jar. Fill jar with vinegar, cover and let set for at least 5 days or up to 2 weeks. Then pour chilies and vinegar into bowl of blender or food processor. Add garlic, salt, sugar, juice and pulp from 1/2 lemon (no rind) and any optional extras. Puree until well blended. Put in saucepan and bring to a boil. Simmer about 1 hour or until consistency of tomato juice. Strain through fine strainer and bottle. Use after 24 hours. Keep in refrigerator after opening.

"SOPPIN" SAUCE FOR SHORT RIBS

2 cloves garlic, chopped
1 small dried red hot pepper
1/2 teaspoon chopped fresh cilantro or 1/4 teaspoon dried coriander
1/4 teaspoon ground cumin
1/2 teaspoon anise seeds
1/2 teaspoon salt
2 tablespoon brown sugar
1 tablespoon worchestershire sauce
1 c cider vinegar
2 c catsup
Hot pepper sauce, optional

In a blender combine garlic, red pepper, cilantro, cumin, anise seeds, salt, brown sugar and worchestershire sauce. Process until smooth. Pour in saucepan and add vinegar and catsup. Simmer uncovered for 30 minutes. Add optional hot pepper sauce. This sauce is perfect for brisket and beef short ribs. The sauce is just for "soppin". Makes 3 cups.

PORK STICKIN' SAUCE

2 tablespoon butter
1 medium onion, finely chopped
2 cloves garlic, minced
juice of 1 orange (about 1/2 c)
1 tablespoon raisins
2 tablespoon cider vinegar
2 tablespoon oil
grated zest of 1 orange
1 c molasses
1 c catsup
2 teaspoon chili powder
pinch of ground cloves
1 teaspoon prepared mustard
1 teaspoon worchestersire sauce
2 teaspoon crushed, dried, hot red peppers
1/2 teaspoon salt

Cook onion and garlic in melted butter, do not brown. In a blender combine orange juice, raisins, vinegar and oil. Process until smooth and add to onions. Stir in remaining ingredients bring to a boil. Lower heat and simmer 15 minutes, uncovered. Slather on pork before and during grilling. Makes about 3 cups.

SAUCE VERDE

1c mayonnaise, divided
1 teaspoon dry mustard
1 c sour cream
1 drop green food coloring
2 tablespoon chives, chopped
2 tablespoon parsley, chopped
2 cucumbers, peeled and chopped

Thoroughly blend 2 tablespoon mayonnaise with the dry mustard. Add remaining mayonnaise and all other ingredients. Serve over salmon patties.

TARRAGON SAUCE I
(Serve with turkey)

1 egg yolk, room temperature
1 teaspoon Dijon mustard, or more to taste room temperature
1 teaspoon white wine vinegar
1 c safflower oil
1/2 teaspoon lemon juice, room temperature
Salt, black pepper and cayenne
1 tablespoon fresh tarragon, blanched and chopped
(blanch by dropping in boiling water for 30 seconds)

Whisk egg yolk with mustard and vinegar. Gradually add oil; then add lemon juice, salt and pepper to taste. Stir in blanched tarragon, adjust seasonings and serve. Makes approximately 1 1/2 cups.

> *Note:* This sauce should be refrigerated for at least an hour before serving. It will keep a day or two in covered container. All ingredients must be room temperature before you begin.

TARRAGON SAUCE II

1/2 c butter, melted
1/4 c dry red wine
1 tablespoon tarragon vinegar
2 tablespoon fresh tarragon, snipped or 2 teaspoon dried
1 tablespoon finely chopped green onion
1/2 teaspoon salt
1/4 teaspoon pepper
dash hot sauce
3 egg yolks, lightly beaten

Heat all ingredients except egg yolks, when hot whisk in egg yolks. Stirring constantly, cook until thickened. Serve while hot with poached eggs, steaks, or stir fried carrots, broccoli and cauliflower, or serve cold as a spread for sandwiches. Makes about 1 cup.

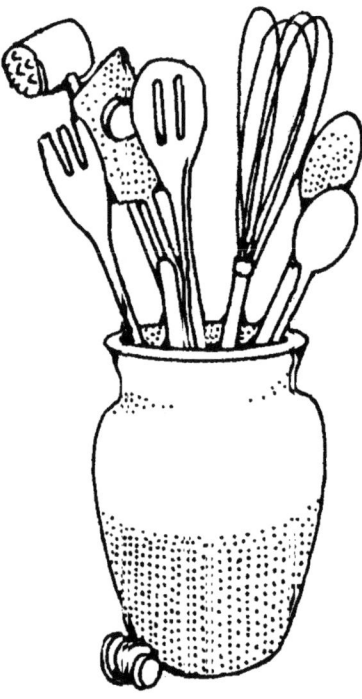

THICK SPAGHETTI SAUCE

1/2 c salad oil
4 medium onions, diced
4 medium garlic cloves, minced
16 lbs tomatoes, peeled and diced
2 (12 oz.) cans tomato paste
1/4 c sugar
1/4 c chopped parsley or 2 tablespoon parsley flakes
2 tablespoon oregano leaves
2 tablespoon salt
2 teaspoon basil
3/4 teaspoon pepper
2 bay leaves

Cook onion and garlic in oil until tender. Add tomatoes and remaining ingredients. Heat to boiling, reduce heat and simmer 2 hours. Discard bay leaves. Makes 10 pints. Each pint is enough to serve over one 8 oz package cooked spaghetti. Freezes well if used within a year.

Other ways to use this sauce:

Red Clam Sauce
Heat 2 pints Thick Spaghetti Sauce and 2 cup diced fresh clams (about 2 dozen large hardshell clams or 3-8 oz. cans minced clams, drained). Heat to boiling, cover and simmer 5 minutes or until clams are tender. Makes enough sauce to serve over one 16 oz. package cooked spaghetti for 4 main dish servings.

Meat Sauce
Cook 1 pound ground beef and 2 tablespoon chopped onion until meat is brown and onion is tender. Drain off fat. Add beef and onion to 2 pints Thick Spaghetti Sauce along with 1/2 teaspoon salt and 1/4 teaspoon pepper. Simmer for 30 minutes. Serve over 16 oz. package of cooked spaghetti. Makes 4 main dish servings.

Mushroom Sauce
In 2 tablespoon margarine cook 1/2 pound thinly sliced mushrooms until tender. Stir in 1 pint Thick Spaghetti Sauce. Simmer 15 minutes. Makes enough sauce to serve over one 8 oz. package cooked spaghetti as four accompaniment servings.

Reunion at W-Hollow.

Ron and Ronnie Clagg help Orville Shultz barbecue chicken while Lori Grizzle and Ora Jean Hill look on at a Hylton Family reunion.

Upper side of table: Carol Abdon, Mary Nelson, Corky Walker.
Lower side of table: Grace Carter, Melinda Arrick and Ronnie Clagg.
Standing: David and Julie Shultz

Reunion at W-Hollow.

Soups & Stews

SOUP SEASONINGS

Use young onions or leeks, carrots and various herbs such as green sage, thyme, marjoram, etc. Celery tops are sometimes included.

A few sprigs of parsley, thyme, celery leaves, or 2 leaves of sage and a bay leaf tied in a bag may be dropped in a kettle of soup for a short time. Remove before serving.

BLACK BEAN SOUP I

1 1/2 c dried black beans
6 to 8 c canned chicken broth
1 c chopped onion
1 c chopped celery
1 c shredded carrots
2 tablespoon butter or margarine, melted
1 c shredded red potatoes
1 bay leaf
2 cloves garlic, minced
1 teaspoon dried whole oregano
1/2 teaspoon black pepper
3 tablespoon fresh lemon juice

Wash and sort beans; put in kettle and cover with water 2 inches above the beans. Let soak over night. Drain beans, add chicken broth. Bring beans to a boil, cover, reduce heat and simmer 3 to 4 hours. Saute onion, celery and carrot in butter until vegetables are tender. Add vegetable mixture, potato, bay leaf, garlic, oregano and pepper to beans. Bring to a boil; cover, reduce heat and simmer 45 minutes or until beans are tender. Remove bay leaf and stir in lemon juice before serving. Garnish each bowl with a slice of lemon, if desired. Makes 8 cups.

BLACK BEAN SOUP II

2 teaspoon olive oil
1 large yellow onion, chopped
2 cloves garlic, minced
1/2 teaspoon dried oregano, crumbled
1/4 teaspoon dried thyme, crumbled
1/4 teaspoon ground cumin
1/8 teaspoon cayenne pepper
1 1/2 c cooked and drained black beans
1 1/2 c chicken broth
4 teaspoon chopped fresh coriander or parsley

Heat olive oil, add onion and garlic and cook until soft. Stir in oregano, thyme, cumin and cayenne pepper; cook 1 minute longer. Place half the beans in blender and puree. Add bean puree, the remaining beans and chicken broth to onion-herb mixture; reduce heat to low and cook 15 minutes. Ladle into bowls and garnish with coriander.

NAVY BEAN SOUP

2 c navy beans
2 1/2 quarts water
1 meaty ham bone
3 med. onions, chopped
2 carrots, diced
2 c celery, chopped with leaves
2 bay leaves
salt and pepper to taste

Cover the beans with water and soak overnight. Or bring to a boil and simmer 2 minutes. Cover and let stand one hour.

Add the ham bone, onions, carrots, celery, bay leaves, salt and pepper to the pot. Cook about 2 hours or until beans are tender. Remove the bay leaves and the ham bone. Remove the meat from the bone and return to the soup.

WHITE BEAN SOUP

6 strips bacon, cut into 1/2 inch pieces
3 cans white beans, drained, rinsed, divided
3 cans reduced-sodium chicken broth
1 medium onion, finely chopped
3 cloves garlic, minced
1 1/2 teaspoon dried thyme leaves
1 1/2 teaspoon dried rosemary leaves

Cook and stir bacon until crisp. Blend 1 1/2 cans beans and broth in blender until smooth. Drain all but 1 tablespoon bacon fat from skillet. Stir in onion, garlic, thyme and rosemary. Reduce heat, cover and cook until bacon is transparent (about 3 minutes). Uncover and cook until onion is tender. Add pureed bean mixture and remaining 1 1/2 cans beans to bacon mixture. Cover and simmer until beans are heated. Makes 4 servings.

BEEF STEW

1 1/2 lb beef, eye of round in 1 1/2 inch pieces
1 tablespoon vegetable oil
1 teaspoon dried thyme leaves
1 can beef broth
1/2 c cooking wine
3 large cloves garlic, crushed
1 1/2 c baby carrots
1 c frozen whole pearl onions
2 tablespoon cornstarch, dissolved in 2 tablespoon water
1 pkg. frozen sugar snap peas

Brown beef in hot oil one half at a time. Pour off drippings. Season with thyme, 1/2 teaspoon salt, and 1/2 teaspoon pepper. Stir in broth, wine and garlic. Cover and simmer 1 1/2 hours. Add carrots and onions; cover again and cook 35-40 minutes until beef and vegetables are tender. Add cornstarch mixture, cook and stir one minute. Stir in sugar snap peas. Cook 3-4 minutes on medium heat or until peas are heated through. Makes 6 servings.

BEEF BARLEY SOUP
(Main Dish Recipe)

1/2 lb ground beef
2 1/2 c cold water
1 (14 1/2 oz.) can stewed tomatoes, cut up
3/4 c sliced carrots
3/4 c sliced mushrooms
1/2 c quick barley, uncooked
2 cloves garlic, minced
1 teaspoon dried oregano leaves
salt and pepper to taste
1/2 lb velveeta cheese, cubed

Brown meat. Drain. Stir in water, tomatoes, carrots, mushrooms, barley, garlic and oregano. Bring to a boil; reduce heat. Cover and simmer until vegetables and barley are tender. Season to taste. Stir in cheese and stir until melted. Makes 6 (1 cup) servings.

BEEF STEW

1 lb trimmed beef chuck, cut into 1 inch cubes
4 oz. carrots, peeled and cut into 1/4 inch slices
4 oz. celery, peeled and cut crosswise into 1/4 inch slices
4 oz. leek, white only, cut across into 1/4 inch slices
2 c tomatoes with juice, crushed
5 cloves garlic, peeled and minced
1/4 teaspoon dried thyme
1/4 teaspoon dried oregano
1 1/2 bay leaves
pinch of pepper
1 c water
2 small potatoes, cut in chunks

Mix all ingredients and bring to a boil. Cover and simmer about one hour or until meat and vegetables are tender. Makes about 3 or 4 servings. Can also be cooked in crock pot.

CHICKEN AND OKRA GUMBO

5 c sliced fresh okra
2 large onions, chopped
2 medium green bell peppers, chopped
2 tomatoes, peeled and chopped
3 tablespoon olive oil
1 frying chicken, cut into serving pieces
2 tablespoon olive oil
1/2 teaspoon fresh black pepper
1/4 to 1/2 teaspoon ground cayenne pepper

Cook okra, onions, green peppers, tomatoes and 1/2 teaspoon salt in 3 tablespoon hot oil about 30 minutes until vegetables are tender. Meanwhile, brown the chicken pieces in 2 tablespoon hot oil about 15 minutes turning once to brown. Drain off fat. Add pepper, red pepper, 4 cups water and 1 teaspoon salt. Bring to boiling, then reduce heat to simmer, cover and simmer for 30-40 minutes until chicken is very tender. Add okra mixture and simmer an additional 30 minutes. Serve over rice and garnish with fresh parsley.

CORN SOUP

7 med ears fresh corn
1 c canned chicken broth
1/4 c butter or margarine
2 c milk
1 teaspoon ground cumin
1 clove garlic minced
1 (4 oz.) can green chilies, undrained
1/8 teaspoon hot sauce, more if desired
1 teaspoon ground white pepper
8 (6 inch) corn tortillas
2 c vegetable oil
1/2 teaspoon salt
1 c shredded monterey jack cheese with jalapeno peppers
1 c diced tomato
2 c diced cooked chicken
1 (8 oz.) jar salsa
1 can sliced ripe olives, sliced and drained
1 (8 oz.) carton sour cream
8 green onions, sliced
1 med. avocado, peeled and diced

Cut corn from cob. Combine corn and broth in electric blender; cover and process until smooth. Melt butter in pan; add corn mixture and simmer 5 minutes, stirring constantly. Stir in milk, cumin and garlic and bring to a boil. Add chilies, hot sauce and white pepper. Reduce heat and simmer uncovered 30 minutes. Stack tortillas and cut in 1 inch pieces. Fry in 2 cups of oil until golden. Drain on paper towels, sprinkle with salt, add cheese to soup, stirring until melted. To serve, place 2 tablespoon tomatoes and 1/4 cup chicken in eight soup bowls. Ladle soup into bowls. Top with tortillas, salsa, sour cream, green onions and avocado. Makes 8 cups.

EASY CRAB CHOWDER

3 tablespoon butter
1/2 c choped onion
1/2 c chopped celery
3 c milk
1 (10 3/4 oz.) can cream of potato soup
1 (8 oz.) can creamed corn
1 (6 1/2 oz.) can crabmeat, drained
1 bay leaf
1/4 teaspoon dried thyme
1/4 teaspoon salt
1/4 c dry sherry, optional
Fresh parsley for garnish

Melt butter in large saucepan over medium heat. Saute onions and celery until softened. Add remaining ingredients except sherry and parsley and continue cooking until heated through and flavors are blended, stirring frequently. Stir in sherry and simmer an additional 15 minutes. Remove bay leaf. Garnish each serving with chopped parsley.

CREOLE SHRIMP GUMBO

1 lg onion, quartered and sliced
1 pkg. (10 oz.) frozen okra
1 yellow pepper, chopped
1 c chopped celery, including leaves
1/4 c minced fresh parsley leaves
4 cloves garlic, thinly sliced
2 bay leaves
2 teaspoon each salt and fresh thyme leaves
1 teaspoon each cayenne and black pepper
1/2 teaspoon ground allspice
1/4 lb bacon, thinly sliced crosswise
vegetable oil
2/3 c unsifted all-purpose flour
1 c (6 oz.) tomato paste
2 qt chicken broth or water
1 can (15 to 16 oz.) whole peeled tomatoes, drained and chopped
2 lb jumbo shrimp, shelled and deveined
1/2 c chopped scallion greens
1 tablespoon distilled vinegar
cooked white rice

Mix vegetables, 1/4 cup parsley and seasonings. Saute bacon, remove bacon and pour fat into glass measure; add oil to measure 2/3 cup. Add flour to fat and cook, stirring until dark. Add vegetable mixture; saute 2 minutes. Blend tomato paste with 1 cup broth, add to pan. Add bacon, tomatoes and remaining broth. Boil; reduce heat. Add 3 shrimp; simmer 1 hour add remaining shrimp and parsley, the scallions and vinegar. Heat through. Remove from heat; cover. Let stand 10 minutes. Serve in bowl over rice. Makes 8 servings.

SEAFOOD GUMBO

1/4 c olive oil
1/4 c all-purpose flour
1 med. onion, thinly sliced
2 cloves garlic, minced
1 sweet green pepper, chopped
1 or 2 jalapeno peppers, seeded and chopped
3 stalks celery, sliced
2 cans (14 1/2 oz.) tomatoes, undrained
1/4 teaspoon red pepper flakes
1 teaspoon paprika
1/8 teaspoon cayenne pepper
5 drops hot pepper sauce or to taste
2 chicken bouillon cubes, dissolved in 9 c water
1 c uncooked white rice
1 lb med size shrimp, deveined and cut in half
1/2 lb scallops
1 pt. oysters
1 teaspoon salt
1/2 teaspoon black pepper

To make roux: Heat oil in Dutch oven. Stir in flour, a tablespoon at a time; cook, stirring, until flour begins to brown, 3 or 4 minutes. Add onion, garlic, green pepper, celery and jalapeno; cook until celery is cooked, 10 to 12 minutes. Add tomatoes, red pepper, paprika, cayenne, pepper sauce, bouillon liquid and simmer, covered for 20 minutes. Add shrimp, oysters, scallops, salt and pepper. Simmer about 3 minutes or util seafood is done.

BRUNSWICK STEW

2 pork chops (about 1 lb)
2 whole chicken breasts
1 lb round steak, cut into bite-size pieces
1 1/2 quarts water
1 can tomato sauce
2 teaspoon hot pepper sauce or to taste
1/2 c vinegar
1/4 c sugar
2 c chopped onion
4 to 5 cloves garlic, minced
2 cans tomatoes with juice, chopped
2 cans cream style corn
2 cans whole kernel corn, drained
1 c toasted bread crumbs
salt and pepper to taste

Put meat in saucepan and cover with water. Cook, covered about 1 1/2 hours or until meat is tender. Strain broth and refrigerate overnight. Place meat in another container and refrigerate after you have removed bones and diced meat. The next day remove fat from stock; add tomato sauce, hot pepper sauce, vinegar, sugar, onions, garlic and tomatoes. Simmer uncovered 45 minutes. Add corn, meat and chicken. Simmer for about 15 minutes. Stir in bread crumbs, season with salt and butter. Makes 6 quarts.

CREAM OF BROCCOLI SOUP

1 c diced broccoli
1/3 c leek, diced
1/3 c onions, diced
3 tablespoon butter
3 tablespoon flour
3 c chicken stock
1 c light cream
1/4 teaspoon thyme
1/4 teaspoon pepper
1/2 teaspoon salt
1/2 c white wine (optional)

Melt butter and add wine; saute vegetables five minutes. Blend in flour and add chicken stock. Season and simmer until vegetables are tender. Add cream and serve.

Chili Recipes

BASIC CHILI CON CARNE

1 lb dried pinto beans (2 1/2 c)
2 qts water
1 1/2 lbs ground chuck
1 lg onion, chopped
2 cloves garlic, minced
1 med. green pepper, seeded and chopped
1 can (1 lb 12 oz.) whole tomatoes
1 (6 oz.) can tomato paste
1 can beef broth
3 tablespoon chili powder
2 tablespoon leaf oregano, crumbled
1 tablespoon ground cumin
1 tablespoon salt

Wash and sort beans. Soak overnight. Next morning bring to a boil and simmer an hour. Brown meat and add onion, garlic and green pepper. Drain fat and add tomatoes (undrained), tomato paste, broth, chili powder, oregano, cumin and salt. Break up tomatoes with wooden spoon and bring to boil. Cover and simmer for an hour. Add beans and 2 1/2 cups of the cooking liquid to meat mixture. Cover and simmer 2-3 hours until beans are tender but not mushy.

Note: If you like very hot and spicy chili, add chopped jalapeno peppers. This is a good basic recipe and can also be used in the following recipes.

CHILI-NOODLE CASSEROLE

4 c basic chili con carne
1 can (1 lb) whole tomatoes
1 can (4 1/2 oz.) sliced mushrooms, drained
2 c uncooked curly egg noodles
1 teaspoon salt
1/4 teaspoon pepper
1/2 c shredded cheddar cheese

Combine chili and tomatoes. Break up tomatoes with a wooden spoon. Bring to a boil and pour into a casserole. Add mushrooms, noodles, salt and pepper. Stir; cover. Bake in 350 degree oven for 45 minutes or until noodles are tender. Sprinkle with cheese and bake 5 minutes more. Makes 6 servings. Delicious served with garlic bread and fruit salad.

WHOLE-MEAL SALAD WITH GUACAMOLE DRESSING

1 sm. head iceburg lettuce
1 bunch radishes
1/2 bunch green onions
1/4 lb cheddar cheese
3 med. tomatoes, peeled and seeded
1 c corn chips

Guacamole Dressing

1 clove garlic, crushed
1 lg avocado, halved, pitted and peeled
1 tablespoon lemon juice
1/2 teaspoon salt
pinch of sugar
Hot pepper sauce to taste
3 tablespoon minced onion
1/4 c sour cream
3 c basic chili con carne

Shred lettuce, slice radishes, chop green onions and tomatoes and shred cheese; chill. Rub salad bowl with garlic and discard garlic. Put avocado in bowl and mash. Add half the chopped tomatoes and sprinkle with lemon juice. Mix onion and sour cream. Cover and chill until serving time. Heat chili. To serve, arrange bowls of vegetables, cheese and chips (in separate bowls). Ladle chili on top of bed of lettuce on each plate; then place whatever else you want, ending with Guacamole dressing.

CORNBURGER LOAF

3 c basic chili con carne
1 long loaf French bread, halved lengthwise
1 can cream style corn
1 c shredded cheddar cheese
1 c sliced olives

Heat chili and cook off excess liquid. Spread hot chili on cut sides of bread. Spoon corn over chili; top with cheese and olives. Place on cookie sheet. Bake in 350 degree oven for 15 minutes or until cheese is melted. Cut into crosswise pieces to serve. Makes 6 servings. Good served with a tossed salad and a fresh fruit dessert.

CHILI CON CARNE

2 lbs lean beef stew meat, cut into 1 1/2 - 2 inch pieces
3 med tomatoes, diced
1 1/2 c water
1 c chopped onion
2 sm garlic cloves, crushed
1 teaspoon salt
1 1/2 c tomato sauce
1 (4 oz.) can chopped green chilies
1 tablespoon chili powder
1 tablespoon ground cumin

Combine meat, tomatoes, water, onion, garlic and

salt and bring to a boil. Reduce heat, cover and simmer, adding water as necessary so meat is always partially covered, until beef is tender enough to shred, about 2 hours. Remove meat and shred. Return meat to pan, add remaining ingredients, cover and simmer 30 minutes stirring often. Serve hot. Makes 6-8 servings.

CHICKEN CHILI

4 bacon strips, chopped
1 c chopped onion
1 c chopped green pepper
2 cloves garlic, chopped
1 3/4 lb ground chicken
1/4 c chili powder
2 c canned crushed tomatoes
1 c chicken broth
2 tablespoon brown sugar
2 tablespoon cider vinegar
1 tablespoon + hot sauce
1 teaspoon salt
2 cans (15 1/4 oz. each) red kidney beans, drained & rinsed

Cook bacon until brown, add onion, green pepper and garlic. Cook until onion is tender, about 5 minutes. Add chicken; cook, stirring to break up lumps until chicken loses its pink color. Stir in chili powder, tomatoes, broth, sugar, vinegar, pepper sauce and salt. Cover and simmer, stirring often until chili is thickened, about 45 minutes. Stir in beans and cook 15 minutes longer. Makes 6 servings.

CHILE WITH PORK

1 (4 lb) boneless pork roast, trimmed and cut in 1/2 inch cubes
1/4 c bacon drippings
8 to 12 dried red chilies, washed and seeded
4 c water
1 clove garlic
1 teaspoon salt

Brown meat in bacon drippings. Combine chilies, water and garlic in electric blender or food processor; process until smooth. Add chile mixture to pork; stir in salt. Bring to a boil; reduce heat and simmer uncovered one hour or until pork is tender, stirring occasionally. Makes 7 cups.

CHILI VERDE

4 fresh poblano peppers
5 tomatillos, peeled and quartered
1 c chopped green onion
1/2 c chopped fresh cilantro
1 can (4 oz.) mild green chilies, drained
2 jalapeno peppers, halved, seeded and chopped
1 tablespoon oil
1 pork butt (about 2 lbs) cut in 1 inch cubes
1 c chopped onions
3 cloves garlic, chopped
1 tablespoon ground cumin
1 teaspoon sugar
1 can (13 3/4 oz.) chicken broth

Broil poblano peppers, turning until blackened, about 15 minutes. Place in bag; close; let stand 15 minutes. Core, seed, peel and coarsely chop. Puree roasted peppers, tomatillos, onion, cilantro, chilies and jalapeno in processor or blender. Heat oil and brown pork; remove pork from skillet and add onion and garlic and cook until tender. Stir in cumin, sugar and salt; cook 1 minute. Combine meat, roasted pepper mixture and broth. Cover and simmer until meat is tender, about 1 hour. Uncover last 15 minutes if chili is not thick enough. Makes 4 servings.

HOT RED CHILI

20 dried red, hot chilies, washed and seeded
4 lbs coarsly ground beef
1 med onion, chopped
4-5 cloves garlic, minced
1 teaspoon vegetable oil
1 1/2 teaspoon salt
1 teaspoon oregano
1 teaspoon ground cumin
1/4 teaspoon pepper
1 can tomato sauce
3/4 c water
2 tablespoon water

Place chilies in saucepan with water to cover; cover and simmer until tender. Drain, reserving 1/4 cup liquid. Put chilies and reserved liquid in blender. Process until smooth. Cook ground beef, chopped onion and garlic in oil in a large pot until meat is brown. Drain. Add pureed peppers, salt, oregano, cumin and pepper. Stir in tomato sauce and 3/4 cup of water. Cover and bring to a boil and simmer, adding water when necessary. Cook mixture until slightly thickened. Makes 8 cups.

RED HOT CHILI

2 tablespoon oil
1 beef brisket (about 2 lbs) cut in 1/4 inch cubes
1 c chopped onion
3 jalapeno peppers, halved, seeded and chopped
2 cloves garlic, chopped
1/4 c chili powder
1 tablespoon ground cumin
1/2 teaspoon salt
1/2 teaspoon ground red pepper
2 cans (14 1/2 oz.) stewed tomatoes
1 can beef broth
1 bottle (12 oz.) beer
1 bay leaf

Heat oil and brown beef, part at a time. Remove from pan and add onion, jalapeno pepper and garlic to drippings in pan, cook until tender. Stir in chili powder, cumin, salt and red pepper and cook 1 minute. Return meat to pot. Stir in tomatoes, broth, beer and bay leaf. Heat to boiling, reduce heat and simmer, covered for 1 1/2 hours. Remove cover for last 20 minutes to let chili thicken. Makes 8 servings.

CORN, TOMATO, & SUMMER SQUASH SOUP

1 tablespoon olive oil
2 cloves garlic, freshly chopped
1 lg onion, chopped
5 c chicken broth
4 med tomatoes, chopped
2 c fresh corn kernels
1 Anaheim chili; seeded and chopped or 2 tablespoon canned mild chopped chile pepper
4 med zucchini, sliced
1/2 c fresh basil, chopped
Garnishes—sour cream and chopped cilantro

Heat oil, add garlic and onion and saute until softened. Add chicken broth, tomatoes, corn and chile pepper and simmer for 15 minutes. Add zucchini and basil and simmer for 5 minutes longer. Serve hot, passing garnishes of sour cream and cilantro. Makes 8 servings.

FISH SOUP WITH MINT

1 lg onion, peeled and cut into 2 by 1/8 inch pieces
4 ribs celery, cut in 2 by 1/8 inch strips
6 carrots (about 1 lb) peeled and cut in 2 by 1/8 inch strips
4 to 5 sprigs fresh mint
4 bay leaves
1/2 c white wine
6 c fish stock

1 lb fresh, firm-fleshed fish, such as cod, scallops, monkfish, flounder, sole or halibut, cut in 1 by 2 inch cubes
salt and white pepper
1/2 c finely chopped fresh mint leaves or 1/4 c crushed dried mint
mint sprigs for garnish

Cook onion, carrots and celery in butter, covered, for 5 minutes. Wrap mint and bay leaves in cheesecloth and tie with string. Add to vegetables with wine and stock. Cook until vegetables are tender. Remove mint-bay leaf bundle and add fish. Cook until fish is done but solid (do not overcook). Season to taste with salt and pepper and add chopped mint. Ladle into bowls and garnish with mint sprigs. Makes 4 servings.

Homemade Fish Stock

1 lb mild fish bones
1 qt water
1 bunch fresh parsley stems
1 med. onion, thinly sliced

Combine all ingredients in large saucepan. Bring to a boil; cover, reduce heat and simmer 2 hours. Pour mixture through a wire mesh strainer, discarding bones, parsley and onion. Makes 2 1/2 cups.

LAMB STEW I

1 1/2 lb lamb shoulders, cut in 1 inch cubes
1/4 c flour
1/2 teaspoon salt
1/8 teaspoon pepper
1 tablespoon salad oil
1 large onion, thinly sliced
3 c water
2 teaspoon minced garlic
1/4 teaspoon dried rosemary
1 (16 oz.) can garbanzo beans, drained
2 med carrots, sliced

Dredge lamb cubes in mixture of the flour, salt and pepper. Saute in hot oil until browned on all sides. Remove from pan. Saute onions until translucent. Return lamb to pan and add water, garlic and rosemary. Bring to a boil then reduce heat, cover and cook about 1 1/2 hours checking occasionally to see that there is enough liquid. Add garbanzos and carrots and continue cooking 20-30 minutes. Use a mixture of flour and water to thicken liquid if necessary.

LAMB STEW II

1 tablespoon salad oil
2 lbs lamb shoulder, cubed
2 c chicken broth
1/2 c chopped tomatoes
1/2 c sliced onion
1/2 teaspoon dried marjoram leaves, crushed
1 (10 oz.) pkg frozen peas and carrots
1/2 c sliced celery
1/3 c water
1/4 c flour
cooked noodles

Brown lamb is hot oil. Add broth, tomatoes with juice, onion, and marjoram. Reduce heat to simmer and cook about 1-1 1/2 hours. Add vegetables and cook another 15-20 minutes or until meat and vegetables are tender, stirring occasionally. Blend water and flour until smooth, slowly stir into sauce. Cook, stirring until thickened. Serve over noodles.

Note: Marjoram is an annual herb which must be sown each year. It has a subtle flavor which can be used alone or combined with most other herbs. On its own it goes well with poultry, fish, eggs, vegetables and sauces. A traditional mix of herbs includes thyme and sage with marjoram.

LAMB AND BARLEY STEW
(For left over lamb)

2 tablespoon butter
2 carrots, chopped
2 celery stalks, chopped
1 onion, chopped
3 lg garlic cloves, chopped
1 c pearl barley, rinsed
4 c canned beef broth
3 c cooked lamb, cut in 1/2 in pieces

Melt butter, add carrots, celery, onions and garlic; saute until vegetables are beginning to soften, about 8 minutes. Add barley; stir until coated, about 2 minutes. Add broth and simmer until all is tender, about 45 minutes. Add lamb and heat through. Makes 4 servings.

OVEN BAKED LAMB STEW

1 c dried white beans
water
2 lbs boneless lamb shoulder, cubed
1/4 c butter
2 onions, sliced
1 garlic clove, minced
1 (19 oz.) can tomatoes
1 bay leaf
1 1/2 teaspoon salt
1/2 teaspoon each pepper and paprika
1/2 teaspoon herb seasoning
1 1/2 c chicken broth
3 tablespoon flour

Wash beans, cover with water and bring to a boil for 2 minutes. Let stand for 1 hour, cover with fresh water and cook until tender. Brown lamb cubes in butter, add onions and garlic, cook a few more minutes. Add drained beans and the rest of the ingredients except flour. Cover and bake in 350 oven for 2 hours. Mix flour and 1/4 cup water until smooth, stir into lamb mixture and bake an additional 15 minutes.

> *Note:* Bay leaves are very spicy and aromatic. They are used primarily in soups, stews, and meat dishes which require longer cooking times. Bay leaves can be used whole or crushed. If used whole they should be removed before serving the food. Bay plants are not inexpensive, a single plant usually costs about $8 or $9 but with care they are very long lived. Bay is not a winter hardy plant and must be brought in during the winter months. The best way to raise a bay plant is to keep it potted and then it is easy to move from the outdoors to inside during cold weather. The plant can reach a height of 30 to 40 feet eventually. Since this is one of the herbs that is as flavorful dried as fresh, buying the leaves is usually more feasible for most people.

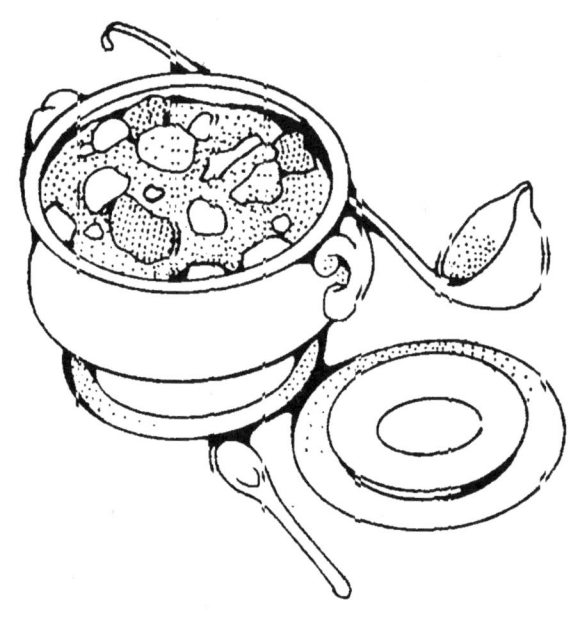

QUICK LAMB STEW

Brown 1 1/2 pounds stewing lamb, cubed (left over lamb roast may be substituted) with 1 sliced onion and 1 sliced green pepper in oil. Add 1 cup water and simmer 20 minutes. Add 2 diced stalks celery with leaves, 1 box frozen limas, 1 bay leaf, 1/2 teaspoon celery salt and salt and pepper to taste. Cook 45 minutes. Add 1 box frozen cut corn; simmer 5 more minutes. Serves 4.

CHILLED PARSLEY AND TARRAGON SOUP

3 tablespoon butter
1 c chopped onion
4 c chicken stock or canned broth
1 bunch fresh parsley, trimmed and chopped
1 lg potato peeled and chopped
3 tablespoon chopped fresh tarragon
1/4 c half and half

Melt butter; add onion and saute 5 minutes. Add stock, 1 bunch chopped parsley, and potato. Bring to a boil. Simmer until potato is tender. Mix in tarragon. Puree in blender in batches. Transfer to bowl. Mix in half and half. Chill at least 3 hours. Season soup to taste with salt and pepper. Ladle into bowls. Sprinkle with parsley and serve. Makes 4 servings.

PORK STEW

2 lbs boneless pork shoulder, well trimmed and cut into 1 1/2 in. pieces
1 tablespoon olive oil
1 lg. onion, coarsely chopped
1 teaspoon salt
1/2 teaspoon black pepper
1 can (28 oz.) tomatoes, undrained, coarsely chopped
1 c picante sauce
2 beef bouillion cubes
1 1/2 teaspoon thyme leaves, crushed
2 bay leaves
1 lb. carrots, sliced 3/4 in. thick

Cook pork in oil until no longer pink; drain. Add onions, cook 2 minutes. Sprinkle with salt and pepper. Add tomatoes, picante sauce, beef bouillon cubes, thyme, and bay leaves. Bring to a boil; cover and simmer 15 minutes. Stir in carrots and potatoes, cover and cook 50 to 60 minutes or until pork and vegetables are tender. Makes about 9 cups of stew.

PORK AND CARAWAY STEW

1 lg head cabbage
2 lb potatoes, diced
1 1/2 lb pork spareribs, in pieces
1 teaspoon salt
1/2 teaspoon pepper
3 c chicken stock
1/2 teaspoon caraway seeds
4 teaspoon chopped celery leaves

Core cabbage and separate the leaves, cut out large ribs and blanch about 1 minute in boiling water. Arrange cabbage leaves, potatoes and spare ribs in layers in a casserole and sprinkle with the salt and pepper. Pour stock over and cover. Bake at 350 for 1 hour. Toward the end of baking time sprinkle on the celery leaves and caraway seed.

SAUSAGE AND POTATO STEW

12 oz. Italian sausage, cut in 1/2 in. slices
2 c water
1 tablespoon + 1 teaspoon all purpose flour
1 lg green bell pepper, cored and cut in bite size pieces
2 lg potatoes, peeled and cut in bite size chunks
1 lg onion, cut in thin wedges
1/2 teaspoon minced garlic
1/2 teaspoon salt
1/4 teaspoon dried thyme leaves

Bring sausage and 1/4 c water to a boil. Cover and simmer 5 minutes until sausage firms up. Uncover and cook about 3 minutes longer until water evaporates. Sprinkle flour with sausage, add remaining water. Add other ingredients, cover and cook until potatoes are barely tender. Uncover and cook until potatoes are tender and sauce is slightly thickened. Serves 4.

SHORT RIB STEW

1 teaspoon salad oil
4 lb beef short ribs, cut into pieces
1 small can mushrooms
1/2 c sliced onions
3 c water
1/2 teaspoon salt
1/2 teaspoon dried thyme
1/2 teaspoon dried basil
1/8 teaspoon black pepper
1 1/2 lb small red potatoes, halved
1/2 c beef stock or water (dry red wine is good)
1/4 c flour

Heat oil in Dutch oven. Brown ribs on all sides and remove. Saute mushrooms and onions until lightly browned, remove and set aside for later. Add water to pan, return ribs, salt, thyme, basil and pepper. Bring to a boil then cover, lower heat to a simmer and cook about 1 1/2 hours until ribs are tender. When ribs are tender, add mushrooms, onions, and potatoes. Cover and cook until potatoes are done. Stir beef stock or water into flour. Gradually add to stew and stir until thickened.

SPICY PORK STEW
(A one pot meal)

1 tablespoon vegetable oil
2 1/2 lbs pork shoulder or boneless country-style spareribs, cut in 1 in. pieces
1 lg. onion, chopped
6 lg. garlic cloves, chopped
1 1/2 tablespoon chopped jalapeno chile
2 (14 1/2 oz.) cans mexican-style stewed tomatoes
1 tablespoon ground cumin
1 tablespoon dried oregano
2 (15 oz.) cans kidney beans, rinsed and drained

Heat oil. Season pork with salt and pepper. Add pork to hot oil and saute until no longer pink. Add onion, garlic and jalapeno and cook 5 minutes longer. Add tomatoes with their liquid, cumin and oregano. Cover pot, reduce heat and simmer until pork is tender, about 1 hour. Mix beans in stew and heat until heated through. Season with salt and pepper. Makes 6 servings.

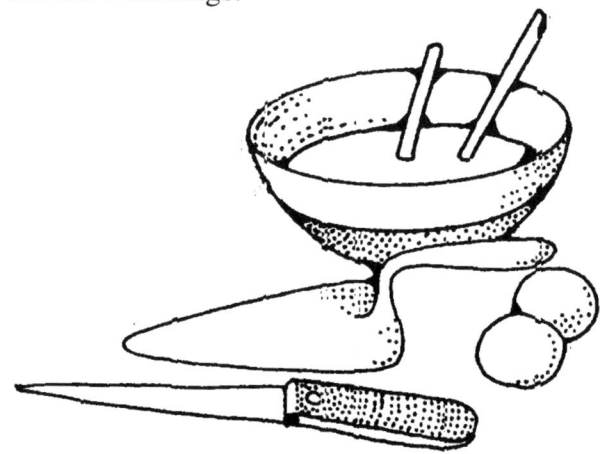

CREAM OF REUBEN SOUP

6 c chicken broth
12 oz. cooked corned beef
8 oz. kraut, drained
1 lg carrot, chopped
1/2 small onion, chopped
1 clove garlic, minced
1/2 teaspoon thyme
1/4 teaspoon white pepper
1/4 teaspoon tarragon
1 bay leaf
3 tablespoon corn starch
1/3 c water
12 oz. Swiss cheese, cut up
1 c Swiss cheese, shredded
1 c half and half
Rye bread croutons

In 4 quart stock pot combine broth, corned beef, kraut, vegetables and seasonings. Bring to a boil, then reduce heat, cover, and simmer 30 minutes. Remove bay leaf. Stir together cornstarch and water until smooth then add to soup. Return soup to boiling and cook another 2 minutes. Reduce heat, stir in cheeses until melted then add half and half. Heat through. Served topped with croutons.

FRESH VEGETABLE SOUP

1/2 c tomato juice
4 c peeled, seeded and chopped tomatoes
1 1/4 c peeled, seeded and chopped cucumber
1/2 c minced green pepper
1/2 c minced onion
2 c tomato juice, chilled
1/3 c olive oil
3 tablespoon vinegar
1 clove garlic, minced
2-3 tablespoon lemon juice
1 teaspoon salt
1/2 teaspoon paprika
1/2 teaspoon pepper
1/4 to 1 teaspoon hot sauce (depends on hotness of sauce)
croutons (optional)
Sour cream (optional)

Pour 1/2 cup tomato juice into ice cube trays (about 6 cubes); freeze. Combine chopped tomato, cucumber, green pepper, onion and 2 cups tomato juice in large bowl. Stir. Add oil and next 7 ingredients; stir. Cover and chill at least 4 hours. To serve ladle into chilled soup bowls, and place a tomato juice cube in each serving. If desired garnish each serving with croutons and a dollop of sour cream. Delicious on a hot summer day. Makes 8 cups.

TOMATO-VEAL STEW

3 lbs veal, cut in 1 1/2 in pieces
1/2 c all-purpose flour
1/3 c salad oil
3 med onions, quartered
1/4 c red cooking wine
1 tablespoon prepared mustard
2 1/2 teaspoon salt
1/2 teaspoon thyme leaves
1/8 teaspoon pepper
2 bay leaves
5 tomatoes, peeled and diced
1 (10 oz.) pkg. frozen peas

Coat veal with flour; reserve left over flour. Brown veal in salad oil and set aside. To fat left in pan add onions and cook about 5 minutes until tender. Blend remaining flour into onion and oil. Stir in wine, mustard, salt, thyme, pepper and bay leaves. Add meat and tomatoes. Cover and simmer 45 minutes or until meat is fork tender. Discard bay leaves. Add peas and heat through. Makes about 10 servings.

OYSTER STEW

1/4 c butter
1 qt. oysters in liquid
1 qt milk
1 c heavy cream
1 teaspoon salt
3 tablespoon chopped parsley
1/4 teaspoon white pepper
2 teaspoon worchestershire sauce
2 dashes tabasco sauce
paprika

Melt butter in heavy saucepan. Saute oysters and 1/2 cup oyster liquid until oysters start to curl around edges. Combine remaining ingredients in another pan and heat until bubbles start to appear; add to oysters. Sprinkle paprika on top when serving.

BARLEY VEGETABLE SOUP

5 1/3 c water
2 teaspoon salt
2 med. tomatoes, cored and chopped
1/3 c barley
1 bay leaf
1/4 teaspoon dried sage, crumbled
1/4 teaspoon dried oregano, crumbled
1 tablespoon olive oil
1 onion, chopped
1 carrot, thinly sliced
2 med. zucchini, quartered and sliced
1 med. yellow squash, sliced
pepper and parmesan cheese
chives, optional

Bring 5 cups water to a boil with salt. Add tomatoes, barley, bay leaf, sage and oregano. Simmer until barley is tender, about 30 minutes. Heat olive oil, add onion and cook 2 minutes. Stir in carrot and celery and cook 3 minutes. Add zucchini and yellow squash and remaining 1/3 cup water; simmer until vegetables are tender and moisture has evaporated, about 10 minutes. Stir vegetables into barley mixture; season with pepper, cover and simmer 10 minutes. Sprinkle with cheese and chives. Makes 4 servings.

MEXICAN CORN SOUP

3 1/2 c fresh or thawed frozen corn
1 c chicken stock
1/4 c butter
2 c milk
1 garlic clove, pressed
1 teaspoon dried oregano
Salt and pepper
2-3 tablespooon rinsed, seeded and finely chopped green chilies
1 c peeled diced tomato
1 c cubed Montery Jack cheese
chopped fresh parsley or cilantro (garnish)

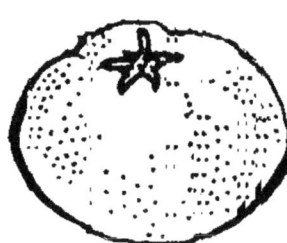

Combine corn and stock in blender and mix to fine puree. Melt butter, add corn and simmer for five minutes, stirring frequently. Blend in milk, garlic, oregano, salt and pepper to taste and bring to a boil. Reduce heat, add chilies and simmer 5 minutes. Remove from heat and stir in cheese until completely melted. Pour over tomatoes. Pour in serving bowls and garnish with parsley. Makes 6 servings.

CHICKEN SOUP

1 carrot
3/4 c celery
1 sweet green pepper
1 onion
3/4 c cooked chicken, chopped
1 apple, peeled and sliced 1/4 inch thick
4 tablespoon butter
1/3 c flour
1 teaspoon curry powder
2 whole cloves
1 sprig parsley
1 c fresh or canned tomatoes
4 c chicken broth (may be made from boullion cubes)
2 1/2 to 3 c milk

Chop celery, carrot, green pepper and onion; fry lightly in butter, stirring often. Add all other ingredients except milk. Cover and simmer for fifty minutes. Add milk; bring to a boil. Serves 6.

GARDEN VEGETABLE STEW

2 tablespoon butter or margarine
1 and 1/2 med onion, chopped
2 med carrots, thinly sliced
3 1/2 c vegetable broth (recipe follows)
2/3 c uncooked brown rice or regular long-grain rice
1 c fresh or frozen whole kernel corn
1/2 med. zucchini, thinly sliced
1/2 med. yellow summer squash, thinly sliced
1 tablespoon chopped fresh or 1 teaspoon dried basil leaves
1 teaspoon chopped fresh or 1/4 teaspoon dried thyme leaves
1/4 teaspoon pepper
4 new potatoes, cut into fourths
1 lg red pepper, cut into strips
1 can (15-16 oz.) garbanzo beans, drained

Cook carrots and onions in margarine until onions are tender. Stir in vegetable broth and rice. Cover and simmer 20 minutes. Stir in remaining ingredients. Cover and simmer 10-15 minutes or until vegetables are tender.

Vegetable Broth

6 c coarsely chopped vegetables--bell peppers, carrots, celery, leeks, mushroom stems, potato, spinach or zucchini
1 med onion, coarsely chopped
1/2 c parsley sprigs
8 c cold water
2 tablespoon chopped fresh or 2 teaspoon dried each basil and thyme
1 teaspoon salt
1/4 teaspoon pepper
2 cloves garlic, chopped
2 bay leaves

Mix all ingredients and bring to a boil. Reduce heat, cover and simmer for one hour; stirring occasionally. Cool slightly. Strain broth and use immediately or cover and refrigerate up to 24 hours or freeze for future use.

Glennis Stuart Liles, Mary Belle Johnson, Nathan Johnson, and Lonnie Johnson putting up the headstone at their grandmother's grave.

Right: Charles Gannon took this photo, the cover photo, and other pictures of herbs and peppers used in the book.

Elizabeth Reffett makes a good supply of herbal vinegar.

Lunch & One Dish Meals

BRUNCH POTATOES

1 (16 oz.) pkg frozen hash brown potatoes, thawed
1 c cooked ham, diced in 1/2 pieces
1 c monterey jack cheese, shredded
1/4 c green onions, chopped
1 (4 oz.) can green chilies, chopped and drained
3/4 c milk
6 eggs
1/4 teaspoon salt
1/8 teaspoon pepper
1/4 teaspoon paprika
1/2 c cheddar cheese, shredded

Heat oven to 350 degrees. Spread potatoes in a 13 x 9 inch greased baking dish. Top with ham, Monterey cheese, green onions and chilies. In medium bowl combine milk, eggs, salt, pepper and paprika; beat until frothy. Pour over potatoes. Bake uncovered for 30 minutes; sprinkle with cheddar cheese and continue baking for about 10 minutes longer or until eggs are set.

LAMPLE PIE

1 (17 1/4 oz.) pkg puff pastry, thawed and cut into two 12 inch circles
1 egg, beaten (glaze)
6 oz. bacon
8 oz. cooked lamb, cut into 1/2 inch dice
1 lg onion, cut into 3/4 inch dice
1 c chicken stock, preferably homemade
1 tablespoon tomato paste
1/2 lb Granny Smith or Golden Delicious apples, peeled, cored and cut into 1 inch dice
12 fresh mint leaves, chopped
1 teaspoon mixed chopped fresh rosemary and sage or 1/2 teaspoon mixed dried crumbled
salt and pepper

Fit one puff pastry into buttered 10 inch pie pan, trim edges. Brush with some of the egg glaze. Prick bottom with a fork; freeze 15 minutes. Bake until just beginning to color, about 15 minutes. Set aside. Fry bacon until crisp, remove and drain on paper towels. Crumble bacon. Heat bacon drippings, add lamb and onion and stir until browned. Do not allow onion to burn. Remove and drain on paper towels. Pour out drippings and return bacon, lamb and onions to skillet. Stir in stock and tomato paste and cook until mixture is consistency of thick stew. Mix in apples, mint, rosemary and sage and cook 5 minutes to blend flavors. Season with salt and pepper. Spoon mixture into baked pastry shell. Cover with second puff pastry circle. Seal edges. Brush remaining egg glaze on pastry. Make 2 or 3 slits in top. Bake 10 minutes at 450 degrees, reduce heat to 350 degrees and continue to bake until pastry is puffed and deep brown, 20-30 minutes. Serve hot. Serves 4 to 6.

HAM WITH STEWED OKRA AND RICE

Wash 1 quart of okra and cut in thin slices. Dice 1/2 pound of cooked ham. Peel and cut 1 pint of tomatoes. Mix all three ingredients in kettle and add 1 pint of chicken broth, 1 red hot pepper, cut in small pieces, and 1 onion cut in slices; cover and simmer for 1/2 hour. While this cooks, cook 1 cup of rice. When the okra is done, add salt and pepper to taste and 1 tablespoon of powdered dry sassafras leaves (called file) and let it heat through. Serve okra mixture over rice.

SCRAPPLE

2 c pork cubed
1 1/2 teaspoon salt
1/8 teaspoon sage
1/8 teaspoon marjoram
1/2 teaspoon pepper
2 c corn meal
2 c whole wheat flour

Boil pork in 4 quarts water until tender. Drain, reserving 3 quarts of the broth. Grind the meat very fine. Bring broth to a boil and add the seasonings. Mix meal and flour and add to boiling broth, stirring briskly while adding. Add ground meat and cook slowly about 30 minutes, stirring frequently. Pour into loaf pans and chill. Slice and fry until brown.

COUNTRY SUPPER CASSEROLE

1/4 c butter or margarine
1 c sliced fresh mushrooms
1/4 c chopped onions
1 1/2 c diced cooked ham
1 c rice
2 c water
1 tablespoon chicken bouillion granules
1/2 teaspoon dried dill weed
1 teaspoon salt
1 c canned tomatoes
1 c grated sharp cheddar
1/2 c buttered bread crumbs

Saute mushrooms, onions and ham in butter. Remove to a 2 quart casserole. Toss rice in saute pan until lightly browned. Put into casserole with mushroom mixture. Combine water and bouillion granules, dill weed, salt and tomatoes. Stir mixture into casserole. Cover and bake at 375 degrees for 45 minutes. Remove cover, stir in cheese and top with crumbs. Brown under broiler for 2-3 minutes.

RED BEANS AND RICE WITH SMOKED SAUSAGE

1 lb dried red beans, rinsed and sorted
1 1/2 lbs smoked sausage, cut in chunks
1/2 lb smoked ham shanks
1 large onion, chopped
1 green bell pepper, seeded and chopped
1 celery stalk, chopped
1 garlic clove, minced
1 teaspoon dried thyme, crumbled
1 teaspoon pepper
1/2 teaspoon ground sage
1 bay leaf
ground red pepper to taste
salt to taste
Freshly cooked rice

Place beans in kettle and cover with water. Let soak 30 minutes. Add all remaining ingredients except rice. Bring to a boil, reduce heat and simmer until beans are done, about 2 1/2 hours, adding more water if needed. Add red pepper and salt to taste. Discard ham bones. Serve hot over rice.

> *Note:* Sage is a hardy shrub-like perennial with soft gray foliage and beautiful leavender flower spikes. It is a traditional herb for poultry stuffing, pork, sausage and cheese. A little pinch of a crushed fresh leaf adds to tomatoes, eggplant or green beans. It is easily dried, just clip the stems, tie together, hang upside down and pick the leaves as you need them.

PORK CHOPS AND RICE

4 med thick pork chops
2 tablespoon vegetable oil
1/4 c sliced celery
2 (8 oz.) cans tomato sauce
1/4 c chopped onions
1 1/2 c water
2 tablespoon brown sugar
1 teaspoon salt
1/2 teaspoon dried basil leaves, crushed
1 c uncooked white rice

Brown chops in hot oil; remove and set aside. Add celery and onions and saute lightly. Drain fat. Stir in remaining ingredients and place chops on top. Bring to a boil. Turn heat to simmer, cover and cook about 30 minutes.

SHEEPHERDER'S BEANS

1 1/2 lb dried red kidney beans
3 c water
1/2 lb smoked sausage, cut in 3/4 inch pieces
2 c beef broth
3/4 lb pork, cut in small pieces
1 onion, peeled and chopped
4 cloves garlic, chopped
1 bay leaf
1 teaspoon dried oregano
1/2 teaspoon salt
1 teaspoon pepper

Combine beans and water. Bring to a boil then simmer 2 minutes. Remove from heat, cover and let stand one hour. In medium skillet cook sausage until brown. Drain. Drain beans and return to the pot. Add broth, pork, onion, garlic, bay leaf, and oregano. Bring to a boil and simmer one hour. Add sausage, salt, pepper, and simmer uncovered about 20 minutes, stirring occasionally, until beans are tender and broth has thickened some.

HERBED PORK PIE

1 lb ground pork
1/2 lb ground beef
1 medium onion, chopped
1 clove garlic, minced
1/2 c water
1 1/2 teaspoon salt
1/2 teaspoon dried thyme leaves
1/4 teaspoon ground sage
1/4 teaspoon pepper
1/8 teaspoon ground cloves
Pastry for 9 inch two crust pie

Heat all ingredients except pastry to boiling, stirring constantly; reduce heat. Cook, stirring constantly until meat is light brown but still moist, about 5 minutes. Pour meat mixture into prepared crust. Cover with 2nd crust, crimp edges and cut slits in top. Bake in 425 degree oven until crust is brown, about 35-40 minutes. Let stand 10 minutes before serving.

DILL QUICHE

8 oz. cream cheese, softened
2 eggs
1/4 teaspoon salt
1/4 teaspoon ground pepper
1/2 c chopped ham
2 tablespoon fresh snipped dill or 2 teaspoon dried dillweed
1 unbaked 9 inch pie shell
1 (8 oz.) pkg. Swiss cheese slices

Preheat oven to 400 degrees, whip cream cheese and egg together until smooth. Add salt and pepper and blend well. Gently stir in ham and dill weed. Spoon into pie shell and top with cheese slices. Bake until golden brown, about 30 minutes. Let stand about 5 minutes before serving.

HAM AND POTATO CASSEROLE

1 c cream-style cottage cheese
2 (3 oz.) pkg cream cheese, softened
1 tablespoon chopped chives
1/2 teaspoon crushed dried basil
1/2 teaspoon paprika
3 c frozen hash brown potatoes, thawed
2 c cooked ham, cubed
1 c shredded mozzarella cheese

In a medium bowl combine cottage cheese, cream cheese and herbs until well blended. In an ungreased 10 x 6 x 2 baking dish place half the hash browns. Spread the cheese mixture over evenly, sprinkle the ham over the cheese layer and half the mozzarella cheese over this. Top with the remaining hash browns. Bake uncovered in a 400 degree oven for 35 to 40 minutes. Top with the remaining mozzarella and return to the oven until the cheese melts. To garnish sprinkle with chopped parsley and tomato slices.

SAUSAGE BEAN CHOWDER

1 lb pork sausage
2 cans (16 oz. each) kidney beans
1 can (1 lb 13 oz.) tomatoes
1 quart water
1 large onion, chopped
1/2 green bell pepper, chopped
1 bay leaf
1 1/2 teaspoon salt
1/2 teaspoon garlic salt
1/2 teaspoon thyme
1/8 teaspoon pepper
1 c diced potatoes

Brown pork sausage. Drain fat. Combine sausage and remaining ingredients except potatoes in large pan. Simmer, covered for 1 hour. Add potatoes and cook an additional 20 minutes. Remove bay leaf, adjust seasonings.

CHICKEN CORN STRATA

1 (8 oz.) can whole kernel corn, drained
1 c cubed cooked chicken
1 1/2 c shredded swiss cheese
12 (1/2 inch thick) French bread slices
4 eggs
2 c milk
1 teaspoon prepared mustard
1 teaspoon finely chopped onion
1 teaspoon Worchestershire sauce
1 teaspoon dried marjoram, crumbled
1/2 teaspoon salt

In 12 x 7 1/2 x 2 inch baking dish, place corn and chicken. Top with 1 1/4 cup swiss cheese. Arrange the bread slices on top in two rows. Beat together the rest of the ingredients except the remaining cheese. Pour over the bread slices and sprinkle on the remaining cheese. Cover and let stand several hours in the refrigerator. Bake in 325 oven for 35 to 40 minutes. Let stand 10 minutes before serving. Garnish with snipped parsley and cherry tomatoes.

> *Note:* Marjoram is an annual herb that is very easy to grow. It is very aromatic and a member of the mint family. Closely related to oregano, marjoram has a more delicate flavor and should be added near the end of cooking when used fresh. Majoram improves the flavor of tomato sauce, bean soup, marinated vegetables and salad dressing. It is the traditional addition to Polish sausage.

LOW FAT CHICKEN POT PIE

1 can (10 3/4 oz.) condensed fat free cream of chicken soup
1 pkg (about 9 oz.) frozen mixed vegetables, thawed
1 c cubed cooked chicken
1/2 teaspoon basil leaves, crushed
1/2 c milk
1 egg
1 c Bisquick reduced fat all-purpose baking mix

Preheat oven to 400 degrees. In pie plate mix basil, soup, vegetables and chicken. Mix milk, egg, and baking mix. Pour over chicken mixture. Bake 30 minutes or until golden. Serves 4.

CHEESY CHICKEN CASSEROLE

1/2 c Miracle Whip dressing
1 1/2 c shredded cheddar cheese, divided
1 1/2 c chopped cooked chicken
1 1/2 c rotini, cooked and drained
2 c mixed frozen vegetables
1/4 c milk
1/2 teaspoon dried basil leaves

Mix all ingredients except 1/2 cup of cheese. Pour into casserole and sprinkle with reserved cheese. Bake at 350 degrees for 30 minutes or until thoroughly heated. Makes 6 servings.

WESTERN CASSEROLE

4 lb lean beef cut in 1 inch cubes
3/4 c flour
2 teaspoon salt
1/2 c vegetable oil
2 cloves garlic, minced
1 (6 oz.) can tomato paste
1 1/4 c dry red wine
3 c water
1 teaspoon dried thyme
2 bay leaves
2 (4 oz.) cans mushroom pieces, undrained
1 (8 oz.) pkg egg noodles, cooked and drained
3 c shredded cheddar

Dredge meat in flour and salt mixture; brown in oil on all sides. Add garlic, tomato paste, wine, water, thyme and bay leaves. Cover and simmer until meat is tender, about 1 1/2 hours. Remove bay leaves. Stir in mushrooms and noodles. Divide in half--pour each into 12 x 8 x 2 inch baking dish. Cool; freeze wrap one and freeze. Bake at 350 degrees for one hour. Uncover, place cheese around edges and bake 15 minutes longer.

REUBEN CASSEROLE

4 slices rye bread, crusts removed
1 can sauerkraut
1/4 lb canned or cooked corned beef
1/4 c sour cream
1/4 c mayonnaise
1 tablespoon catsup
4 square slices Swiss cheese, cut in half diagonally

Tear bread into cubes and place in buttered 8 or 9 inch square baking dish. Dot with 1-2 tablespoon butter. Drain sauerkraut well. If not chopped already, coarsely chop. Place over bread cubes. Crumble or coarsely chop corned beef and mix with sour cream, mayonnaise and catsup. Spoon on casserole. Bake at 350 degrees for 25 minutes. Place cheese triangles over top of casserole and return to oven 5 minutes or until cheese melts. Makes about 6 servings.

SLOPPY JOES

1 1/2 lb ground beef
1 onion, chopped
1/2 c ketchup
1 tablespoon mustard
1 can chicken gumbo soup
1 c water
1 (3 oz.) can mushroom pieces
1 teaspoon hot pepper sauce
salt and pepper to taste

Cook meat and onion until lightly brown, breaking into small pieces with fork. Add remaining ingredients. Cover, bring to a boil then simmer about 30 minutes. Serve on toasted rolls.

BAKED REUBEN CASSEROLE

6 slices rye bread
2 tablespoon thousand island dressing
6 oz. thinly sliced corned beef
1 1/2 c kraut, drained and rinsed
2 dill pickles, chopped
1/2 teaspoon caraway seed
2 c Swiss cheese, shredded
3 eggs
1 1/2 c milk
1 tablespoon yellow mustard

Butter an 11 x 7 inch baking dish. Arrange 3 slices bread in bottom cutting to fit. Spread 1/2 dressing on bread. Cover with half the corned beef, kraut, pickles and caraway seed. Sprinkle with 1/2 the cheese. Repeat layers. Beat together the eggs, milk and mustard. Pour over casserole. Let stand while heating oven to 350 degrees. Bake about 40 minutes or until set in the center and is golden brown.

COMPANY ROAST BEEF & VEGETABLES

1/2 teaspoon dried parsley flakes
1/2 teaspoon garlic powder
1/2 teaspoon dried whole basil
1/2 teaspoon dried whole oregano
1/4 teaspoon pepper
1 (4 1/2 lb) beef roast
vegetable cooking spray
2 c water
12 new potatoes (about 2 1/2 lbs large potatoes cut)
12 small boiling onions (about 1 1/4 lbs large onions--cut in fourths)
12 carrots, scraped and cut in half

Combine first 5 ingredients in small bowl and mix well. Divide herb mixture in half and set aside. Trim fat from roast, place roast on rack coated with cooking spray; place rack in broiler pan.

Sprinkle half of herb mixture over roast and bake at 325 degrees for 50 minutes. Pour water into broiler pan. Arrange vegetables around roast in single layer; cover with aluminum foil. Bake at 325 degrees for 25 minutes. Remove foil, sprinkle remaining herb mixture over vegetables; cover and bake an additional 45 minutes or until vegetables are tender and meat is desired doneness. Transfer to serving platter. Let roast stand 10 minutes before slicing. Arrange vegetables around roast. Yeild: 12 servings.

COUNTRY RIBS
(with hot sauerkraut and potatoes)

2 tablespoon salad oil
2-3 lb beef chuck flank-style ribs
2 c white grape juice
4 teaspoon salt
1/2 teaspoon pepper
12 small red potatoes
2 qts. hot tomato sauerkraut, drained and rinsed

Cook beef ribs in oil until browned on all sides. Stir in grape juice, salt and pepper; heat to boiling. Reduce heat to low, cover and simmer 1 1/2 hours, turning ribs occasionally. Peel 1/2 inch wide strip around center of potatoes. Skim off fat from liquid in pan. Add potatoes, and kraut. Cover and simmer until meat and potatoes are tender. Makes 8 servings.

SAUCY STEAK SKILLET
(one dish dinner)

1 lb round steak, cut in serving pieces
1/4 c all-purpose flour
1 tablespoon vegetable oil
1 lg onion, chopped
1 can whole potatoes, drained (reserve liquid)
1/4 c catsup
1 tablespoon worchestershire sauce
2 teaspoon bell pepper flakes
1 teaspoon instant beef bouillion
1 teaspoon salt
1/2 teaspoon dried marjoram leaves
1/4 teaspoon pepper
1 pkg (10 oz.) frozen Italian green beans
1 jar (2 oz) sliced pimento, drained

Coat beef pieces with flour; pound flour into beef. Brown beef in oil in skillet; push beef to side. Cook and stir onion in oil until tender in other side of skillet. Drain. Add enough water to potato liquid to make 1 cup. Mix potato liquid, catsup, worchestershire sauce, pepper flakes, bouillon, salt, marjoram and pepper. Pour on beef and onion. Heat to boiling; reduce heat. Cover and simmer until beef is tender, 1 1/4 to 1 1/2 hours. Rinse frozen beans under running cold water to separate. Add potatoes, beans and pimento to skillet. Heat to boiling; reduce heat. Cover and simmer until beans are tender, 10 to 15 minutes. Makes 4 servings.

TORTILLA CHIP CASSEROLE

2 lbs lean ground beef
1 med. onion, chopped
1 garlic clove, minced
1 c sour cream
1 (8 oz.) can tomato sauce
1 (6 oz.) can tomato paste
2 (4 oz.) can green chilies
8 oz. tortilla chips
3/4 lb Monterey Jack cheese, shredded
2 med size green onions, minced
Hot salsa

Brown beef with onion and garlic. Pour off drippings. Stir in sour cream, tomato sauce, tomato paste and chilies. Cook until heated through, about 5 minutes. Cover bottom of casserole dish with half of tortilla chips. Spoon beef mixture over and top with remaining chips. Sprinkle with cheese. Bake until heated through, about 20 minutes. Garnish with minced green onions. Serve with salsa.

SPICED BEEF WITH CHILIES AND VEGETABLES

1 tablespoon olive oil
1 lb ground beef
1 sm onion, chopped
4 garlic cloves, minced
1 (14 1/2 oz.) can diced peeled tomatoes
12 oz. potatoes, peeled and diced
1 c canned beef broth
1 lg carrot, diced
2 serrano chilies or jalapeno chilies, minced
2 teaspoon dried oregano
2 teaspoon chili powder
1 teaspoon ground cumin
1/2 teaspoon ground allspice

Heat oil; add beef, onion and garlic and saute until beef is cooked through, breaking up beef with fork or spoon. Add remaining ingredients and bring to a boil. Cover and simmer until vegetables are tender. Uncover and cook until liquid thickens. Delicious spooned on warm corn or flour tortillas and topped with salsa. Makes 4 servings.

SAUSAGE LASAGNA

1 clove garlic, crushed
1 1/2 tablespoon olive oil
1 (15 oz.) can tomato sauce
1 (6 oz.) can tomato paste
1/2 c water
1 bay leaf
1/2 teaspoon sugar
1/2 teaspoon salt
1/4 teaspoon pepper
1/2 teaspoon dried marjoram, crumbled
2 c ricotta cheese
1 egg
1/2 lb lasagna noodles, cooked and drained
1/2 lb sweet Italian sausage, cooked and sliced
1/2 lb hot Italian sausage, cooked and sliced
3/4 lb sliced Mozzarella cheese
1/4 c grated Parmesan and Romano cheese

Saute garlic in oil until golden. Add tomato sauce, tomato paste, water, sugar, salt, pepper, bay leaf and marjoram. Cover and simmer stirring frequently about 1/2 hour. Combine ricotta and egg in large bowl and mix well. Spoon sauce to cover bottom of 13 x 9 x 2 inch baking dish (about 1/2 cup). Arrange 1/3 noodles over sauce, spoon 1/3 cup ricotta mixture over, then 1/3 sausage slices and 1/3 of mozzarella slices. Repeat layers until all ingredients are used, ending with tomato sauce and mozzarella. Bake at 350 degree for 35 minutes. Sprinkle with Parmesan Romano cheese.

PIZZA PITAS, QUICK AND EASY
(Microwave)

3/4 lb ground beef
1 small onion, chopped
1 teaspoon sugar
3/4 teaspoon chili powder
1/2 teaspoon garlic salt
1 (8 oz) bottle salsa
1 (4 oz.) can chopped green chili peppers, drained
1 (2 1/4 oz) can sliced ripe olives
1 c shredded Monterey Jack cheese
4 large or 8 small pita bread rounds

Combine beef and onion. Cook on high, covered, for 4-6 minutes or until no pink remains. Drain. Stir in sugar, chili powder and garlic salt. Spread salsa on each pita. Top with meat mixture, chili peppers, olives and cheese. Place half the pitas on microwave safe plate. Cook, uncovered, on high for 2-3 minutes or until hot and cheese is melted. Repeat with remaining pitas. Makes 4 servings.

ENCHILADA CASSEROLE

1 lb ground beef
1 teaspoon salad oil
1 (1 lb) can tomatoes
1 (8 oz.) can tomato sauce
1/4 c chopped chili pepper
1/2 teaspoon vinegar
1/2 teaspoon sugar
1 teaspoon salt
1/4 teaspoon oregano
1/4 teaspoon cumin
1 clove garlic, crushed
12 oz. shredded cheddar
1 large onion, chopped
12 tortillas
1/2 c shortening

Brown meat in 1 teaspoon oil. Add tomatoes, tomato sauce, chilies, vinegar, sugar, salt, oregano and garlic. Simmer 45 minutes. Fry the tortillas for about 30 seconds on each side. Drain on paper towels. Alternate layer of tortillas, meat sauce, cheese and onion in casserole, topping with cheese and onion. Bake at 350 degrees for 35-40 minutes. Serve with salsa and sour cream.

NEW ENGLAND MEAT PIE

1 lb lean ground beef
2 (8 oz) cans tomato sauce
1/4 c finely chopped onions
1 egg
1/4 c dry bread crumbs
1 teaspoon salt
1 (10 oz.) pkg frozen mixed vegetables, thawed
1/2 teaspoon crushed dried thyme
1/2 teaspoon pepper
1 (12 oz.) pkg frozen hash brown potatoes, thawed
3 tablespoon vegetable oil
6 slices cheese, cut into 1/2 inch strips

Combine beef, 2 tablespoon tomato sauce, onions, egg, bread crumbs and salt; shape into 1 inch balls. Lightly brown in skillet; drain fat. Stir in rest of tomato sauce, mixed vegetables, thyme and pepper. Simmer 5 minutes. Press thawed potatoes in bottom of 10 x 6 x 2 inch baking dish, drizzle with the vegetable oil and place under broiler until lightly browned. Spoon meatball mixture over potatoes, arrange strips of cheese in lattice pattern over top. Bake at 375 degrees for about 30 minutes.

ZIPPY BEEF CASSEROLE

1 1/2 lbs ground beef
1 med onion, chopped
1 clove garlic, minced
1 1/2 teaspoon chili powder
1 teaspoon salt
1/4 teaspoon pepper
1/4 teaspoon cumin
1 can refried beans
1 (8 oz.) can tomato sauce
1 (4 oz.) can chopped chilies, drained
1/2 c shredded Monterey Jack cheese
cornmeal biscuits, recipe follows

Cook ground beef, onion and garlic until meat is no longer pink. Drain drippings. Stir in chili powder, salt, pepper, cumin, refried beans, tomato sauce and chilies. Cook about 15 minutes, stirring occasionally. Remove from heat and stir in cheese. Transfer to baking dish. Prepare biscuits and place on top of casserole and bake at 400 degrees 15 to 20 minutes or until biscuits are brown. Makes about 8 servings.

Cornmeal Biscuits

1/2 c flour
1/2 c yellow cornmeal
2 teaspoon baking powder
1/2 teaspoon salt
1/2 teaspoon chili powder
3 tablespoon shortening
1/2 c milk

Combine flour, meal, baking powder, salt and chili powder. Cut in shortening to texture of cornmeal. Stir in milk just until combined. On lightly floured surface roll out dough to 1/2 inch thickness. Cut with 2 1/2 inch biscuit cutter.

HOT SAUERKRAUT AND MEATBALLS

1 lb ground beef
1/2 lb ground pork
1/2 c finely chopped onion
3/4 c fine dry bread crumbs
1 tablespoon snipped fresh parsley
1 1/2 teaspoon salt
1/8 teaspoon pepper
1 teaspoon worchestershire sauce
1 egg, beaten
1/2 c milk
2-3 tablespoon oil
1 can hot sauerkraut, undrained
1/3 to 1/2 c water, optional

Combine first 10 ingredients in a mixing bowl; shape into 18 two inch balls. Heat the oil in a skillet; brown the meatballs. Remove meatballs and drain fat. Put sauerkraut in skillet; top with meatballs. Cover and simmer for 15-20 minutes or until meatballs are done. Add water if necessary. Garnish with fresh parsley.

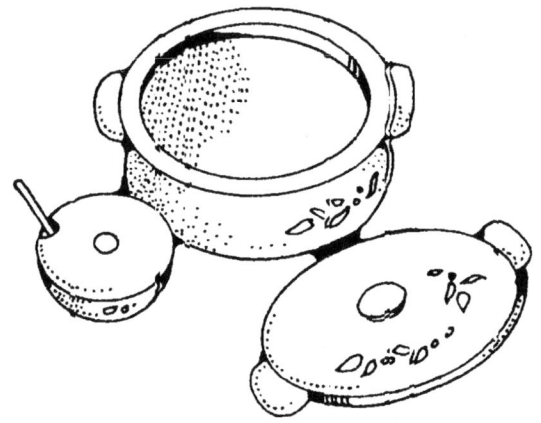

BEEF, ZUCCHINI AND RICE

1 1/2 lb ground beef
5 c sliced zucchini
1/2 c chopped sweet red pepper
3/4 c chopped onions
1 (4 oz.) can sliced mushrooms, drained
1 clove garlic, minced
1/2 teaspoon salt
1/2 teaspoon basil leaves
1/2 teaspoon oregano leaves
1/8 teaspoon black pepper
3 beef bouillon cubes
1/2 c dry red wine
3 c hot cooked rice

In large skillet, cook beef stirring to crumble; drain. Add remaining ingredients except rice. Cover and simmer 30 minutes or until zucchini is tender. Serve over rice.

STEAK POTATO CASSEROLE

1 1/2 - 2 lb round steak
2 tablespoon flour
3 tablespoon margarine or butter
4 med. potatoes, halved
1 onion chopped
1 tablespoon parsley, chopped
1 teaspoon thyme or marjoram crumbled
1/2 teaspoon salt
1/4 teaspoon pepper
2 (8 oz.) cans tomato sauce

Cut steak into serving pieces and dredge in flour. Brown on both sides in butter in Dutch oven. Add potatoes, sprinkle herbs, salt and pepper over all and pour tomato sauce over top. Cover and bake at 350 degrees for about 1 1/2 hours.

SPARE RIBS AND SAUERKRAUT

3 lbs spare ribs, cut into serving portions
2 lbs sauerkraut
2 cloves garlic, chopped
1 onion, chopped
1 teaspoon caraway seed
10 peppercorns tied in cheesecloth bag (optional)

Brown the spare ribs in a skillet. Drain the sauerkraut and put in Dutch oven along with the garlic, onion, caraway seeds and black pepper. Add enough water to barely cover the sauerkraut. Add the spare ribs and cover. Simmer one to two hours, piling the sauerkraut on top of the ribs as they cook.

James Stuart

Nick McGuire visiting Deane Stuart in Florida.

J.K. O'Hare

John O'Hare with J.K.

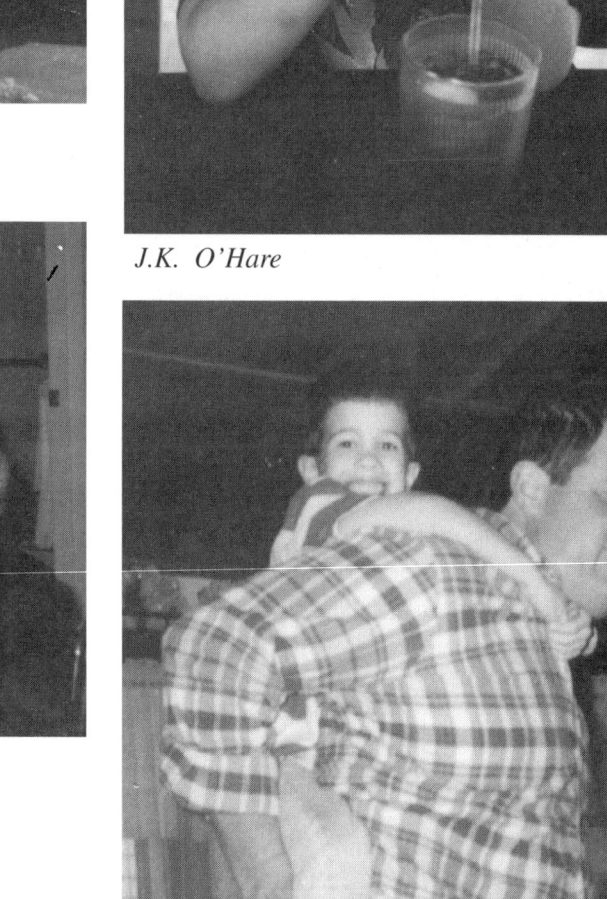

Glennis and Herbert Liles and Deane Stuart

Whitey and Glennis Liles at Whitey's retirement Party from Ashland Inc.

Mary Stuart Nelson, Sophie Keeney, James Stuart, and Glennis Liles

"The Ladies" of Greenup Christian Church. First Row — Norma Stapf, Clara Baker, Ruth Cordell. Sec. Row — Martha Callihan, Patty Gibson, Hazel Baker. Third Row — Kathryn Reed, Faye Johnson, Marty Hancock, Ethel McBrayer, Eunice Eastham.

Glennis Liles, daughter Anne O'Hare, Herbert Liles

Anne and J.K. O'Hare

Melissa and Glennis Liles

Salads

BLACK BEAN, CORN, & BELL PEPPER SALAD

1 c dried black beans
1 (10 oz) frozen corn, thawed
1 medium green pepper, chopped
1 medium sweet red pepper, chopped
1 jalapeno pepper, seeded and chopped
3 green onions, thinly sliced
2 tablespoon minced fresh parsley
2 tablespoon olive oil
3 tablespoon fresh lime juice
salt and pepper to taste

Sort and wash beans; place in a pan and cover with water 2 inches above beans; let soak over night. Drain beans and cover with fresh water; cook until tender. Drain and let beans cool. Combine beans, corn, all peppers, onions, tomatoes and parsley. Combine salt and pepper, olive oil and lime juice. Pour over vegetables and mix. Makes 6 servings.

SALAD SPARKLES

Cut an unpeeled cucumber into medium thick slices, then cut slices in half. Soak them in beet juice about 1 hour. Slices come out red with a green rind resembling a mini watermelon slice. Add a sprig of fresh mint for decoration.

FOUR BEAN SALAD

1-16 oz can kidney beans
1-16 oz can Garbanzo (chick peas)
1-16 oz can cut green beans
1-16 oz can yellow wax beans
2 sweet onions, thinly sliced
1/4 c sugar
2/3 c tarragon vinegar
1/3 c salad oil
salt and pepper to taste

Drain beans and put into glass bowl. Add onions. Mix remaining ingredients well and pour over the beans. Best if refrigerated over night to blend flavors.

BEAN SALAD WITH PESTO DRESSING

1-15 oz can red kidney beans, drained
1-15 oz can garbanzo beans, drained
1/2 c celery, sliced
1/2 c onions, thinly sliced
4 tablespoon grated Parmesan cheese
Pesto Dressing, below
chopped fresh parsley for garnish

Combine beans, celery, onions and cheese in bowl. Pour dressing over and toss to combine.

PESTO DRESSING

1/4 c oil
1/4 c white wine vinegar
1 tablespoon fresh chopped basil
1/2 teaspoon salt
1/2 teaspoon minced garlic

In electric blender, blend until smooth.

COLE SLAW WITH CARAWAY DRESSING

4 c shredded cabbage
1/2 c mayonnaise
2 tablespoon lemon juice
1 tablespoon grated onion
1 teaspoon caraway seeds
1 teaspoon sugar
1/2 teaspoon salt
1/8 teaspoon black pepper

Combine all ingredients except cabbage, mixing well. Pour over cabbage and stir in. Garnish with paprika.

> *Note:* Caraway is a biennial plant which must be sowed each year to guarantee a steady supply. The seeds are produced the second year and should be harvested as soon as they darken and ripen. Let some ripen and fall to the ground and you will have next year's crop already sowed. Caraway has a distinctive licorice flavor. Caraway goes particularly well with beets, potatoes, cabbage, cheese and in bread. Caraway seeds are the ones found in rye bread.

TEX-MEX COLESLAW

1/2 c cilantro (coriander) leaves
1 large garlic clove
1 jalapeno pepper, halved and seeded
1 small onion, quartered
1 1/3 c vegetable oil
1/2 c red wine vinegar
2 teaspoon sugar
1 teaspoon salt
3 lbs cabbage

Shred cilantro, garlic, jalapeno and onion; mix in oil. Shred cabbage. Pour dressing over cabbage and toss. Makes about 8 servings.

SPICY PEPPER SLAW

3 large red bell peppers, thinly sliced
2 jalapeno peppers, finely chopped
2/3 c olive oil
1/2 c red wine vinegar
3 tablespoon sugar
large head cabbage, shredded

Toss peppers and chilies in large bowl. Put oil, vinegar and sugar in saucepan and bring to a boil over medium heat, stirring to dissolve sugar. Pour over peppers in bowl and toss together. Cool. Add to cabbage, season with salt and mix well.

MEXICAN SALAD BOWL

1 medium size head lettuce
3 tomatoes, cut into eighths
3/4 c sliced pitted ripe olives
1/3 c thinly sliced green onions
Avocado Salad dressing

Break the lettuce into bowl. Add tomatoes, olives and onion. Add the avocado dressing and toss lightly to blend.

AVOCADO DRESSING

1 avocado, mashed
1 tablespoon lemon juice
1/2 c sour cream
1/3 c salad oil
1 clove garlic, crushed
1/2 teaspoon sugar
1/4 teaspoon chili powder
1/2 teaspoon salt
1/4 teaspoon Tabasco sauce

Combine all ingredients and blend well.

BILL THOMPSON'S FAMOUS CAJUN COLE SLAW

1 head of cabbage, cut fine with a knife
1/2 lb bacon, fry crisp, let cool and crumble
1 cucumber, chopped
2 small bunches green onions, sliced
1 tomato, chopped
5 or 6 large radishes, sliced thin
2 (or more) hot banana peppers, diced
1 tablespoon mayonnaise *(Bill uses Miracle Whip)*

Chop and slice all vegetables by hand. Mix and refrigerate. Slaw will be juicy, so not much mayonnaise is needed. Better if made several hours ahead and stirred occasionally.

CORN RELISH

3 c corn, cut from cob
1 large onion, chopped
2 medium zucchini, unpeeled and cubed
1 bunch green onions, sliced
1 red sweet pepper, chopped
1 green sweet pepper, chopped
1/4 c minced fresh parsley
1 clove garlic, minced
1/4 teaspoon salt
1/8 teaspoon pepper
1/4 c sugar
1 teaspoon ground cumin
2 teaspoon Dijon style mustard
1/2 to 1 teaspoon hot sauce
2/3 c vegetable oil
1/3 c white vinegar

Cook corn, covered in boiling water to cover 8-10 minutes. Drain and cool. Combine corn and next six ingredients and set aside. Combine garlic and remaining ingredients, stirring well. Toss gently with vegetables. Chill at least 8 hours.

CUCUMBERS IN SOUR CREAM I

2 teaspoon salt
1/4 teaspoon Tabasco
1 tablespoon lemon juice
2 teaspoon fresh dill, chopped
1 tablespoon chives, chopped
3 cucumbers, peeled and sliced

Combine all ingredients and serve well chilled.

Note: Chives is a hardy perennial and very easily grown. It is a member of the onion family. The leaves are finer and it has blooms resembling clover blooms so it is very pretty. Chives are best used when fresh or freeze dried. They are good when just a hint of onion flavor is wanted. They are good in salads, egg dishes, in cottage cheese and cheese dishes.

CUCUMBERS IN SOUR CREAM II

2 medium cucumbers
1 large onion, sliced in rings
1 1/2 teaspoon salt
3/4 c water
3/4 c vinegar
1 teaspoon sugar
1/2 c sour cream
hot pepper sauce to taste
pepper

Peel one of the cucumbers; thinly slice both cucumbers and sprinkle with salt. Combine water, vinegar and sugar; pour over cucumbers. Let stand at room temperature for 1 hour. Drain thoroughly. Add remaining ingredients to cucumbers. Toss gently, cover and chill 1 hour or more. Makes 6 servings.

CUCUMBER SALAD I

Fresh mint gives this salad a cool & refreshing taste.

4-5 cucumbers (about 2 1/4 lbs)
1 teaspoon salt
5 tablespoon olive or vegetable oil
1 tablespoon white vinegar
1 tablespoon lemon juice
1 teaspoon Dijon mustard
1/4 teaspoon pepper
1/2 c sour cream
2 tablespoon finely chopped fresh mint
2 tablespoon finely chopped fresh chives or parsley

Score cucumbers skins with tines of fork. Cut in half lengthwise. Remove seeds with tip of spoon. Cut into 1/8 inch slices; place in a colander and sprinkle with 1 teaspoon salt. Stir to mix and let stand half an hour. Rinse cucumbers under running water. Pat dry on paper towels. Beat olive oil, vinegar, lemon juice, mustard and pepper in bowl with whisk or fork. Add sour cream, mint, chives or parsley. Add the cucumbers. Toss. Taste to see if additional salt is needed. Chill at least four hours. Makes about 8 servings.

CUCUMBER SALAD II

2 large cucumbers
vinegar
salt and pepper
chopped green onions, or chopped mint, or chopped fresh dill (according to your taste and rest of menu).

Peel & quarter cucumbers, remove seeds. Slice 3/4 inch layer into glass bowl. Sprinkle with vinegar, salt & pepper, green onions or mint or dill. Repeat until all cucumbers are used. Weigh down with plate or saucer. Chill. Drain before serving & add additional onion, mint or dill. Makes 6-8 servings.

GREEN BEAN AND TOMATO SALAD

2 (10 oz) pkgs frozen green beans (Frenched or the fancy whole ones)
oil
vinegar
salt and pepper
6 green onions
mint, 5 sprigs fresh or 2 tablespoon dried
2 large fresh tomatoes, peeled

Cook beans according to package directions. Drain. Add oil, vinegar, salt and pepper according to taste. Add green onions and mint leaves. Toss, cover and refrigerate overnight or longer. Makes 8 servings.

Variations: Add thin sliced fresh or canned mushrooms before marinating. Or use leftover dill pickle juice to cook beans and substitute fresh dill for mint in seasoning.

JALAPENO COLESLAW

1/3 c sour cream
1/3 c mayonnaise
2 tablespoon red wine vinegar
2 tablespoon vegetable oil
1 garlic clove, minced
1/4 c chopped jalapeno pepper
1/4 teaspoon salt
1/8 teaspoon pepper
1 (16 oz) bag coleslaw mix or mix your own

Combine first 8 ingredients. Add coleslaw mix, tossing to coat. Cover and chill. Makes 4-6 servings.

LENTIL SALAD

2 c water
1 c lentils
1 c dry red wine
3 scallions, minced
3 tablespoon red wine vinegar
2 roasted peeled green chilies, minced
2 large cloves garlic, minced
1 tablespoon olive oil
salt and pepper to taste

Combine water, lentils and red wine. Bring to a boil and simmer until lentils are just tender, about 25-30 minutes. Drain and transfer lentils to a bowl. Add scallions, vinegar, green chilies, garlic and olive oil. Add salt and pepper to taste and mix well. Chill for 3 hours or overnight. Let salad come to room temperature before serving and mound it in a salad bowl lined with romaine. Serves 4-6.

HEARTY LUNCH SALAD

1 small head lettuce
1/2 bunch watercress
1/2 head romaine lettuce
3 small tomatoes, peeled
2 roasted chicken breasts
6 strips crisp bacon
1 avocado
3 hard-boiled eggs, chopped
1 teaspoon fresh chives, chopped (1/2 teaspoon dried)
1/2 c Roquefort cheese, grated
1 c French dressing

Chop lettuce, watercress and romaine very fine. Toss and arrange in large bowl. Cut tomatoes in quarters, dice and arrange in a strip across the salad. Dice chicken breasts and arrange over top of salad greens. Crumble bacon and sprinkle on top of salad. Cut avocado in long, thin strips and arrange around outer edge of salad. Sprinkle chopped eggs, chives and grated cheese over salad. Pour French dressing over all. Toss before serving. Serves 4-6.

Note: This hearty salad makes a very good lunch served with your favorite crackers.

MARINER'S SALAD

1 1/4 lb cod fish fillets
1 1/4 lb small shrimp, precooked
1 c chopped celery hearts
1 c mayonnaise
1/4 c fresh minced onion
1 tablespoon lemon juice
1/4 teaspoon sugar
1 teaspoon prepared mustard
salt as needed
1 teaspoon hot sauce

Cook cod fillets in hot water with 1 1/2 teaspoon salt. Simmer until fish flakes easily when tested with a fork. Drain fish and chill. Flake cod in large pieces. Add shrimp, celery and onions. Mix mayonnaise, lemon juice, sugar, mustard, salt and hot sauce. Pour mixture over fish and toss lightly until well blended. Keep chilled. At serving time place on a bed of lettuce, dust with paprika. Garnish around salad with quartered hard boiled eggs, ripe olive slices, tomatoes, etc. depending on your own taste. Serves 12.

MEXICAN CHEF SALAD

1 red onions, sliced thin
4 medium tomatoes, coarsely chopped
1 head lettuce, shredded
4 oz cheddar cheese, grated
Tabasco to taste
1-6 1/4 oz bag Doritos corn chips, slightly crushed
1 large avocado, peeled and chopped
1 lb ground beef, browned and drained
1-15 oz can red kidney beans, drained
1/4 teaspoon salt
chili powder to taste
1/2 c black olives, sliced
1-8 oz bottle Green Goddess Salad dressing

Combine all ingredients except dressing, mix well. Then toss with salad dressing. Garnish with tomato slices and whole Doritos chips.

MARINATED KRAUT

1 lb can sauerkraut
1 c bell pepper, chopped
1 c onion, chopped
1 small can pimentos, chopped
1 jalapeno pepper, chopped and seeds removed
1 c sugar
1 c white vinegar

Drain kraut and mix with vegetables. Heat sugar and vinegar to boiling until sugar is dissolved. Pour over kraut mixture. Toss thoroughly. When cool, store in covered bowl in refrigerator. Keeps well for several days.

MACARONI AND MOZZARELLA SALAD

1 c uncooked elbow macaroni
1/2 c mayonnaise
1/4 teaspoon leaf oregano, crumbled
pinch of dried thyme
1 teaspoon dry mustard
2 teaspoon salt
1/8 teaspoon white pepper
2 tablespoon minced onion
2 tablespoon minced, green pepper
1 tablespoon minced, drained pimiento
3/4 c finely diced celery
1/3 c finely diced, peeled, seeded cucumber
1 c coarsely shredded Swiss or Cheddar
3 hard boiled eggs, peeled and chopped

Cook macaroni and drain. Mix mayonnaise, herbs, onions, green peppers and pimento. Place macaroni, celery and cucumber in a large bowl. Add mayonnaise mixture and stir gently to mix. Add cheese and eggs and toss just enough to mix. Chill before serving.

MIXED BEAN SALAD

1 (1 lb) can red kidney beans
1 (1 lb) can white kidney beans
1 (10 oz) pkg baby lima beans (very lightly cooked)
1 slice bread
2 green onions, chopped
1/2 c walnut meats
1 c strong chicken broth
salt and pepper
dash of hot sauce (or to taste)
1 tablespoon lemon juice
1 small bunch parsley, chopped
1 red onion, chopped
3 stalks celery, chopped

Drain canned beans. Cook limas very lightly and drain. In blender, blend bread until it crumbs. Add onions, nuts, chicken broth, salt and pepper, hot sauce and lemon juice. Blend at high speed for 1 minute. Mix beans and dressing and toss; add chopped parsley, onion and celery and toss. Cover and refrigerate. Serve in lettuce lined bowl. Makes 8 servings.

FESTIVE PASTA SALAD

4 oz rotini pasta, uncooked
1/2 small zucchini
3 oz provolone cheese, cubed
4 oz cooked ham, diced
1/2 c broccoli florets, chopped
1/2 c finely chopped sweet red bell peppers
1/2 c finely chopped sweet green bell peppers
1/2 small red onion, thinly sliced
3 tablespoon grated Parmesan cheese
3 tablespoon snipped fresh parsley
3 tablespoon sliced pitted ripe olives
1/2 c Italian salad dressing
1/2 teaspoon oregano

Cook the pasta according to directions on package. Drain well and place in large bowl. Cut the zucchini lengthwise into quarters, then thinly slice. Add to pasta. Add the cheese, herbs and vegetables and stir well. Pour over the dressing and toss until mixture is coated. Cover and chill in refrigerator about 2 hours to blend the flavors.

POTATO SALAD WITH MINT

1 c one-step potato salad dressing
1 tablespoon chopped fresh mint or 1 teaspoon dried mint
1 clove garlic, minced
1 1/2 lb small red potatoes, cooked and cut in 1/2 inch cubes
2 medium cucumber, peeled, seeded and cut in 1/2 inch cubes
1/2 c chopped green onions
fresh mint leaves, for garnish

In large bowl combine salad dressing, chopped mint and garlic. Add potatoes, cucumbers and green onions; toss to coat. Spoon into serving bowl; garnish with mint leaves. Makes 8 servings.

PERUVIAN POTATO SALAD

6 medium potatoes, peeled and cubed
2 hard-boiled eggs
1 oz shredded cheddar
1 small onion, chopped fine
1 jalapeno pepper, chopped fine
1 teaspoon salt
2 tablespoon olive oil
1/2 c light cream
lettuce

Cook potatoes in boiling salted water until tender. Drain. Return to pan and toss over low heat until dry. Place in large bowl. While potatoes cook, mash eggs in small bowl; stir in cheese, onion, peppers and salt. Stir in olive oil until well blended then add cream and mix. Pour over potatoes and toss until evenly coated. Chill about an hour to blend flavors. Serve with lettuce leaves.

SHRIMP SALAD WITH MUSTARD SAUCE

1/2 c creole mustard
1/2 c prepared mustard
1/2 c catsup
1/4 c white vinegar
1/4 c horseradish
1/4 c Worcestershire sauce
3 tablespoon paprika
2 c finely minced celery
1 1/2 c minced green onion
1/3 c oil or olive oil
5 eggs, lightly beaten
1 bunch parsley, minced
4 bay leaves
1 lemon, seeded and diced
2 tablespoon garlic powder
1 tablespoon salt
1 teaspoon hot pepper sauce
juice of 1 lemon
boiled shrimp, well chilled (peeled and deveined)
shredded lettuce

Combine first 7 ingredients in food processor and blend. Add remaining ingredients except shrimp and lettuce and mix well. Cover and chill overnight. About 2 hours before serving place shrimp in shallow bowl and cover with some of the sauce, let marinate until serving time. Line individual serving plates with lettuce, top with shrimp. Add a little extra sauce and serve immediately. Serves 6. Leftover extra sauce will keep for up to 3 weeks, sealed and refrigerated.

SALMON SALAD

1 lb canned salmon
1/2 c diced celery
1 can (20 oz) peas, drained
2 tablespoon lemon juice
1 teaspoon minced onion
1/2 teaspoon salt
1/2 teaspoon pepper
1/2 teaspoon snipped dill weed
1 c sour cream
lettuce, chopped chives and lemon wedges

Drain and flake salmon. Add celery and peas. Combine next six ingredients to make dressing. Pour over salmon and mix with fork. Chill for several hours. Serve in lettuce cup and garnish with chopped chives and lemon wedges, if desired.

SALMON AND PASTA SALAD WITH LEMON-DILL VINAIGRETTE

1 tablespoon Dijon mustard
1/2 c lemon-dill vinegar (recipe in condiment section)
salt and white pepper to taste
1 c peanut or safflower oil

To make lemon-dill vinaigrette whisk the above ingredients together, dribbling oil in last while continuing to whisk. Set aside.

Salmon and Pasta Salad

1 1/2 lbs fresh salmon steak or fillet
1/4 c lemon-dill vinaigrette, recipe precedes
salt and pepper
4 quarts water
1 1/2 teaspoon salt
3/4 lb fresh spinach fettuccine
2/3 c diced red onion
1/2 c chopped fresh, leafy dill

Arrange salmon in shallow baking dish. Add enough water to half cover salmon. Add lemon-dill vinegar and season with salt and pepper, place in a 400 preheated oven and bake about 10-12 minutes until just barely done. Allow to cool in its own juices. Bring 4 quarts water to a boil. Add fettuccine, stir to separate strands and cook 3-5 minutes until tender but still firm. Drain and rinse. Place in large bowl. Add 1/2 cup of onion and 1/4 cup dill. Pour half the lemon-dill vinaigrette over pasta and season with salt and pepper and toss well. Arrange pasta on a serving platter and mound salmon in center. Drizzle with any remaining vinaigrette before serving. Makes 6-8 servings.

Note: Avoid refrigerating salad. If necessary, refrigerate salmon and pasta separately. Allow to return to room temperature and toss well before arranging on platter.

TANGY SPINACH SALAD

1 lb fresh spinach, torn into bite size pieces
1/4 lb bacon, fried and crumbled

Dressing:
2 tablespoon bacon drippings
1/4 c red wine vinegar
3 tablespoon tarragon vinegar
1 or 2 cloves garlic, crushed
2/3 c olive oil
1 teaspoon Worcestershire sauce
1 teaspoon salt
1/4 teaspoon pepper

Mix all dressing ingredients together. Toss with bacon over spinach. This is best when the dressing is made a few hours ahead.

SERRANO-CUCUMBER RELISH

2 medium cucumbers, diced
2 serrano chilies, diced
1/2 medium red onion, diced
1/2 c sugar
1 c white vinegar
1/2 teaspoon salt
2 tablespoon diced scallions
2 tablespoon chopped fresh cilantro

Combine cucumber, chilies, onion, sugar, vinegar, salt, scallions and cilantro in serving bowl. May be made up to 2 hours ahead and chilled. Bring to room temperature before serving.
Makes about 2 cups.

SHRIMP AND JICAMA SALAD WITH CHILE VINEGAR

5 c water
1 lb unpeeled small fresh shrimp
chile vinegar
2 c peeled, shredded jicama
4 large tomatoes, sliced
4 large fresh tomatillos, husked and sliced
fresh cilantro sprigs, optional

Bring water to a boil; add shrimp and cook 3-5 minutes. Drain and rinse in cold water. Peel and devein shrimp. Pour 1/3 cup chile vinegar over shrimp. Pour 1/3 cup chile vinegar over jicama and toss. Arrange tomato slices and tomatillos on individual salad plates; top evenly with jicama mixture. Place shrimp over jicama mixture. Pour remaining chile vinegar over salads. Garnish with cilantro. Makes 4 servings.

Chile Vinegar

3/4 c white wine vinegar
1/4 c sugar
1/8 teaspoon salt
3 tablespoon fresh cilantro
2 tablespoon seeded, minced jalapeno pepper

Combine all ingredients; stir with a whisk until well blended.

SPAGHETTI SALAD

8 oz spaghetti, cooked and drained
1 lb sharp cheese, cut in small pieces
1 medium onion chopped
1 medium green pepper, chopped
1 c chopped celery
1/2 c chopped dill pickle
1 small jar chopped pimento
1 small jar stuffed olives, sliced
4 hard-boiled eggs, chopped
3 medium tomatoes, cubed (drain and fold in last)
2 tablespoon marjoram (fresh)
1 teaspoon celery seed
1/2 teaspoon dry mustard
salt and pepper to taste
mayonnaise to moisten

Cook spaghetti, drain and put 3 tablespoon vinegar over it. Dry chopped pickle, celery, olives, and pimento on paper towels. Add all ingredients to spaghetti except tomatoes, fold them in last. Serves 12.

> *Note:* This is also good to use poppy seed dressing from Krogers as the dressing. You can cut down fat by eliminating eggs.

SPINACH SALAD

10 oz fresh spinach, stemmed
5 strips lean bacon, cut into 1 inch pieces
1/2 teaspoon dried oregano, crumbled
1/4 teaspoon dried tarragon, crumbled
1/4 teaspoon dried rosemary, crumbled
3 tablespoon red wine vinegar
2 tablespoon olive oil
2 teaspoon sugar
1 teaspoon Dijon mustard
1 teaspoon Worcestershire sauce
pepper to taste

Wash spinach, pat dry and place in salad bowl. Cook bacon until crisp; drain. Discard bacon drippings. Add oregano, tarragon and rosemary to warm skillet. Stir in vinegar, oil, sugar, mustard and Worcestershire sauce. Whisk over medium heat until hot (2-3 minutes). Add peppers to taste. Pour dressing over spinach. Cover bowl with inverted skillet and let steam about 15 seconds. Toss salad with dressing and reserved bacon pieces. Serve immediately. Makes 2 servings.

FIRE AND ICE TOMATO SALAD

6 tomatoes, cut in thick wedges
1 large sweet pepper, cut in rings
1 large red onion, sliced in rings
1 cucumber sliced thin
1 tablespoon chopped parsley

Dressing:

   1/2 c vinegar
   1/3 c water
   1 teaspoon celery seed
   1 1/2 teaspoon mustard seed
   1/2 teaspoon salt
   1 tablespoon sugar
   hot sauce to taste
1/8 teaspoon pepper
1 avocado cubed, optional for garnish

Put the tomatoes, peppers, and onions in alternate layers in a salad bowl, reserving cucumber in a separate bowl. Combine dressing ingredients in saucepan. Bring to a boil and cook 1 minute. Pour over vegetables. Chill. Just before serving add the sliced cucumbers and sprinkle with parsley over top of vegetables. Garnish, if desired. Makes 6-8 servings.

STIR-FRY CHERRY TOMATOES AND HERBS

1 pint or about 3 dozen cherry tomatoes, stemmed, washed and patted dry
1 tablespoon butter
1 tablespoon olive oil
1 clove garlic, minced
2 scallions, minced
1/3 c chopped fresh basil
1 tablespoon chopped fresh oregano
salt and pepper

Heat butter and oil; add garlic and scallions and saute 2 or 3 minutes. Add tomatoes and herbs, shaking pan continuously for 2-3 minutes until heated through. Do not overcook. Season with salt and pepper to taste. Serve immediately. Makes 4 servings.

STUFFED CHERRY TOMATOES

24 cherry tomatoes (about 1 pint)
1/2 c plain yogurt cheese (see below)
3 tablespoon nonfat cream cheese
1/2 teaspoon dried dill weed
1/4 teaspoon dry mustard
1/8 teaspoon onion powder
shredded parmesan cheese

Cut off tops of tomatoes. Scoop out and discard pulp. Set shells aside. Combine cheeses, dill weed, mustard and onion powder. Spoon or pipe mixture into tomatoes. Sprinkle tops with parmesan cheese. Chill. To make yogurt cheese. Line mesh strainer with 3 paper towels. Place strainer over bowl. Spoon yogurt into strainer and cover with plastic wrap. Let drain overnight in refrigerator. Discard liquid. Store in closed container until used.

TOMATO ASPIC

7 medium tomatoes, cut into bite size chunks
2 medium celery stalks, sliced
1 medium onion, sliced
2 1/2 teaspoon salt
1 bay leaf
1/2 c water
2 envelopes unflavored gelatin
3 tablespoon sugar
2 tablespoon lemon juice
1/2 teaspoon Worcestershire sauce
1/2 teaspoon hot pepper sauce
vegetable cooking spray
1 (8 oz) container plain yogurt (1 cup)
2 tablespoon chopped fresh dill or 2 teaspoon dill weed
1 teaspoon grated lemon rind or peel
lettuce leaves for garnish

Cook tomatoes, celery, onion, salt and bay leaf until vegetables are tender, about 20 minutes. Mix water and gelatin and let stand 5 minutes to soften gelatin. Blend tomato mixture in blender until pureed; then press through a coarse sieve. Discard seeds and skins. Stir sugar, lemon juice, Worcestershire sauce, hot pepper sauce and gelatin mixture into tomato sauce. Cook until gelatin is completely dissolved. Pour into lightly sprayed bundt pan or mold, cover and refrigerate until set. Unmold gelatin onto lettuce leaves serve with dressing made by mixing yogurt, dill and lemon peel. Keep leftovers of aspic and dressing both refrigerated (covered) until used.

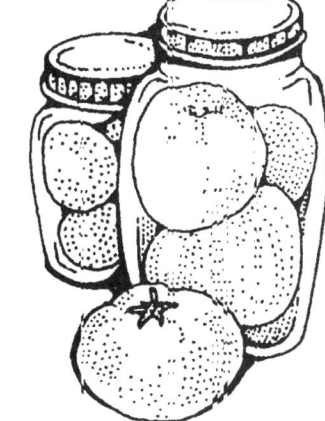

MARINATED TOMATOES

5 or 6 fresh tomatoes, peeled and quartered
1 large onion, finely chopped
6 large fresh basil leaves, cut into strips
1/2 c olive oil
1/3 c herb vinegar (one which complements basil)
1 clove garlic, crushed
1 tablespoon minced oregano leaves
2 tablespoon honey
salt and pepper

Layer tomatoes in jar with onions and basil strips. Make a dressing of the remaining ingredients and pour over tomatoes. Store in refrigerator overnight or at least 6 hours.

TOSSED SALAD WITH PARSLEY-GARLIC DRESSING

Combine 3 tablespoon olive oil, 2 tablespoon chopped parsley, 2 tablespoon sliced green onions, 1 tablespoon red wine vinegar and 1 teaspoon minced garlic. In salad bowl combine 8 cups greens, 1 head Belgian endive (separated into leaves) and 1 cup cherry tomatoes. Stir dressing well; pour over salad and toss.

TORTELLINI SALAD WITH RED WINE-HERB VINAIGRETTE

Red Wine-Herb Vinaigrette
3 tablespoon Dijon mustard
1/2 c + 1 tablespoon Red-Wine-Herb Vinegar (Recipe in condiment section)
salt and black pepper
1 1/2 c light olive oil
3 cloves garlic, peeled and crushed

Whisk mustard and Red-Wine-Herb vinegar in a bowl. Season with salt and pepper. Slowly dribble in olive oil while whisking. Add garlic and let vinaigrette stand at least an hour. Remove garlic and whisk again before using.

Tortellini Salad

6 quarts water
1 1/2 tablespoon salt
1 1/2 lb fresh cheese--filled tortellini
1/2 c chopped red onion
3/4 c chopped Italian (wide leaf) parsley
1 c diced red bell pepper (about 2 medium)
1 c large black olives
1/4 lb thinly sliced salami or other hard sausage, julienned

Bring water to a boil, stir in salt and tortellini and cook until tender about 7-12 minutes (taste test). Drain well. Combine tortellini, chopped onion, parsley and 1 cup vinaigrette. When cool add diced bell pepper, olives and sliced salami or sausage. Season to taste with salt and pepper and add additional vinaigrette if necessary. Toss again before serving. Makes 6-8 servings.

Note: Avoid refrigerating pasta salads for extended periods. If necessary, do so no more than 1 or 2 hours and bring to room temperature before serving.

HOT TUNA-SHRIMP SALAD

2 cans tuna
1/2 lb cooked, peeled, deveined shrimp cut up
1/4 c minced green pepper
1/4 c minced green onion
1 c minced celery
1/2 c sour cream
1 c mayonnaise
hot sauce to taste
1/3 c fine dry bread crumbs
2 tablespoon melted butter

Drain, and separate tuna chunks. Mix carefully with all ingredients, except last 2. Turn into greased casserole. Combine butter and bread crumbs and sprinkle over top. Bake at 400 for 15 minutes or until heated. Serves 6. Makes a good lunch or supper.

TURKEY PECAN & BLUE CHEESE SALAD WITH HONEY-HOT SAUCE DRESSING

1/2 c vegetable oil
1/2 c chopped onion
1/4 c white wine vinegar
1/4 c honey
4 teaspoon hot sauce
6 c assorted greens
2 c bite-size pieces curly endive
8 oz smoked turkey, diced
2/3 c crumbled blue cheese
2/3 c coarsely chopped pecans, toasted
1 avocado, peeled, pitted and diced

Combine first 5 ingredients in blender and puree. Season to taste with salt and pepper. Can be made 4 hours ahead and let stand at room temperature. Combine greens and endive in salad bowl. Toss with enough dressing to coat. Add remaining ingredients. Drizzle with more dressing; toss gently.

CRISP VEGETABLE SALAD

1/4 c red wine vinegar
4 shallots, minced
3 cloves garlic, minced
2 tablespoon Dijon mustard
1 tablespoon minced fresh tarragon or 1 teaspoon dried
1 tablespoon minced fresh basil or 1 teaspoon dried
1 teaspoon salt
1/4 teaspoon pepper
1 c olive oil
Romaine leaves
1/2 lb carrots, peeled, shredded
2 small zucchini, cut in 1/4 inch slices
1 red bell peppers, stemmed, seeded, cut in 1 inch slices
3 green onions with tops, cut in 2 inch strips
1 pint cherry tomatoes, cut in half
1/2 lb mushrooms, sliced

Combine first 8 ingredients and gradually whisk in oil. Refrigerate in tightly covered jar for 1 hour or overnight. At serving time line serving bowl with romaine leaves; arrange vegetables on lettuce. Shake dressing to blend. Pour over vegetables. Makes 6-8 servings.

MARINATED VEGETABLE MEDLEY

1 medium bunch broccoli (1 lb)
1 medium head cauliflower (1 lb)
1 small red onion, sliced and separated
1 large green pepper, cored, seeded and cut into strips

Marinade:
1 c crisco oil
2/3 c dry white wine
1 tablespoon Dijon mustard
1/2-1 teaspoon dried dill weed
1 teaspoon salt
1 teaspoon sugar
1/8 teaspoon pepper

Mix marinade and pour over vegetables; cover and refrigerate 1-2 days, stirring occasionally. For milder flavor and less crunch parboil broccoli and cauliflower 2 minutes and rinse in cold water before marinating.

COLESLAW DRESSING

1/2 c sour cream or yogurt
1/4 c mayonnaise
1 teaspoon lemon juice
3 teaspoon olive oil
2 pinches salt
1 teaspoon tarragon vinegar

DILL DRESSING

1 c sour cream
2 cloves garlic, mashed
1 teaspoon salt
1 teaspoon dill weed, finely chopped

Combine ingredients. Good on cucumbers or raw slice summer squash. Also good served warm on boiled potatoes, broccoli or cauliflower.

MUSTARD DRESSING

In small bowl with wire whisk or fork, beat 1/3 cup water and 1/4 cup prepared mustard until well blended. Gradually stir in 1 cup salad or olive oil, 1 teaspoon lemon juice, 1/2 teaspoon salt, 1/2 teaspoon tarragon and 1/4 teaspoon coarsely ground black pepper. Beat until well mixed. Store in tightly covered jar in refrigerator. Stir before using. Serve with a green salad or cooked ham.

THOUSAND ISLAND DRESSING

Good with seafood, egg, vegetable, or mixed - green salads.

Mix 1 cup mayonnaise, 1/2 cup chile sauce, 2 tablespoon minced green peppers, 3 tablespoon chopped stuffed olives, 1 minced pimento, 1 teaspoon grated onion or 2 teaspoon chopped chives. Make about 2 cups.

SHARP-CHEDDAR DRESSING

Good for fruit, vegetables, or pasta salads.

Finely shred 1/2 lb sharp cheddar cheese; soften at room temperature. Add 1 cup mayonnaise, 2 tablespoon vinegar, 1 minced clove garlic, 1/2 teaspoon salt, dash cayenne pepper, and 2 teaspoon Worcestershire sauce. Beat until blended. Makes about 2 cups.

HERB DRESSING

Good on meat or seafood salads.

To 3/4 cup French dressing add 2 teaspoon chopped fresh dill, marjoram, rosemary, or summer savory.

SALAD DRESSING

1/4 c half and half
1/4 c water
2 tablespoon flour
2 tablespoon sugar
1/2 teaspoon salt
pinch cayenne pepper
2 egg yolks, beaten
1/4 c cider vinegar
2 tablespoon vegetable oil
1/4 c sour cream
1 1/2 teaspoon horseradish
1 teaspoon Dijon style mustard
1/2 teaspoon Worcestershire sauce
dash hot sauce

Mix half and half, water, flour, sugar, salt and pepper. Heat, stirring constantly until thickened. Add oil. Remove from heat, cover and let cool slightly. Add other ingredients, mix well. Taste to adjust seasonings. Cover and refrigerate until cold. Use on spinach salad, potato salad, hard boiled eggs, on sandwiches, or a dip for fresh vegetables. Make abut 1 1/4 cups.

BLUE CHEESE DRESSING

2 c olive oil
1 c vinegar
juice of 1 lemon
2 teaspoon paprika
dash Worcestershire sauce
1 teaspoon grated onion
1/8 teaspoon cayenne pepper
1 teaspoon salt
8 oz Blue cheese, mashed

Mix all ingredients well and place in quart jar. Shake well before using. Keeps a long time in refrigerator.

CREAMY PARSLEY SALAD DRESSING

1/2 c salad oil
1/3 c minced fresh parsley leaves
3 green onion, chopped
1/2 teaspoon salt
1/2 teaspoon black pepper
2 tablespoon sour cream

Combine all ingredients except sour cream in blender or food processor and mix well. With machine running, slowly add sour cream to blend thoroughly. Refrigerate in a jar with the lid on until ready to use.

YOGURT SALAD DRESSING

1 c plain yogurt
1/2 c mayonnaise
1/2 teaspoon garlic powder
2 teaspoon minced chives
1 tablespoon finely chopped parsley
1 teaspoon lemon juice

Mix all ingredients together. Let stand about 6 hours before using (in refrigerator) to blend flavors. Delicious on green salads or as a dip for raw vegetables.

FRENCH DRESSING

1/2 c lemon juice
1 1/2 c olive oil
3 clove garlic, mashed
2 teaspoon salt
1/4 teaspoon pepper
1 teaspoon dry mustard
dash of cayenne
1/3 c chili sauce
1 tablespoon ground horseradish
1 teaspoon paprika

Mix all ingredients thoroughly. Put into a covered container. Refrigerate. Shake until well blended before using.

Note: Parsley — There are two main types of parsley, the curly one used as a garnish and widely available in supermarkets and the Italian flat leaf parsley which has a better flavor and much better to use in cooking. Parsley is good both fresh and dried. It can be added to almost any meat, poultry, seafood or vegetable dish while cooking and is very good when minced finely and sprinkled over tomatoes, green salads, scrambled eggs, in fact, almost anything.

It is a mistake to think of parsley only as a garnish or an addition to recipes for its flavor and appearance. Parsley is rich in vitamins A, B, C and niacin so be sure to eat the garnish on your plate and be liberal in adding it to your cooking.

ITALIAN CREAM DRESSING

1 can tomato soup
1/2 c olive oil
1/4 c vinegar
1/4 c grated Parmesan
1 teaspoon basil leaves, finely chopped
1 teaspoon oregano leaves, finely chopped
1/8 teaspoon garlic salt

In covered jar, combine ingredients; chill. Shake well before using. Good with a tossed green salad.

BASIL SALAD DRESSING

1 c salad oil
1/3 c vinegar
1/2 teaspoon salt
1 clove garlic, crushed
1 1/2 teaspoon dried basil leaves

Measure all ingredients into a jar and stir thoroughly. Store in refrigerator. Makes about 1 1/3 cup dressing.

CREAMY YOGURT DRESSING

1/2 c olive oil
1/2 c apple cider vinegar
1 tablespoon prepared mustard
1 tablespoon lemon juice
1 clove garlic, minced
1 tablespoon soy sauce
1/4 teaspoon dill weed
1/2 c plain low-fat yogurt

Mix all ingredients until thoroughly blended.

HERB DRESSING

1/4 c olive oil
1/4 c apple cider vinegar
1 tablespoon prepared mustard
1 tablespoon lemon juice
1 tablespoon chopped parsley
1 tablespoon chopped chives
1/2 teaspoon basil
1/8 teaspoon cayenne pepper
1 clove garlic, minced
6 oz V-8 juice or tomato juice

Combine all ingredients and mix thoroughly. Makes about 1 1/2 cups. Thirty-three calories per tablespoon.

HOMEMADE MAYONNAISE

2 eggs
2 tablespoon lemon juice
1/2 teaspoon salt
1/2 teaspoon sugar
4-5 drops hot sauce
1 1/2 c crisco oil

Combine first 5 ingredients; beat until smooth while adding oil slowly. Beat until thick and smooth.

BLUE CHEESE DRESSING

1 recipe home made mayonnaise (above)
4 oz blue cheese
1 pkg (3 oz) cream cheese
1 clove garlic, minced
1/4 teaspoon pepper
1/4-1/3 c milk

Crumble blue cheese with a fork; blend in cream cheese. Add other ingredients and mix well. Mix in milk to desired consistency.

FRESH TOMATO SALAD DRESSING

3 tomatoes, peeled, seeded and finely chopped
1/3 c tomato juice
1 clove garlic, finely chopped
2 green onions, finely chopped
3 tablespoon chopped parsley
1/2 c chopped fresh basil
1 tablespoon lemon juice
4 tablespoon red wine vinegar
1/4 teaspoon sugar
1/2 c olive oil
salt and pepper to taste

Combine all ingredients, adding salt and pepper to taste.

HERBED CROUTONS

1/4 grated Parmesan cheese
2 tablespoon oregano
2 tablespoon garlic powder
1 tablespoon sweet basil
1/2 teaspoon salt
1/2 teaspoon black pepper
4-5 c dry bread cubes
3 tablespoon olive oil or plain salad oil

In a small bowl mix cheese, oregano, garlic powder, basil, salt and pepper. In a large bowl, toss bread cubes with oil; then toss with cheese mixture. Spread on ungreased cookie sheet. Bake in a 225 oven 1 hour, or until dry and light golden. Stir occasionally. Cool. Makes 4-5 cups. Store in plastic bag. Will keep about a month in pantry; longer in freezer.

Kyle, Jared, and Steve Arnold enjoying family dinner at Orville and Helen Shultz's.

Eggs & Cheese

BACON AND DOUBLE CHEESE QUICHE

10 strips lean bacon
4 large eggs
1 1/2 c light cream
1/4 teaspoon dried thyme
1/4 teaspoon white pepper
1/2 c shredded Gruyere cheese
1/2 c shredded white cheddar cheese
9 inch pie crust, baked until lightly golden

Cook bacon until crisp, transfer to paper towel to drain. In a small bowl, whisk together the eggs, cream, thyme and pepper. Pour into crust. Crumble the bacon. Sprinkle the egg mixture with the bacon and cheeses. Bake at 375 until golden and custard is set. Serve while warm.

> *Note:* Thyme is a very versatile herb which goes well with mild flavored foods such as seafood, chicken, lamb and dried beans. There are two main varieties that are best for use, English thyme and lemon thyme. Of the two the lemon thyme has a milder flavor and a much prettier appearance in the herb garden. Just a smidgen is enough to flavor foods. It can be used alone or combine it with other herbs such as basil and oregano. It enhances the flavors of soups, most vegetables and dressings.

CHEESE PUFF

5 c grated sharp cheddar cheese
4 c grated Monterey Jack cheese
2 medium tomatoes, seeded and chopped
1 (7 oz) can diced green chilies
1 (2 1/4 oz) can sliced black olives, drained
1/2 c all-purpose flour
6 eggs, separated
1 (5.33 oz) can evaporated milk
1/2 teaspoon salt
1/2 teaspoon dried oregano leaves, crumbled
1/4 teaspoon ground cumin
1/4 teaspoon pepper
1/4 teaspoon cream of tartar

Combine first 5 ingredients with 2 tablespoon flour and mix well. Spoon into greased casserole dish. Beat egg yolks. Gradually blend in remaining flour and milk and beat until smooth. Add salt, oregano, cumin and pepper. Mix well. Beat egg whites until foamy, add cream of tartar and continue beating until stiff peaks form. Fold egg whites into yolk mixture, blending thoroughly. Spoon over cheese. Bake until top is golden brown and firm, about 1 hour. Let stand 15 minutes before serving.

CHEESE, SAUSAGE, & EGG CASSEROLE

1/2 c butter
1 lb bulk pork sausage
6 slices French bread, cubed
2 teaspoon dried basil
1 teaspoon dill
1/2 c shredded cheddar cheese
6 eggs, beaten
2 c milk

Melt butter and pour in baking pan. Brown sausage and set aside. Layer half bread cubes in baking pan and sprinkle with basil, dill and cheese. Sprinkle browned sausage over herbs and cheese. Layer rest of bread. Beat eggs and add milk. Pour over contents of baking pan. Bake at 350 for 1/2 hour or until set. Cut into squares and serve hot.

COTTAGE CHEESE & CHIVE OMELET

6 eggs
1 carton (8 oz) creamed cottage cheese
1/2 teaspoon salt
1/8 teaspoon pepper
2 tablespoon chopped chives
1 1/2 tablespoon butter

Beat all ingredients, except butter, until fluffy. Heat butter in skillet, and pour in egg mixture. Cook over low heat until firm and browned on bottom. Put under medium heat in broiler until browned on top. Cut in wedges. Makes 4 servings.

CORN OMELET

2 large ears of corn (1 c canned corn can be substituted)
6 slices bacon
4 tablespoon butter
1 large onion, thinly sliced
1 c diced green pepper
6 eggs
1 teaspoon salt
1/4 teaspoon black pepper
few drops hot pepper sauce

Scrap corn from cob. Cook in small amount of salted water 3-5 minutes. Drain. Cook bacon until crisp. Crumble and add to corn. Pour off fat; return 1 tablespoon to skillet. Add 2 tablespoon butter to bacon fat and heat until butter is melted. Saute onion in fat until tender and add to corn. Beat eggs with hot sauce, salt and pepper. Add the corn mixture. Wipe skillet clean with paper toweling. Heat the remaining 2 tablespoon butter with 1 tablespoon bacon fat. Add the egg mixture and cook until bottom is set, but top is still liquid. Transfer skillet to 325 oven and bake 2 minutes. Or until set. Delicious made with fresh corn from the garden. Makes 4 servings.

EGGS BENEDICT

Cilantro Cream:
1/4 c + 2 tablespoon sour cream
3 tablespoon whipping cream
2 tablespoon chopped fresh cilantro

Salsa:
2 tomatoes, seeded and chopped
1/2 medium red onion, chopped
1/4 c chopped fresh cilantro
1/4 c fresh lime juice
1 jalapeno chili, seeded and minced

Sausage and Eggs:
1 1/2 lb bulk hot pork sausage
4 garlic cloves, minced
2 tablespoon chopped fresh chives
1 tablespoon chopped fresh parsley
1 tablespoon chopped fresh thyme or 1 teaspoon dried
2 tablespoon olive oil
1/4 c distilled white vinegar
8 eggs
4 corn, tortillas, warmed

For cilantro cream: Mix all ingredients. Season with salt and pepper.

For salsa: Mix all ingredients. Season with salt and pepper.

For sausage and eggs: Combine pork, garlic and herbs. Season with salt and pepper. Form into 8 (1/2 inch) patties. Heat olive oil. Add sausage patties and brown 2 minutes per side. Cover and cook until cooked through. Bring wide shallow pot of water to a boil. Add vinegar. Crack eggs into water. Simmer about 3 minutes until whites are set. Using slotted spoon remove eggs to paper towels. Place 1 tortilla on each plate. Place 2 sausage patties atop each. Top sausages with eggs. Spoon cilantro cream and salsa over eggs. Makes 4 servings.

EGG AND OLIVE LOAF

2 envelopes unflavored gelatin
2 teaspoon salt
1/4 c lemon juice
1/2 teaspoon hot sauce
2 c mayonnaise
1 tablespoon grated onion
1 c diced celery
1/2 c chopped stuffed green olives and pitted ripe olives mixed
8 hard cooked eggs, chopped

Soften unflavored gelatin in 1 cup cold water. Place over boiling water to dissolve. Add salt, lemon juice, hot sauce. Cool. Gradually stir in onion, celery, olives and hard-cooked eggs. Turn into large loaf pan. Chill until firm. Makes 8 servings.

EGG AND OLIVE MOLD

1 envelope unflavored gelatin
1/2 c cold water
1/2 teaspoon salt
juice 1 lemon
1 c mayonnaise
hot sauce
small amount grated onion
3/4 c diced celery
1/4 c chopped onions
4 hard-cooked eggs, chopped
salad greens

Soften gelatin in cold water. Dissolve over hot water. Add salt, lemon juice and hot sauce; cool. Stir mixture slowly into mayonnaise. Add remaining ingredients, except salad greens, and pour into mold. Chill until firm. Unmold onto salad greens. Makes 4 servings.

EGGS WITH ONION-TOMATO-PIMENTO SAUCE

1 clove garlic, minced
2 onions, chopped
3 tablespoon butter
1 or 2 dried hot red peppers
1 pimento, chopped
1 can (28 oz) tomatoes
salt
8 eggs

Cook garlic and onion in 2 tablespoon butter until lightly browned. Add crumbled hot pepper, pimento and tomatoes. Simmer about 45 minutes or until thickened. Add salt to taste. Fry eggs in remaining butter. Serve with the sauce. Makes 4 servings.

HERB CUSTARD EGGS

4 eggs
3/4 teaspoon salt
dash pepper
1/4 teaspoon each marjoram, thyme, and sage
1 1/3 c milk

Slightly beat eggs, seasoning, herbs, and milk in top of well-greased double boiler. Cook, covered, over boiling water, without stirring 20 minutes or until just set. After 15 minutes remove cover and if eggs have set discontinue cooking. Spoon carefully onto hot plates.
Makes 4 servings.

SHRIMP DILLED DEVILED EGGS

6 eggs
1/4 c mayonnaise
4 1/2 oz can medium shrimp, rinsed and drained
2 tablespoon chopped green onion
1 tablespoon chopped fresh dill weed
pinch of pepper
1 tablespoon lime juice
2 teaspoon country-style Dijon mustard
1/4 teaspoon hot pepper sauce
fresh dill weed

Cover eggs with cold water in saucepan. Cook over high heat until water comes to a full boil. Cover and turn off heat; let stand 20 minutes. Cool eggs in cold water; peel and cut in half crosswise. Remove yolks from whites. Set whites aside. Mash egg yolks with a fork; add mayonnaise, shrimp, onion, 1 tablespoon dill, pepper, lime juice, mustard and hot sauce. Stir to blend. Spoon egg yolk mixture into egg whites. Garnish with sprig of fresh dill. Place in egg carton to transport; refrigerate until used.

THE INCREDIBLE OMELET

1 (8 oz) jar taco sauce (mild or hot)
8 eggs
1/2 c water
1/4 c undrained chopped chilies
1/2 teaspoon salt
1/4 c butter
1 c shredded cheddar cheese

Heat sauce and keep hot. Beat together eggs, water, chilies and salt. For each omelet melt 1 tablespoon butter on medium high heat. Pour about 2/3 cup egg mixture in butter which should set around edges immediately. With pancake turner move set edges to center while tilting pan slightly so uncooked eggs can flow to bottom. While top is still moist sprinkle 1/4 cup cheese on half of omelet. Slip turner under unfilled side and fold over filling. Turn omelet on heated plate and keep warm until you cook other three omelets. Pour about 1/4 cup hot sauce over each omelet. Makes 4 servings.

MEXICAN STYLE SCRAMBLED EGGS

6 flour tortillas
8 eggs
1/4 c water
2 tablespoon chopped green chilies
2 tablespoon taco sauce
1/4 teaspoon salt
dash of pepper
vegetable cooking spray
3/4 c taco sauce, divided
1/2 c + 1 tablespoon shredded cheddar cheese, divided

Wrap tortillas in foil and bake at 350 for 7 minutes. Set aside and keep warm. Combine next 6 ingredients and mix with wire whisk. Cook in spray coated skillet on medium heat, stirring often, until eggs are firm but still moist. Spoon 1/6 of mixture on each tortilla; top with 1 tablespoon taco sauce and 1 tablespoon cheese. Fold opposite side over. Garnish each with 1 tablespoon taco sauce and 1/2 tablespoon cheese.

MUSHROOM EGG PIE

2 tablespoon package bread crumbs
3/4 lb small mushrooms
1/4 c butter
1 c chopped onion
2 tablespoon all-purpose flour
1/2 c grated Swiss cheese
3 eggs
3 egg yolks
2 c light cream or half-and-half
1 1/4 teaspoon salt
1/8 teaspoon hot pepper sauce or to taste
1 tablespoon melted butter
3 egg whites
1/4 teaspoon cream of tartar

Butter pie plate generously. Coat with bread crumbs. Set aside five mushrooms for garnish; slice remaining mushrooms. Melt butter, saute sliced mushrooms and onion 3 minutes. Stir in flour until blended. Spoon mixture over pie plate. Sprinkle with cheese. Beat eggs and egg yolks, add cream, salt and hot pepper sauce. Pour over mushroom mixture. Bake 25 minutes at 375. Cut reserved mushrooms in half and toss in 1 tablespoon butter. Beat egg whites and cream of tartar until stiff. Spoon egg whites around outside of pie. Arrange mushrooms in center. Bake about 10 more minutes until knife inserted comes out clean. Makes 6 servings.

SLICED TOMATO AND EGG FRANCAISE

1 c mayonnaise
1/4 c milk
2 1/2 teaspoon lemon juice
1 teaspoon tarragon or sage leaves
3/4 teaspoon salt
1/2 teaspoon sugar
1/4 teaspoon pepper
4 hard-cooked eggs
4 medium tomatoes

Use wire whisk to mix mayonnaise, milk, lemon juice, tarragon, salt, sugar and pepper. Slice eggs and tomatoes; arrange slices alternately on platter. Spoon dressing over tomatoes and eggs. Makes 8 accompaniment servings.

TANGY BAKED EGGS

6 English muffins, split, toasted and buttered
1 can condensed cream of celery soup
1/2 c sour cream
1 can condensed cream of mushroom soup
6 tablespoon chopped green onions
2 tablespoon Worcestershire sauce
1/4 c dry Sherry
2 tablespoon Dijon mustard
4 teaspoon chopped pimento
1/2 teaspoon liquid hot pepper sauce
1/2 teaspoon dried basil
1/2 teaspoon dried oregano
12 extra large eggs
1 c grated Parmesan cheese
1/2 teaspoon paprika

Mix soups, sour cream, green onions, Worcestershire sauce, Sherry, mustard, pimento, hot pepper sauce, basil and oregano. Spread this mixture into two 9 x 13 inch baking pans. Break eggs onto the mixture and sprinkle with cheese and paprika. Bake, uncovered in 325 oven until whites are set, about 25 minutes. Lift eggs out and place each on a muffin half (muffins should be warm). Spoon sauce on top and serve immediately. Makes 12 servings.

FRESH TOMATO TART

Serve with green salad and fresh French bread to mop up the juices.

1 (9 inch) pie shell, pre-baked 5 minutes
3-4 medium tomatoes, cored and cut into thick slices
salt and pepper
1 tablespoon olive oil
1 clove garlic, finely chopped
1 medium onion, finely chopped
1/4 c freshly grated Parmesan cheese
2 eggs
1 c whole milk
1/2 c grated Fontina or Monterey Jack cheese
1/2 c chopped basil
2 tablespoon chopped parsley
2 tablespoon chopped chives

Pat tomato slices dry with paper towels. Sprinkle with salt and pepper. Heat oil; saute garlic and onion until softened. Cool. Sprinkle 3 tablespoon of the Parmesan cheese on crust. Top with onion mixture and lay tomato slices on next. Beat eggs, milk, Fontina or Jack cheese, basil and parsley until mixed. Pour over tomatoes in crust. Sprinkle with additional cheese and chives. Bake 35 minutes or until puffed and golden in 375 oven. Let cool on a wire rack a few minutes before cutting and serving. Makes 6 servings.

JALEPENO PIE

Pastry for 9 inch pie
1-12 oz jar whole pickled jalepeno peppers drained and seeded
2 c shredded Monterey Jack cheese
4 large eggs
1/4 teaspoon salt
2 tablespoon chopped fresh cilantro

Put pastry shell into pie plate. Cut jalepeno lengthwise into thin slices and arrange on the bottom and sides of pie shell. Sprinkle cheese over pepper slices and press gently into pepper strips. Combine remaining ingredients until well blended. Pour over cheese. Bake uncovered at 350 for 25-30 minutes or until set and lightly browned. Let stand 5 minutes then sprinkle with fresh cilantro.

HOT CHEESE DIP

My sister-in-law, Ina V. Black, gave me this recipe several years ago. This is something I try to keep on hand all the time. It is so good, and not just with chips. I like it added to cream of tomato soup, heated and used on taco salad, or as a topping for baked potatoes.

2 pounds Velveeta cheese
2 cups Hellmann's Mayonnaise
2 medium onions, grated
Juice of 2 medium lemons
1 tablespoon sugar
1/4 cup minced Jalapeno peppers (canned)
1 clove garlic, minced

Melt cheese and add all other ingredients. Mix well with mixer. Store in refrigerator. Frito corn chips are very good with this.

Vegetables

SPRINGTIME ASPARAGUS

2 lbs. asparagus
1/4c. dried bread crumbs
1/3c. margarine
1 tablespoon chopped fresh parsley

Prepare asparagus stalks. Cook in boiling, salted water just until tender. Saute bread crumbs in margarine until golden; add parsley. Drain asparagus and top with buttered crumbs.

ASPARAGUS WITH PARSLEY SAUCE

2 tablespoon butter
2 tablespoon flour
1 c chicken stock
1/2 c light cream
3/4 teaspoon salt
1/8 teaspoon pepper
2 egg yolks
3/4 c finely chopped fresh parsley
2-2 1/2 lbs fresh asparagus, cooked

Melt butter; remove from heat and blend in flour. Stir in chicken stock and 1/4 cup of the cream. Return to heat and cook, stirring, over medium heat until mixture begins to thicken about 5 minutes. Add salt and pepper. Beat egg yolks, mix with remaining cream and stir into the sauce. Cook over low heat only until hot, about two minutes. Just before serving, add parsley and heat about 30 seconds. Serve over the hot asparagus.

ASPARAGUS VINAIGRETTE

2 lb. asparagus
6 tablespoon vegetable oil
3 tablespoon wine vinegar
1 teaspoon dry mustard
1 teaspoon finely chopped parsley
1 teaspoon finely chopped chives
1/2 teaspoon salt
1/8 teaspoon pepper
1/2 teaspoon finely chopped tarragon
1/4 clove garlic, mashed
1 tablespoon finely chopped hard cooked egg white (optional)

Trim and wash asparagus; cook in boiling salted water just until tender, about 10-12 minutes. Drain well. Place in glass dish and chill well. Combine remaining ingredients and chill. Pour dressing over asparagus and chill an additional 30 minutes. Serve on lettuce if desired.

HERBED GREEN BEANS

1lb fresh green beans, cut in 1 in pieces or 1 16 oz pkg frozen cut green beans
1/2 c chopped onion
1/4 c chopped celery
2-3 tablespoon butter or margarine
1 clove garlic, minced
1/4 c dried rosemary, crushed
1/4 teaspoon dried basil, crushed
salt to taste
bacon pieces for garnish

Cook fresh green beans, covered, in small amount of boiling water until crisp tender. Drain well. Stir in remaining ingredients, cover and cook over low heat until vegetables are tender. May need to add a little more liquid. Garnish with bacon bits.

COMPANY LIMA BEANS

1 lb dried lima beans
2 quarts boiling water
1 large onion, chopped
4 stalks celery, sliced
1 tablespoon salt
1/2 teaspoon marjoram
1/4 c butter
3 tablespoon cream
3 drops tabasco
2 tablespoon chopped parsley

Cover the beans with boiling water, bring to boil again and boil 2 minutes. Remove from heat and let stand 1 hour. Add onion, celery, salt, marjoram and butter. Bring to a boil, reduce heat and simmer over low heat for about 45 minutes. Stir in cream, tabasco and parsley.

BAKED BEANS SOUTHERN STYLE

1 lb dried white beans
6 c water
2 cloves garlic, minced
1 onion, sliced
1 small dried hot red pepper
1 bay leaf
3/4 lb salt pork, sliced
3 tablespoon molasses
1/4 c catsup
1 teaspoon dry mustard
1/2 teaspoon ginger
1 1/2 teaspoon Worcestershire sauce
1/2 teaspoon salt
1/4 c brown sugar, packed

Cover beans with water, bring to a boil and boil for 2 minutes. Cover and let stand 1 hour. Add next 5 ingredients and cook until beans are tender. Drain, reserving 2 cups liquid. To reserved liquid add remaining ingredients except sugar. Put beans in shallow 2-quart baking dish. Remove bay leaf and pork slices. Arrange pork slices on top of beans. Add the liquid and sprinkle sugar over top. Bake uncovered at 400 degree for 1 hour.

DRIED WHITE BEANS WITH SAVORY

1 lb. dried white beans
water
salt and pepper to taste
2 tablespoon butter or meat drippings
1/2 teaspoon dried savory
1 medium onion, minced (optional)

Soak beans overnight in 2 quarts of water or boil for 2 minutes, cover and let stand one or two hours. Drain and discard water. Add water to cover and bring to a boil. Add salt, pepper, savory and shortening. Bring to a boil again, cover and lower heat to simmer until beans are tender, about 2 1/2 to 3 hours. Adjust seasonings.

Note: SAVORY — There are 2 kinds of savory, the winter savory which is a hardy perennial shrubby plant and the summer savory which needs to be planted each year. Summer savory is preferred by most cooks because it is not as strong tasting as the winter type. Savory has a peppery, aromatic taste which resembles thyme though it is not as strong. The nickname for savory is the "bean herb" because of its close affinity for beans. Its use should not be limited to beans because it also goes well with soups, stuffings and in meat dishes. Crushed leaves mixed with bread crumbs make a tasty coating for fish or pork before frying. Savory is easily dried for winter use and it also freezes well.

BEETS WITH PARSLEY BUTTER

6 medium sized fresh beets (1 1/4 lbs)
boiling water
2 tablespoon butter
1/2 teaspoon crumbled basil leaves
1/2 teaspoon salt
1/8 teaspoon black pepper
1 1/2 tablespoon chopped fresh parsley

Leave the beets whole with roots and about 2 in. of the tops. Cook in boiling water until tender, 25-30 minutes. Remove from heat, slip off skins and trim off tops and roots. Slice 1/4 inch thick and place in saucepan with butter, basil, salt and pepper. Cook until hot. Turn into a serving dish and sprinkle with chopped parsley.

BEETS WITH CARAWAY SEEDS

2 cups cooked and sliced beets, drained
2 tablespoons butter
1 tablespoon lemon juice
1/2 teaspoon salt
dash of black pepper
3/4 teaspoon caraway seeds
1/4 cup sour cream (optional)

Place all ingredients in a saucepan and heat but do not boil. Serve hot.

HERBED BROCCOLI

2 heads broccoli, cut into flowerettes
2 c chicken stock
1 small onion, chopped
1 teaspoon leaf marjoram, minced
1 teaspoon leaf basil, minced
3 tablespoon melted margarine

Prepare broccoli. In large skillet, combine chicken stock, onion, marjoram, basil and broccoli. Cover and cook just until tender. Drain. Drizzle with margarine.

COUNTRY SPROUTS

1 pint Brussel sprouts
1 tablespoon sugar
1 tablespoon cider vinegar
1 tablespoon water
1 teaspoon dried tarragon leaves, crushed

Cut sprouts into halves. Cook covered in salted boiling water until tender. Drain and sprinkle with remaining ingredients. Toss lightly to mix.

CREAMED SAVORY CABBAGE

1 medium head cabbage
water to cover
salt to taste
2 tablespoon butter
2 tablespoon flour
1 c milk or half & half
1/2-1 teaspoon chopped fresh savory

Remove the core and outer leaves of cabbage and shred it fine. Put the cabbage into rapidly boiling water seasoned to taste with salt. Cook about 10 minutes until the cabbage is crisp-tender. Drain.

Meanwhile melt the butter and stir in the flour. Add the milk stirring as you do. When the sauce is thick and smooth add the savory. Continue cooking for 5 minutes stirring occasionally. Combine the cabbage with the sauce and heat through.

DILLED CARROTS AND GREEN BEANS

1 lb carrots
2 cans (1 lb each) blue lake green beans, vertical pack
2 cloves garlic, split in half
1 1/2 c wine vinegar
1 1/2 c water
4 tablespoon salt
2 tablespoon crushed hot red pepper
1/2 cup snipped fresh dill or 2 tablespoon dill weed

Peel carrots, cut in strips and cook until limp; drain. Drain liquid from beans and pack with carrots, 1/2 garlic clove into 4 hot, sterilized 1-pint jars. Bring last 5 ingredients to a boil, pour over vegetables, seal with sterilized lids or can be stored in refrigerator.

SAUTEED RED CABBAGE

1 large onion, chopped
1/2 c bacon drippings or vegetable shortening
1 medium head red cabbage, shredded
3 medium tart apples, chopped
1 bay leaf
1 1/2 teaspoon salt
1/8 teaspoon black pepper
1/4 c red wine vinegar
1 tablespoon sugar

Saute onion in fat until golden brown. Add cabbage, apples, bay leaf, salt and pepper; mix well. Cover and cook over low heat about 20 minutes, stirring occasionally. Combine vinegar and sugar; add to cabbage. Cook 5 minutes more.

HERBED CREOLE CABBAGE

1 medium head cabbage
boiling water
1/4 c chopped onion
1 c chopped green pepper
3 tablespoon butter
2 c canned tomatoes
3/4 teaspoon oregano
2 1/2 teaspoon salt
1 1/2 teaspoon sugar
2 teaspoon lemon juice

Shred cabbage, cover and cook in small amount of boiling water. Cook the onion and green pepper in butter until they are wilted. Add the tomatoes and simmer 15 minutes. Drain cooked cabbage, add the tomato sauce and the remaining ingredients and serve hot.

GLAZED CARROTS

9-12 medium carrots-about 1 1/2 lbs
4 tablespoon butter or margarine
2 tablespoon brown sugar
2 tablespoon lemon juice
1 tablespoon medium hot sauce

Peel carrots and cut in half lengthwise. Cook in salted water until tender; drain well. Melt butter in heavy skillet; add lemon juice, brown sugar and hot sauce. Stir until mixture thickens. Add carrots; stir until well glazed and heated through. Make 6 servings.

MINTED CARROTS

7 c carrots, sliced
1/4 c firmly packed brown sugar
2 teaspoons cornstarch
1/2 teaspoon salt
1/4 c fresh mint, minced
Fresh mint leaves optional

Pour water to a depth of 1/2 inch in large saucepan; add carrots. Bring to a boil; cover and let simmer about eight minutes or until crisp tender. Drain, reserving 3/4 cup cooking liquid. Set carrots aside and keep warm. Combine next 3 ingredients, gradually add reserved liquid and place over heat, stirring constantly. Cook until thickened. Add carrots and mint and toss gently to coat. Garnish with mint leaves. Makes 10 servings.

HERBED CREAMED CAULIFLOWER

1 medium head cauliflower
1 tablespoon lemon juice
1/3 c mayonnaise
2 tablespoon milk
1/2 teaspoon sugar
1/2 teaspoon fines herb

Break cauliflower into flowerets. Stir lemon juice into small amount of boiling salted water. Add cauliflower, cover and cook until tender. Drain well. Heat remaining ingredients in a small pan, stirring constantly, until heated through but not boiling. Serve sauce over warm cauliflower and sprinkle with the fines herbes.

PRINCESS' PEAS

2 c frozen peas
1/2 teaspoon sugar
2 tablespoon butter
3/4 teaspoon dried marjoram, crushed

Cook peas with sugar, drain well. Melt butter in pan and stir in marjoram. Heat, stirring until butter starts to bubble. Pour over peas and mix well.

CHILI RELLENO CASSEROLE (LOW FAT)

1 (32 oz) can fat-free refried beans
1 teaspoon chili powder
2 (4 oz) cans diced green chilies
1 lb fat-free shredded Monterey Jack Cheese
1 c fat-free egg substitute
4 tablespoon flour
1 c skim milk

Season the refried beans with chili powder and spread over the bottom of 9 x 13 inch baking dish, lightly spray with cooking spray. Layer chilies and cheese on top of beans. Mix eggs, flour and milk and blend well. Spread egg mixture on top of cheese. Bake at 350 degree for 30-45 minutes until egg mixture is set and lightly browned. Makes 8 servings.

Note: FINES HERBES — Fines Herbes is a blend of chervil, parsley, chives and tarragon. It is available in dried form or you can make your own by tieing springs of each herb in a bundle and drop into food as it is being cooked or when using fresh, snip a few leaves and mix together to sprinkle on food.

CORN SOUFFLE

1/4 c butter
1/4 c flour
1 c milk
1 can (1 lb) cream style corn
4 eggs, separated
1/2 teaspoon salt
1/2 cup finely grated cheddar cheese
1 teaspoon caraway seed

Melt butter in heavy saucepan, add flour and stir to mix completely; add milk and corn. Cook, stirring constantly until it thickens. Remove from heat. Add salt, cheese and caraway seeds then blend in well beaten eggs. Fold in stiffly beaten egg whites. Place in a greased 2 quart casserole and bake at 325 degree about 45 minutes.

JALEPENO CORN PUDDING

1 1/2 c cream style corn
1 c yellow corn meal
1 c butter or margarine, melted
1/4 c buttermilk
2 medium onions, chopped
2 eggs, beaten
1/2 teaspoon baking soda
1 1/2 c grated cheddar
3 jalepeno peppers, fresh or canned, diced

Combine first 7 ingredients in large bowl and mix well. Turn 1/2 batter into greased 9 inch baking pan. Cover with 1/2 cheese and all the jalepeno then remaining cheese. Top with remaining batter. Bake at 350 for 1 hour. Cool about 15 minutes then cut into squares to serve.

CAJUN CORN

6 ears fresh corn
1/2 c heavy cream
2 slices bacon
6 scallions, white bulbs and green ends chopped separately
1 red bell pepper, seeded and chopped
2 ripe tomatoes, seeded and chopped
1/2 teaspoon sugar
pinch fresh thyme or dried
2 teaspoon chopped fresh basil or 1/2 teaspoon dried
salt and pepper

Cut the corn kernels from 2 ears of corn and place in bowl. Using a sharp knife, cut corn from the remaining 4 cobs by slicing halfway into the kernels down the full length of the cob to release milk. With the back of the knife, rub up and down each cob to remove all pulp and juice. Add to the kernels in the bowl. Stir in cream. Saute bacon until crisp. Remove, drain on paper towels and set aside. Add chopped white bulbs of scallions and chopped red pepper to skillet and cook until soft, about 5 minutes. Add tomatoes, sugar, thyme and basil. Cook for 5 minutes. Add corn-cream mixture and cook, stirring constantly until corn is done and mixture is creamy, about 10 minutes. Add salt and pepper to taste. Sprinkle with green scallions and crumbled bacon. Makes 4 servings. Very good served with turkey at Thanksgiving.

CORN CASSEROLE

1 can (16 oz) mexican style corn (with sweet peppers), drained
1 (16 oz) can cream style corn
4 large eggs, at room temperature
1/2 c all-purpose flour
1 tablespoon granulated sugar
1 1/2 c (6 oz) shredded jalapeno Jack Cheese

(Monterey Jack with chili peppers)
1/2 c heavy whipping cream
1/2 c chopped scallions
1 garlic clove minced
1/4 teaspoon hot pepper sauce, or to taste

Bring both corns to a simmer and transfer to a mixing bowl. Whisk eggs into corn, one at a time. Whisk in one cup of the cheese, cream, scallions, garlic, and hot pepper sauce. Spread evenly on top of corn casserole. Bake at 375 degree until casserole is set; about 50 minutes. Sprinkle top with remaining 1/2 cup cheese and bake until cheese has melted. Remove from oven and let stand 5 minutes before serving. Makes 4 to 6 servings.

CORN ON THE COB WITH SHALLOT-THYME BUTTER

1 stick butter, room temperature
2/3 c chopped shallots (about 3 oz)
2 tablespoon chopped fresh thyme or 2 teaspoon dried
6-9 ears fresh corn, shucked and silked
olive oil

Melt 2 tablespoon butter, add shallots and cook until brown. Combine remaining butter and thyme. Add shallot mixture and blend. Season to taste with salt and pepper. Butter can be prepared 2 days ahead. Cover and refrigerate. Bring to room temperature before serving. Corn may be cooked in two different ways: Prepare barbecue grill, medium high heat. Brush corn with olive oil. Grill corn away from direct heat just until cooked and beginning to turn brown in a few places, turning frequently. Alternative, omit brushing with oil and cook in a large pot of boiling water until tender, about 6 minutes. Drain. Serve corn with shallot-thyme butter. Makes 6 servings.

CORN PUDDING

2 tablespoon butter
1 small onion, chopped
1 garlic clove, minced
4 1/2 c fresh corn kernels or frozen corn, thawed
3 eggs
3 eggs whites
3 tablespoon all-purpose flour
1 tablespoon chopped fresh parsley
1 tablespoon sugar
1/2 teaspoon salt
pinch of cayenne pepper
1 c whipping cream
1 c half and half

Melt butter, add onion and garlic and saute until tender, about 5 minutes. Cool. Puree 2 3/4 cup corn in blender. Whisk eggs and egg whites to blend. Mix in corn puree and corn kernels. Mix in flour, parsley, sugar, salt and cayenne. Stir in cream and half and half and a generous amount of pepper. Pour into baking dish. Place baking dish into large pan; add enough hot water to make 1 inch upon baking dish. Place in 350 degree oven and bake until pudding is set, about 1 hour. Makes 8 servings.

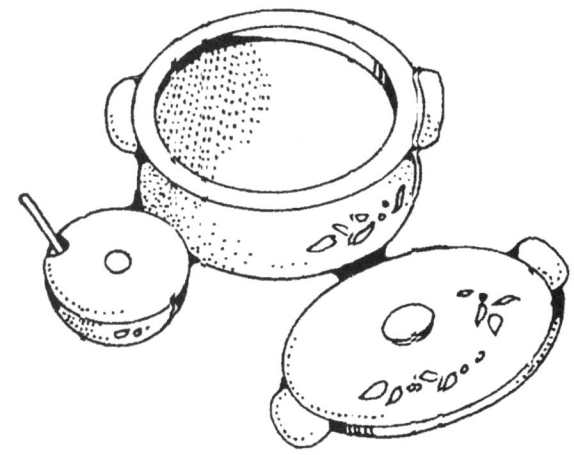

SPICY EGGPLANT

1 eggplant, peeled, and diced in 1/2" cubes
1 large onion, halved, and sliced in rings
1 large red sweet pepper, sliced in thin strips
3 cloves of garlic, finely minced
1 tablespoon of olive oil
1 can of whole tomato Rotel
salt and pepper to taste
2 tablespoon finely chopped fresh cilantro

In a large, non-stick skillet, heat oil until wavy on high heat. Add eggplant and toss until lightly browned. Add onions and garlic, and then saute for 2 or 3 minutes, stirring constantly to prevent burning. Add sliced peppers, and stir for about 1 minute. Add can of Rotel, crushing tomatoes. Stir mixture constantly over high heat until liquid is almost absorbed, about 3-5 minutes. Add salt and pepper to taste, sprinkle with cilantro, and serve.
Note: Submitted by Katrina Reffett

EGGPLANT CASSEROLE

1 large eggplant
2 tablespoon flour
2 tablespoon butter
1 can tomato sauce
1 can water
1 clove
2 teaspoon hot sauce
2 bay leaves
1 bell pepper, chopped
1 onion, chopped
1 teaspoon salt
1/2 c grated cheese
1/2 c bread crumbs

Cut eggplant in cubes; cook in boiling water for 8 minutes, drain. Place butter and flour in skillet; when blended, add tomato sauce and water; stir until smooth. Add clove, bay leaves, bell pepper, onion, pepper sauce, and salt. When sauce thickens, remove clove, fold in eggplant and sprinkle with cheese and bread crumbs. Bake for 1/2 hour at 350.

ROASTED EGGPLANTS WITH CHILIES

2 lbs eggplant
1/2 c olive oil
2 c finely chopped onions
1 c ripe tomatoes, peeled, seeded and cut into wedges
1/2 c finely shredded fresh ginger
1 1/2 teaspoon salt
1/2 c or more fresh chili peppers, shredded
1 tablespoon paprika
1/2 teaspoon black pepper
1/2 c chopped fresh parsley or coriander

Grill the whole eggplants over hot coals or in broiler, turning from time to time, until they collapse. Let cool enough to handle, then cut them open and scrape pulp into a skillet with the oil. Add onion and cook 10 minutes, stirring frequently. Add tomatoes, ginger, salt, peppers, paprika and black pepper. Cook, stirring often, for 10-15 minutes. Be careful not to let it burn. When done, stir in parsley or coriander. Serves 4-6. This dish can be made ahead and served at room temperature. Very tasty.

BAKED EGGPLANT

2 medium eggplants
1 tablespoon salt
2 tablespoon packaged bread crumbs
2 tablespoon minced parsley
1 teaspoon oregano, crumbled
1 1/2 teaspoon basil, crumbled
2 cloves garlic, minced
6 tablespoon olive oil

1/2 teaspoon salt
1/8 teaspoon pepper
2 tablespoon water
1 medium tomato, thinly sliced

Cut eggplants in half lengthwise. Cut deep, long slits in each cut half. Sprinkle 1 tablespoon salt and let drain, cut side down, on paper toweling for 1 hour. Combine bread crumbs, parsley, oregano, basil and garlic. Add 1 tablespoon of the oil, the 1/2 teaspoon salt and pepper and mix thoroughly. Wipe as much moisture from the eggplant as possible. Divide bread crumb mixture among eggplant halves, pressing deep into slits. Arrange in baking dish. Pour the water and 4 tablespoon of the oil around them. Arrange the tomato slices, slightly overlapping, on the eggplant and drizzle with remaining oil. Bake in 375 degree oven, basting several times with pan juices. Sprinkle with fresh basil if you wish. Makes 4 servings.

BAKED STUFFED EGGPLANT

1 large eggplant, unpeeled
1/2 c olive oil
3/4 c onion (2 sm), chopped
1 clove garlic, minced
2 medium tomatoes, peeled, seeded and chopped
1 tablespoon tomato paste, optional
1 teaspoon oregano
1/2 c fine, fresh bread crumbs
1/2 c sharp cheddar cheese, grated
1 tablespoon parsley, minced
1 medium potato, sliced in 1/4 inch rounds and blanched
3 eggs

salt and pepper to taste
4 tablespoon parmesan cheese, optional

Cut eggplant in half lengthwise, and with sharp knife, cut around the edge 1/4 inch from the skin. Scoop out pulp and chop. Heat 4 tablespoon olive oil and add onion. Cook for about 8 minutes and add garlic and eggplant pulp. Cook for 3-4 minutes longer. Add more oil if necessary. Add tomatoes, tomato paste, oregano, bread crumbs, cheddar cheese, parsley and potatoes. In separate bowl heat eggs, season with salt and pepper and stir into eggplant mixture. Spoon into eggplant shells, drizzle with remaining oil and top with parmesan. Bake at 350 degree in preheated oven for 1 hour or until potatoes are tender. Makes 4-6 servings. For a different taste replace potatoes with lightly browned sweet Italian sausage.

FENNEL WITH MINT

4 large bulbs fennel
2 tablespoon softened butter
salt and pepper
1 c chicken stock
1/2 c fresh chopped mint or 2 tablespoon dried, crushed

Cut fennel into halves or quarters. Coat a 2 quart baking dish with butter and layer fennel pieces in it. Season with salt and pepper. Add enough stock to come just below half-way up bulbs. Be careful not to add to much liquid. Bake in a preheated 350 oven for about 1 hour, until fennel can be pierced all the way through with a fork. Add chopped mint and stir gently. Serve with roasts or grilled meats. Makes 8 servings.

EGGPLANT PARMIGIANA

2 tablespoon oil
1/2 c chopped onion
1 clove garlic, crushed
1/2 lb ground chuck
1 can (2 lb 3 oz) Italian tomatoes, undrained
1 can (6 oz) tomato paste
2 teaspoon dried oregano leaves
1 teaspoon dried basil leaves
1 1/2 teaspoon salt
1/4 teaspoon pepper
1 tablespoon brown sugar
1 large eggplant
2 eggs, lightly beaten
1/2 c Italian-flavored bread crumbs
1 1/4 c grated parmesan cheese
1/3 c oil
1 pkg (8 oz) mozzarella cheese, sliced

Saute onion, garlic and chuck in 2 tablespoon oil until meat is no longer red. Add tomatoes, tomato paste, oregano, basil, salt, pepper and sugar; bring to boil, cover and simmer 45 minutes. Do not peel eggplant, slice crosswise 1/4 inch thick slices. Combine eggs and 1 tablespoon water. Dip slices in egg mixture then in crumb mixture. Saute slices in 1 tablespoon oil, more if needed, until brown. Drain on paper towels and place in bottom of baking dish. Sprinkle with half parmesan cheese top with half of mozzarella cheese, then half of the tomato sauce. Repeat. Bake at 350 until cheese melts and top is brown(uncovered).

OKRA PIQUANT

1 10 oz pkg frozen okra
1/4 c chopped green onions
2 tablespoon margarine
2 tablespoon lemon juice
1/4 teaspoon dried lemon thyme

Cook okra, covered, in 1 inch boiling salted water 10 minutes; drain. Saute onions in margarine until soft but not brown, add lemon juice and thyme, toss lightly with okra.

STEAMED ONIONS IN VINAIGRETTE SAUCE

boiling water
30 small white onions, unpeeled
chicken broth or bouillon
vinaigrette sauce (see below)

Pour boiling water over onions and let stand five minutes. Peel the onions and place them in a saucepan with stock one inch deep. Bring to the boiling point and cook, uncovered, six minutes. Cover and continue cooking until the onions are crisp tender, about 15 minutes. Drain and serve with vinaigrette sauce.

VINAIGRETTE SAUCE

3 tablespoon wine vinegar
3/4 c olive oil
1/2 c chopped parsley
1 tablespoon finely chopped chives
1 tablespoon chopped, drained capers
1/2 teaspoon finely chopped onions
1 teaspoon finely chopped sour pickle (optional)
salt and pepper to taste

Combine all the ingredients and beat until well blended. Chill sauce if it is to be used with chilled vegetables or shrimp. Heat to lukewarm if used with hot boiled beef, fish, chicken or pig's feet.

SPICY BLACK-EYED PEAS

1 (16 oz) bag dried black-eyed peas
5 c water
2 tablespoon minced green onions

1 tablespoon creole seasoning
1 teaspoon dried parsley flakes
1 teaspoon garlic powder
1 teaspoon chili powder
1 teaspoon coarsely ground pepper
3 chicken-flavored bouillon cubes

Sort and wash peas; place in large kettle. Add water to cover peas about 2 inches; let soak 8 hours. Drain peas and return to kettle. Add 5 cup water and remaining ingredients. Bring to a boil, cover and simmer until tender, about 1 hour. Stir occasionally. Makes 8 to 10 servings.

CREAMED PEAS AND POTATOES

2 pounds small red potatoes, peeled
1 1/2 tablespoon butter
2 teaspoon flour
1 1/2 cups heavy cream
1/4 teaspoon salt
1/8 teaspoon ground cayenne pepper
2 packages (10 oz each) frozen peas

Cook potatoes in boiling salted water until tender. Drain thoroughly and cut into quarters. While potatoes are cooking melt butter in heavy saucepan; when butter is bubbly whisk in flour and cook over low heat about 3 minutes, stirring frequently. Slowly whisk in cream and heat to boiling. Simmer 5 minutes, stirring occasionally. Add salt and cayenne pepper. Heat peas over low heat until they are hot then drain thoroughly. Just before serving combine potatoes, peas and cream sauce and reheat over low heat until vegetables are heated through.

CHILLED DILLED PEAS

1 c sour cream
1 bunch fresh chives, snipped
1/2 c fresh snipped dill
1 teaspoon curry powder
salt and pepper to taste
1 (16 oz) can tiny French peas, drained

Combine sour cream, chives, dill, curry powder, salt and pepper to taste. Add peas and mix gently. Place in serving bowl and chill before serving. Makes 4-6 servings.

PARSLEY PEAS

3 tablespoon butter
1/4 c chopped onion
1-10 oz pkg frozen peas, thawed
1 tablespoon chopped fresh parsley
1/2 teaspoon salt
1-1 1/2 c chopped lettuce
3 tablespoon chicken stock

Melt butter in small saucepan. Add onion and saute until tender. Add peas, parsley, and salt. Cover and cook, stirring frequently about 5 minutes. Stir in lettuce and chicken stock. Reduce heat and simmer until heated through, 2 minutes.

MINTY PEAS AND ONIONS

2 large onions, cut into 1/2 inch wedges
1/2 c chopped sweet red pepper
2 tablespoon cooking oil
2 pkgs (16 oz each) frozen peas
2 tablespoon minced fresh mint or 2 teaspoon dried mint

Saute onions and red pepper in oil until onions just begin to soften. Add peas; cook, uncovered, stirring occasionally, for 10 minutes or until heated through. Stir in mint and cook for 1 minute. Makes 8 servings.

ROSEMARY-MINTED SUGAR SNAP PEAS

2 sprigs fresh rosemary or 2 teaspoon dried rosemary
1 c water
1/2 teaspoon salt
2 lbs sugar snap peas, trimmed
1 tablespoon butter or margarine
1/4 c blanched slivered almonds
1/2 c fresh mint, chopped or 2 teaspoon dried mint
1/8 teaspoon black pepper

Place rosemary in cheesecloth and tie closed. Bring water salt and rosemary in pan over high heat. Add peas, cover and cook 8-10 minutes or until desired doneness. Melt butter add almonds and mint. Saute until almonds are golden. Drain peas, remove rosemary bag, toss with butter mixture and pepper. Serve immediately.

HOPPIN JOHN SOUTHWESTERN STYLE

1 c presoaked black eyed peas
2 slices bacon, in 2 inch dice
1 onion, chopped fine
2 1/2 cup water
1/2 lb ground beef
salt to taste
1 small can chopped green chilies
1 cup grated cheese
3 cups cooked rice

Combine peas, bacon, water and onion and bring to a simmer. Cook about 1 hour. Saute ground beef and add it along with the salt and chilies to the peas. Continue cooking for 30 minutes. Drain the mixture and combine with the rice, adding enough of the pea broth to moisten. Top with grated cheese and bake in 350 degree oven for about 15-20 minutes.

PARSLEY-STUFFED PEPPERS

6 large green peppers
1 c boiling water
2 3/4 teaspoon salt
1/2 clove garlic, finely chopped
2 tablespoon finely chopped onion
1/4 c butter
1 3/4 c fine bread crumbs
3/4 teaspoon ground thyme
1/8 teaspoon black pepper
4 c finely chopped fresh parsley

Cut a thin slice off top of pepper and remove seeds. Place in pan of boiling water and 1 1/2 teaspoon salt. Cover and boil 5 minutes. Remove from water and drain. Saute onion in butter until limp, about 5 minutes. Add bread crumbs, remaining salt, thyme, and black pepper. Toss lightly. Blend in parsley. Spoon into drained peppers. Place in casserole dish and bake 375 degree oven, cover and bake 30 minutes. Remove cover and bake 10 minutes longer.

FRIED BANANA PEPPERS

hot banana peppers (wear gloves)
1 1/2 c milk
1 1/2 c flour
1/2 c cracker meal

Split peppers in half lengthwise and remove seeds. Dip peppers in milk, then in 1 cup of the flour. Let peppers stand 10 minutes. Redip peppers in milk and coat with 1/2 cup flour and 1/2 cup cracker meal. Fry in hot fat until brown on both sides. Onion ring mix may also be used instead of the above. Follow package directions for coating onion rings.

PERUVIAN POTATO SALAD OR YAM BALLS

4 lbs yams, baked and peeled
1 fresh jalapeno pepper or 1 tablespoon canned diced chili
2 cloves garlic, minced
1-2 tablespoon fresh lemon juice
salt
1/2 c minced onion
1/3 c minced pimiento-stuffed olives
1/4 c minced fresh parsley
1/4 c olive oil
1/4 c wine vinegar
salt and pepper

Combine yams, jalapeno, garlic and lemon juice, and mash until mixture is smooth. Season with salt to taste. Shape into 1 inch balls and arrange in a single layer in large serving dish.  Combine remaining ingredients and mix until well blended. Pour mixture over yam balls. Cover and chill overnight. Serve slightly chilled. Makes 6-8 servings. Excellent with grilled poultry or lamb.

POTATO FANS

4 medium potatoes, peeled
3/4 c butter or margarine
1/2 teaspoon salt
1/4 teaspoon cayenne pepper
3 tablespoon fresh herbs such as parsley, thyme or herb of your choice
2 tablespoon shredded cheddar cheese
2 tablespoon grated Parmesan
1 tablespoon bread crumbs

Slice potatoes 3/4 inch way through at 1/4 inch intervals to make fans. Melt butter in baking dish and roll potatoes in butter to coat. Place in dish cut side up. Sprinkle with salt, cayenne and which ever herb you choose. Bake at 350 degree for 45 minutes basting with butter in dish a couple of times. Blend cheese and bread crumbs, sprinkle over potatoes and bake 10 minutes longer.

BAKED POTATOES WITH HOT PEPPER

1/3 cup margarine, melted
1/2 teaspoon salt
1/4 teaspoon chili powder
1/8 teaspoon black pepper
8 c baking potatoes, sliced 1/4 inch
1 medium onion, sliced 1/4 inch and separated into rings
1 cayenne or jalepeno pepper, diced very small
1 1/2 c monterey jack cheese, shredded

Heat oven to 400 degree. In 13 x 9 inch baking dish stir together butter and seasonings. Add potatoes, onion and diced peppers, stir to coat. Bake, stirring or turning occasionally for about 1 hour or until potatoes are fork tender. Sprinkle with the cheese and bake 1-2 minutes longer until cheese is melted. Garnish with fresh parsley and serve with salsa.

HERBED PAN-ROASTED POTATOES

Boil peeled medium potatoes 10 minutes. Drain, arrange around roast of meat 1 hour before meat is done. Turn occasionally, and baste with drippings in pan. When done remove roast to platter. If potatoes are not brown enough put under broiler in same pan, turning to brown. Sprinkle with paprika, crumbled thyme or marjoram, minced parsley, and arrange around roast.

HERBED SCALLOPED POTATOES

3 leeks, washed, trimmed and diced (white part)
2 tablespoon butter or margarine
2 cloves garlic, chopped
1 teaspoon dried thyme or 1 tablespoon fresh
2 tablespoon all-purpose flour
1 teaspoon salt
1/4 teaspoon black pepper
1 c skim milk
2 lbs potatoes, peeled and thinly sliced
1/4 c dry bread crumbs
2 tablespoon grated Parmesan cheese

Saute leeks in 1 tablespoon butter until tender. Remove half the leeks. Add garlic and thyme to first half and saute 2 more minutes. Whisk together flour, salt, pepper, and milk. Stir into leek mixture and cook until thickened. Arrange half of potatoes in casserole. Spread leek sauce mixture over potatoes. Top with remaining potatoes. Bake, covered, in 350 degree oven for 1 hour or until potatoes are tender. Remove from oven and sprinkle reserved leeks around outside edge. Melt remaining butter over low heat. Stir in crumbs and Parmesan. Sprinkle this mixture on top of casserole. Broil 2-3 minutes or until golden.

HOT, HOT POTATO WEDGES

1/2 c vegetable oil
4 lg. garlic cloves, pressed
3 tablespoon fresh lime juice
2 teaspoon hot sauce
1 teaspoon chopped fresh thyme or 1/4 teaspoon dried
2 lg. potatoes, cut into 8 wedges

Whisk first five ingredients to blend. Season with salt. Arrange potatoes in baking dish. Set aside 1/4 cup dressing. Pour remainder over potatoes and toss to coat. Let stand 30 minutes. Roast potatoes in 400 degree oven, turning occasionally, about 1 hour. Drizzle reserved 1/4 cup dressing over potatoes.

BAKED CRISPY POTATO WEDGES

4 medium potatoes, cut into large wedges
1 tablespoon vegetable oil
1/4 teaspoon ground black pepper or dash of hot sauce
1/8 teaspoon salt
2 cloves garlic, minced
ketchup

Place wedges in cold water to cover for 15 minutes. Preheat oven to 425 degree. Spray cooking sheet with cooking spray. Drain potatoes and place them on paper towels. Cover with a second layer of paper towels and press to dry potatoes. Place wedges in a bowl and sprinkle with oil, pepper (hot sauce) and salt and toss. Place in a single layer on baking sheet. Bake for 20 minutes. Turn with spatula and sprinkle with garlic. Bake until golden, about 20 more minutes. Serve with ketchup. Serves 4.

HERBED POTATOES

Scrub 2 lbs. small red potatoes. Peel ring around centers. Boil about 20 minutes or until done. Cook 2 green onions, sliced, 1 tablespoon chopped fresh parsley, 1 teaspoon snipped fresh chives, 1/2 teaspoon salt, and 1/8 teaspoon pepper in 1 tablespoon butter for 3 minutes. Add to potatoes and mix.

BUTTERNUT SQUASH WITH THYME

1 large butternut squash
1 tablespoon butter
1 tablespoon skim milk
1 teaspoon honey
dash of cinnamon or nutmeg
1 tablespoon fresh thyme leaves or 1 teaspoon dried

Cut squash in half lengthwise. Scoop out seeds. Place squash in pan with 1 inch of water. Cover and cook in 350 degree oven until easily pierced with a fork, about 35-40 minutes. Be careful that water does not boil away. With a spoon, remove pulp from squash, mash well. Add remaining ingredients to pulp. Whip until fluffy.

YELLOW SQUASH CASSEROLE

1 quart cooked yellow squash
1/2 c diced green pepper
1 medium onion, chopped
1 stick margarine
1 c Pepperidge Farm Herb dressing
shredded cheddar cheese

Saute the onion and pepper in margarine. Add to squash and blend in dressing. Pour into greased casserole dish. Sprinkle shredded cheese on top. Bake in 350 degree oven for 30-45 minutes until lightly browned.

SQUASH RIBBONS WITH CHILI PEPPERS

1 1/2 lbs. summer squash
1 red onion, thinly sliced
1 teaspoon finely chopped red or green chili pepper
2 teaspoon lime or lemon juice
1/8 teaspoon each salt and pepper

Trim squash. With vegetable peeler shave squash into long strips. Place ribbons over onions in steamer basket and steam about 3 minutes or until tender. Transfer to a bowl, add chili pepper, lime juice, salt and pepper and toss to coat. Cover and let stand for a few minutes.

STUFFED TOMATOES

2 firm large tomatoes, unpeeled
1/4 c dry bread crumbs
1 teaspoon butter, melted
1/2 teaspoon grated Parmesan cheese
1/2 teaspoon finely diced ham
1/8 teaspoon leaf basil, crumbled
1/8 teaspoon leaf oregano, crumbled
1 teaspoon minced parsley
pinch salt

Preheat oven to 350 degree. Cut tomatoes in half. Mix remaining ingredients and press on top of tomato halves. Place in shallow baking dish and bake for 15-25 minutes or until tomatoes are softened (time will depend on firmness of tomatoes). Topping should be lightly browned. Makes 4 servings.

MARINATED TOMATOES

1 clove garlic, minced
1/4 c green onions and tops, sliced
1 teaspoon salt
1/4 teaspoon pepper
1/4 c parsley, fine cut
1/2 teaspoon thyme leaves, fine cut
6 fresh tomatoes, peeled and cut in thick slices
2/3 c olive oil
1/4 c vinegar

Combine first 6 ingredients and sprinkle over tomatoes. Mix oil and vinegar and pour over tomatoes. Cover and chill several hours. Spoon dressing over tomatoes 2 or 3 times while chilling. Drain before serving.

MARINATED TOMATOES WITH BASIL

4 ripe tomatoes, sliced 1/2 inch thick
1/4 c finely chopped green basil
3 tablespoon olive oil
2 tablespoon lemon juice
1 teaspoon sugar
salt and pepper to taste

Arrange tomatoes on a platter in single layer. Sprinkle basil evenly over. Mix remaining ingredients and spoon over tomato slices. Let stand at room temperature about 1 hour before serving.

BROILED TOMATOES

3 medium tomatoes
hot sauce to taste
salt
sugar
butter
Parmesan cheese
fine dry bread crumbs
parsley, chopped

Wash tomatoes, cut out stem ends and half crosswise. Sprinkle cut side with small amount of hot sauce, salt, pepper and sugar. Dot with butter. Place under broiler, four inches away from source of heat. Broil 10-12 minutes. Combine small amount of butter with parmesan cheese and bread crumbs. Sprinkle tomatoes with crumb mixture during last 3 minutes of broiling time. Sprinkle with chopped parsley. Makes 6 servings.

GREEN TOMATO CASSEROLE

6 green tomatoes, sliced
onions, sliced thin
salt
herb seasoning
Romano grated cheese
bacon, cut in one inch pieces
herb seasoned stuffing

Grease casserole with small amount of olive oil. Layer green tomatoes then a layer of onions. Sprinkle with salt, seasoning and grated cheese. Add another layer of tomatoes and onions. Again sprinkle with salt, seasoning and cheese. Top with stuffing and bacon. Bake at 350 degree for 1 hour and 15 minutes.

ROASTED TOMATOES AND HERBS

4 ripe tomatoes
1 tablespoon olive oil
1 tablespoon chopped parsley
1 tablespoon chopped fresh basil or 1 teaspoon dried
2 cloves garlic, finely chopped
1/8 teaspoon pepper

Preheat oven to 375 degree. Remove the stem end from the tomatoes and halve each tomato crosswise. Brush each half with oil and arrange cut side up in roasting pan. Roast about 8 minutes or until slightly soft. Sprinkle with herbs, garlic and pepper and roast 5-10 minutes longer or until very soft.

VEGETABLE MEDLEY WITH BASIL

3 c broccoli florettes
2 medium zucchini, cut into 1/4 inch thick slices
1 medium red bell pepper, cut into strips
1 medium onion, sliced thin
1 clove garlic, minced
1 1/2 teaspoon snipped fresh basil leaves
3 tablespoon margarine or butter
1 c crushed Ritz crackers (about 20)
1 c shredded Mozzarella cheese

Melt 1 tablespoon butter in large skillet and cook

vegetables til tender-crisp. Place in 2 quart casserole. Melt remaining butter, combine with crackers and cheese. Sprinkle evenly over vegetables. Bake uncovered, at 350 for 20-25 minutes.

FRESH VEGETABLES WITH HORSERADISH-MUSTARD DIP

1 (8 oz) container plain nonfat yogurt
3 tablespoon chopped fresh chives or green onion tops
1 tablespoon prepared horseradish
1 tablespoon dijon mustard
1 tablespoon chopped fresh dill
assorted vegetables such as carrot, celery, cucumber, bell peppers, cherry tomatoes, broccoli and cauliflower.

Mix first 5 ingredients, season with salt and pepper. Refrigerate until ready to serve (can be made 2 days ahead). Place dip in center of platter, surround with vegetables and serve.

HERBED CREAMED VEGETABLES

1/4 c butter
1/4 c flour
2 c half and half
1/4 c chicken broth
1/2 teaspoon each sage, thyme, parsley flakes, garlic powder, dried rosemary, salt and pepper
1 (16 oz) jar pearl onions, drained
1 (16 oz) pkg frozen peas
1 (14 oz) pkg frozen baby carrots

Melt butter, stir in flour. Gradually add cream, broth and seasonings. Bring to a boil, stirring constantly until thickened and bubbly. Add onions, peas and carrots. Cover and simmer on very low heat for 30 minutes, stirring often to prevent sticking. Yield 12-14 servings.

BAKED ACORN SQUASH

2 medium acorn squash
1 teaspoon salt
1/4 c melted margarine
1/4 c corn syrup
2 tablespoon brown sugar
1/2 teaspoon tabasco sauce

Halve squash lengthwise. Remove seeds and stringy portion with teaspoon. Sprinkle cut surface with salt and place cut side down in greased baking pan. Bake at 400 degree for 25 minutes. Combine remaining ingredients. Turn squash cut side up and fill each cavity with butter mixture. Bake 30 to 35 minutes or until tender. If desired sprinkle pecan chips over butter mixture before baking.

ZIPPY ZUCCHINI

4 c thinly sliced zucchini
3/4 c chopped celery
1 lg. onion, chopped
1/2 c sliced sweet red or green pepper
2 tablespoon olive oil
1/2 c picante sauce
1 1/2 teaspoon dried whole basil, crushed
1 teaspoon salt
1/2 teaspoon pepper
1 c shredded Monterey Jack cheese

Saute zucchini, celery, onion and sweet peppers in oil 3 minutes, stirring constantly. Add picante sauce, basil, salt and pepper; cover and cook 3-5 minutes or until vegetables are tender. Add cheese, stirring until it melts. Serve immediately. Makes 6 servings.

BAKED ZUCCHINI

butter
4 tablespoon butter
1/4 c chopped onion
1 clove garlic, minced
2 medium zucchini, sliced and quartered
4 oz cheddar cheese, shredded
1/2 teaspoon dill seed
1/8 white pepper
1/2 c dry bread crumbs

Butter 1 1/2 quart baking dish. Melt 2 tablespoon butter. Add onion and garlic and saute until golden, stirring constantly. Blend in cheese, zucchini, dill seed and white pepper and toss. Put in prepared dish. Melt remaining butter, add bread crumbs and saute until golden. Spoon over zucchini. Cover and bake until zucchini is tender, about 25 minutes. Uncover and bake 10 minutes. Makes 4 servings.

ZUCCHINI-TOMATO CASSEROLE

1/4 c oil
1 clove garlic, finely minced
4 medium zucchini, cut into 1/4 inch pieces
1/4 teaspoon oregano
1/4 teaspoon basil
1/2 c grated cheddar cheese
1/4 c freshly grated Parmesan cheese
4 medium tomatoes, peeled and sliced
salt and pepper to taste
1/2 c bread crumbs
2 tablespoon melted butter

Cook garlic in oil long enough to flavor oil. Remove and discard garlic. Saute the zucchini slices in flavored oil. Combine the oregano, basil, cheddar and parmesan cheeses. Place alternate layers of zucchini and sliced tomatoes in a buttered casserole. Sprinkle each layer lightly with salt and pepper and with the cheese mixture. Combine bread crumbs with melted butter. Sprinkle on top of casserole and bake, uncovered, until crumbs are brown, about 20-25 minutes.

SKILLET ZUCCHINI AND POTATOES

1 medium onion, sliced
2 tablespoon olive oil
2 c sliced zucchini
2 medium potatoes, peeled and sliced
1 medium tomato, peeled and chopped
1 teaspoon dried oregano, crumbled
1/2 teaspoon salt
grated Parmesan cheese

In skillet, cook onion in oil until translucent. Stir in vegetables, oregano, salt, and 1/8 teaspoon black pepper. Cook covered, until potatoes are tender, about 15 minutes. Serve with the grated cheese.

Note: Oregano and marjoram have similar flavors with oregano being somewhat stronger. Oregano is a popular herb to use in pizza and spagetti sauces. It is a hardy perennial and will spread rapidly. The Greeks think it is the only herb worth drying. Oregano is good in salads, soups, casseroles, pastas and dressings. It is easily dried and maintains its aroma and flavor very well.

Pasta & Rice

MEXICAN HOMINY

2 large cans hominy
1 (8 oz) can chopped green chilies
1 1/2 c sour cream
1/4 c grated Parmesan cheese
1/2 lb Jack cheese, cubed
2 to 4 tomatillos chopped
1/2 c cilantro, minced
2 teaspoon garlic, pureed
salt and pepper to taste
cumin to taste

In large bowl, mix all ingredients. Place in greased 2 1/2 quart casserole. Bake 30 minutes at 350.

Note: Garlic is one seasoning about which there is no middle ground. It is prized and disdained in just about equal measure. It is a member of the onion family and very easily grown and is also widely available in dry powdered form or freshly minced in most grocery stores. Moderation is the key word in cooking with garlic. A simple method to add the flavor is using garlic salt. A garlic clove rubbed around a salad bowl or saucepan will flavor the food prepared in it. Over 2 million dollars worth of garlic is grown in the United States each year. Most of it is used in cooking but some turns up in health foods and in insect repellants for organic gardening.

MAC "N" CHEESE
(with a double dose of heat)

1 1/2 c elbow macaroni
2 teaspoon vegetable oil
1/3 c minced red onion
1/3 c finely chopped red pepper
1/2 teaspoon cumin
1 tablespoon butter
1/4 c all-purpose flour
3 c skim milk
1 teaspoon salt
1/4 teaspoon pepper
1/4 teaspoon hot pepper sauce
1/2 c shredded sharp cheddar cheese
1 can chopped green chilies (4 1/2 oz)
1/2 c plain dry bread crumbs
2 tablespoon chopped fresh parsley
cooking spray

Cook macaroni according to package directions. Rinse and drain. Heat oil, add onion and cook until translucent. Add red pepper and cumin. Cook 2 minutes more and set aside. Melt butter, add flour and salt, pepper and pepper sauce. Cook and whisk for 1 minute. Remove from heat add cheese, chopped chilies and onion mixture. Stir in macaroni. Spoon into 2 quart baking dish. Combine bread crumbs and parsley and sprinkle on top. Spray with cooking spray. Bake 20 minutes at 375 or until golden. Makes 6 servings.

CAULIFLOWER & MACARONI AU GRATIN

1 medium head cauliflower, cut into florets
12 oz elbow macaroni
4 tablespoon butter
3 tablespoon all-purpose flour
2 c milk, heated
1/2 teaspoon salt
1/2 teaspoon hot pepper sauce or more
2 1/2 c (10 oz) shredded sharp cheddar cheese
1/2 c fresh bread crumbs
1/2 c grated Parmesan cheese

Cook cauliflower in boiling salted water until just tender, about 8 minutes. Transfer to a colander and drain well. Rinse under cold water and pat dry on paper towels. In same boiling water cook macaroni just until tender, about 8 minutes. Drain well. Melt 3 tablespoon of butter and whisk in flour; stir constantly until browned, about 2 minutes. Whisk in hot milk, salt and hot pepper sauce. Simmer, whisking often, until thickened. Remove from heat and stir in cheddar cheese until smooth. Toss cauliflower, macaroni and sauce until well combined. Pour in casserole. Sprinkle top with Parmesan cheese and dot with the remaining 1 tablespoon butter. Bake in 375 oven until bubbly and top is browned, about 25 minutes. Serves 6-8.

EGGPLANT AND MACARONI CASSEROLE

1 lb eggplant, peeled and cut into 1/2 inch slices
2 tablespoon butter
1 medium onion, diced
1 (28 oz) can tomatoes, seeded and chopped (reserve liquid)
1 bay leaf
1/4 teaspoon dried thyme, crumbled
salt and pepper
8 oz elbow macaroni, cooked and drained
8 oz mozzarella cheese, coarsely grated
2 tablespoon grated Parmesan cheese

Grease baking sheet. Arrange eggplant slices in single layer. Bake at 375 until tender and lightly browned, turning once. Set aside. Melt butter; and onion and cook until tender. Stir in tomatoes, with liquid, bay leaf and thyme. Season with salt and pepper. Simmer, stirring occasionally until liquid has evaporated. Combine tomato mixture, macaroni and mozzarella cheese. Mix. Layer half eggplant slices in greased casserole. Cover with half of the tomato mixture. Repeat layers; then sprinkle with Parmesan cheese. Bake until cheese is melted and mixture is heated through. Makes 6 servings.

EASY NOODLES ROMANOFF

1 pkg regular noodles (8 oz)
1 c cream style cottage cheese
1 c sour cream
1/2 c grated Parmesan
1 teaspoon grated onion
1/4 teaspoon dried marjoram, crumbled
1 teaspoon hot pepper sauce

Cook noodles according to directions; drain. Stir in remaining ingredients, mix well. Spoon into greased 6 cup baking dish. Bake at 350 for 30 minutes. Sprinkle with fresh, snipped parsley and serve.

PASTA PRIMAVERA

12 oz uncooked lasagna mini noodles
2 c fresh broccoli flowerets
6 oz fresh mushrooms, sliced (2 cups)
1 medium yellow squash, cut in 1 1/2 x 1/4 inch strips
1 medium zucchini, cut in 1 1/2 x 1/4 inch strips
1 medium carrot, sliced
2 1/2 c water, divided
1 c nonfat dry milk powder

2 tablespoon all-purpose flour
2 large garlic cloves, minced
2 teaspoon dried oregano leaves
1 teaspoon dried basil leaves
1/2 - 1 teaspoon fennel seed, crushed
1/2 teaspoon salt
1/2 teaspoon pepper
1 c shredded nonfat or part-skim mozzarella cheese
1 tablespoon snipped fresh parsley

Cook noodles as directed on package. Rinse. Let stand in warm water. Combine broccoli, squash, carrot, mushrooms and 1/2 cup water. Cover and cook 5-7 minutes or until vegetables are crisp tender. Drain. Set aside. Combine dry milk, flour, garlic, oregano, basil, fennel, salt and pepper and remaining 2 cups water. Cook until sauce thickens, stirring constantly. Add mozzarella cheese, remove from heat and stir until cheese melts. Combine sauce, noodles (drained), and vegetables. Toss. Sprinkle with parsley. Makes 10 servings.

SALMON OR TUNA AND NOODLES

8 oz uncooked medium noodles
1 1/2 c dairy sour cream
1 1/2 c creamed cottage cheese
1/2 c finely chopped onion
1 clove garlic, minced
1-2 teaspoon Worcestershire sauce
dash of hot sauce
1/2 teaspoon salt
1 can (16 oz) salmon, drained, or 2 cans (6 1/2 oz each) tuna, drained
1/2 c sharp cheddar cheese (about 2 oz)

Cook noodles according to package directions. Drain. Mix noodles, cottage cheese, sour cream, onion, garlic, worcestershire sauce, hot sauce, salt and salmon (or tuna). Place in greased 2 quart casserole. Bake in 325 oven for about 40 minutes. Makes 5-6 servings.

NOODLES 'N THYME

4 tablespoon margarine or butter, softened
2 tablespoon snipped parsley
1 teaspoon dried thyme
1/8 teaspoon pepper
1 8 oz package cream cheese, softened
1/2 cup boiling water
8 oz fettucini or medium noodles
3/4 c shredded Parmesan cheese

In saucepan, combine margarine, and herbs. Blend in cream cheese; stir in boiling water and blend well. Keep warm. Cook noodles in boiling salted water until tender; drain. Turn into bowl and sprinkle with 1/2 cup of the Parmesan. Serve noodles on plate topped with the hot herbed cheese sauce. Pass the remaining Parmesan to sprinkle over all.

THAI NOODLES WITH JULIENNED VEGETABLES

1 tablespoon olive oil
2 Thai hot peppers, chopped
1 tablespoon minced fresh ginger
2 carrots, julienned
2 small zucchini, julienned
16 oz noodles or linguine, cooked and drained
1 tablespoon teriyaki sauce
4 scallions, chopped

Noodles can be cooked ahead and tossed with 1 tablespoon of olive oil to coat, then refrigerated. Pour 1 tablespoon olive oil in wok or skillet. Add chilies and ginger and stir-fry for 30 seconds. Add carrots and zucchini and fry 2 minutes or until vegetables are tender. Add the noodles and teriyaki sauce and toss to coat. Transfer to serving dish and top with scallions.

ZIPPY SPAGHETTI

1/3 c salad oil
3 large onions, chopped fine
1 lb ground round steak
3 cloves garlic, minced
1 teaspoon salt
1/2 teaspoon pepper
1 quart can tomatoes
1 small can hot green chilies or 6 fresh ones
1 small can mushrooms
1 c olives, chopped
1 lb spaghetti
1 bay leaf
1/2 lb grated American cheese

Brown the onions and steak in oil, drain. Add the chilies, garlic, tomatoes, salt and pepper, and simmer slowly for about 2 hours. The tomato liquid should be allowed to evaporate, to make the sauce rich and thick. During the last 1/2 hour add the olives and mushrooms. In the meantime, cook the spaghetti with the bay leaf in boiling salted water, when tender, drain. Pile on a platter, cover with cheese. Pour the sauce on top and let stand in the oven for a few minutes. Serves 12.

CHICKEN AND PASTA

1 lb skinless, boneless chicken breasts, cut up
1 tablespoon vegetable oil
1 can condensed cream of mushroom soup
2 1/4 c water
1/2 teaspoon dried basil leaves, crushed
2 c frozen vegetables combination (broccoli, cauliflower, carrots)
2 c uncooked corkscrew pasta

In skillet brown chicken in oil. Set aside. Add soup, water, basil and vegetables to skillet and heat to boil. Add uncooked pasta. Cook for 10 minutes, stirring often. The pasta will cook in the soup. Add browned chicken and cook 5 more minutes or until pasta is done. Serve with Parmesan cheese, if desired. Serves 4.

HERB PASTA

5 tablespoon butter
1/4 c minced fresh parsley
1 teaspoon dried oregano, crumbled
1 teaspoon dried rosemary, crumbled
1 small garlic clove, minced
1/4 lb mushrooms, sliced
1/2 lb cooked spaghetti
3 tablespoon freshly grated Parmesan cheese

Melt 4 tablespoon butter and add parsley, oregano, rosemary and garlic. Remove from heat and let steep. Melt remaining tablespoon butter in another skillet and saute mushrooms about 4 minutes or until tender. Put all in mixing bowl, add Parmesan cheese and toss gently. Makes 2-4 servings.

RAVIOLI PRIMAVERA

1 pkg (25 oz) frozen cheese or beef ravioli
1/4 c olive oil
2 cloves minced garlic
1 pkg (16 oz) frozen Italian vegetables
1/4 c dry white wine
1/4 c chicken broth
2 tablespoon fresh Italian parsley or 2 teaspoon dried
1/4 teaspoon each salt and pepper

Prepare frozen ravioli according to package directions. Heat 1/4 cup olive oil, add garlic and cook for 1 minute. Add frozen vegetables and cook 4 minutes. Add wine and and chicken broth and cook for another 3 minutes. Stir in parsley, salt and pepper. Cook for 1 minute. Drain ravioli, pour primavera over ravioli. Sprinkle with Romano or Parmesan cheese and serve.

PASTA & RICE

DILLY PASTA SALAD

8 oz spiral pasta, cooked and drained
2 cans water packed tuna, drained
2 medium tomatoes, diced & some of seeds removed
1 medium cucumber, quartered and sliced
1 small onion, thinly sliced
1/2 c olive or salad oil
1/4 c lemon juice, fresh if available
1 1/4-2 teaspoon fresh dill weed, finely snipped
1 garlic clove, minced
salt and pepper to taste

Toss pasta, tuna and vegetables together in a large bowl. In another bowl combine remaining ingredients, pour over pasta mixture, toss to combine. Chill and serve over lettuce leaves.

Note: THE HERB DILL — If you were playing the word association game and the word was dill, almost everyone would respond with pickle. Dill is not just for pickling, its distinctive pungency and flavor can add to many recipes. Its feathery foliage is very aromatic and when a recipe specifies dill weed this is what is meant. It is very flavorful with poultry, fish and some vegetables dishes. It makes a great addition to some salad dressings and dips for vegetables. The seeds of the plant are used ground or whole in pickling.

JALAPENO CHEESE GRITS

4 1/2 c water
1 teaspoon salt
1 1/2 c quick cook grits
4 c (1 lb) sharp cheddar, shredded
1/4 c butter
2 cans jalapeno peppers, seeded and chopped
2 tablespoon chopped pimento
1 teaspoon salt
3 eggs, beaten

Combine water and 1 teaspoon salt and bring to a boil. Gradually stir grits into water, cover, reduce heat to low and cook 5 minutes, stirring occasionally. Add cheese and butter, stir until melted. Stir in peppers, pimento and 1 teaspoon salt. Add small amount of hot grits to eggs, stirring well. Stir mixture into all of grits. Pour into lightly greased 12 x 8 x 2 inch baking pan. Bake, uncovered, at 350 for 30 minutes.

PUFFY CHEDDAR GRITS

2 tablespoon butter
1 teaspoon salt
3 1/2 c milk
1 1/4 c quick-cooking grits
8 oz (2 c) shredded cheddar cheese
1 teaspoon hot pepper sauce
1/4 teaspoon pepper
5 large eggs

Heat butter, salt, 1 1/2 cup milk and 2 cups water to boiling. Gradually stir in grits, whisking constantly to prevent lumping. Reduce heat to low, cover and cook 5 minutes, stirring occasionally. Grits will be very stiff. Remove from heat; blend in cheese. In separate bowl, with wire whisk, mix hot pepper sauce, pepper, eggs and 2 cups milk until blended. Gradually stir grit mixture into egg mixture. Pour grit mixture into greased baking dish. Bake 325 for 45 minutes, uncovered, or until knife inserted comes out clean. Makes 12 main dish servings.

Note: Make this the day before and bake the morning of the brunch—just add 20 extra minutes to the baking time.

BEANS AND RICE

1 can kidney beans
1 can tomato sauce, small
1 onion, chopped
2 cloves garlic, mashed
salt and pepper
1/2 teaspoon oregano
3 sprigs parsley
diced ham or pork, browned
2 c water
2 c converted rice
3 leaves cilantro

Fry onions, garlic, oregano, cilantro, parsley, tomato sauce, salt and pepper until tender. Add water, bring to a boil. Add beans. Wash converted rice, add to sauce, bring to a boil again. Cook until rice is tender. Add ham or pork. If there is any liquid left simmer until all the water is absorbed.

RED BEANS AND RICE

1 lb red beans
2 quarts water
1 meaty ham bone
1 lb hot sausage, thinly sliced
2 c chopped onion
2 stalks celery, chopped
1 green pepper, chopped
4 bay leaves
pinch of thyme
salt and pepper to taste
hot pepper sauce
freshly cooked rice

Rinse beans, place in pot and add water. Place on medium heat and add next 8 ingredients. Bring to a boil, reduce heat and simmer about 3 hours. Using a wooden spoon mash about 1/2 of the beans against side of pan to give a creamy smoothness. Season with salt, pepper and hot sauce to taste. Serve over rice. Makes 8-10 servings.

ITALIAN FRIED RICE

2 tablespoon vegetable oil
2 medium onions, chopped
6 Italian sweet or hot sausages, casings removed
2 carrots, diced (about 1 cup)
1 bunch broccoli florets
4 c cooked brown rice
1 tablespoon tamari sauce
3 eggs, beaten
1 teaspoon worcestershire sauce
hot pepper sauce

Heat 1 tablespoon oil until hot but not smoking. Add onions and saute until golden, stirring frequently. Remove from skillet and set aside. Add sausage and cook until no longer pink, breaking chunks with fork. Remove to plate and drain fat from skillet. Add 1 tablespoon oil and heat. Add carrots and broccoli and cook until crisp tender. Stir in sausage, onions and rice. Whisk tamari sauce into beaten eggs and add to skillet, mix thoroughly. Blend in worcestershire and hot sauce to taste. Make 4 servings.

CONFETTI RICE WITH BASIL

1 c uncooked rice
10 oz package frozen corn, thawed
1/2 c finely chopped celery
1/4 c chopped basil
1 red sweet pepper, finely chopped
2 tablespoon chopped parsley
2 green onions, finely chopped
3 tablespoon finely chopped sweet basil
1/4 c lemon juice
1/3 c salad oil
1/2 teaspoon salt
1/4 teaspoon pepper

Cook rice in boiling salted water according to package. Do not overcook. Drain. Cook corn two minutes, drain, combine with rice. Combine remaining ingredients in a jar. Shake until well mixed. Pour over rice mixture.

> *Note:* Basil is a herb much favored by cooks. Its flavor and aroma lend an added dimension to everything from main dishes to desserts. The exact flavor of basil is hard to describe, it has a hint of clove, mint, cinnamon or allspice. It can be used both raw or in cooking. In cooking it should be added toward the end of the cooking period to prevent losing its flavor and aroma. The regular sweet basils are the ones most used in cooking. Basil has a special affinity for tomatoes and rivals oregano as an ingredient for pizza or sphagetti sauce. Basil is a tender annual which is very easy to grow and if it is kept cut to prevent blooming it will produce all summer long. Use scissors to cut the basil as chopping with a knife will bruise the leaves and they become discolored.

HERBED RICE (MICROWAVE)

2 c water
1 c long-grain rice
6 medium mushrooms, sliced
2 tablespoon butter
2 tablespoon chopped chives
2 beef bouillon cubes
1/2 teaspoon dried basil, crumbled
1/2 teaspoon dried marjoram, crumbled
pepper to taste

Combine all ingredients in microwave safe dish. Cover and cook on high 15 minutes. Let stand 8-10 minutes. Fluff with fork and serve. Makes 4-6 servings.

PILAF

2/3 c chopped onion
   3 tablespoon butter
   1 c rice
   1 teaspoon marjoram, crumbled
   1 teaspoon rosemary, crumbled
   1/2 teaspoon savory, crumbled
   3 c chicken broth

Saute onion in butter until soft. Add rice, and herbs; cook stirring constantly until rice starts to brown. Add chicken broth, simmer until rice is tender and liquid is absorbed.

HERBED RICE

1 c uncooked rice
2 beef bouillon cubes
1/2 teaspoon salt
1/2 teaspoon dried rosemary
1/2 teaspoon dried marjoram leaves
1/2 teaspoon dried thyme leaves
1 teaspoon dried green onion flakes
2 c cold water
1 tablespoon butter

Mix all ingredients except water and butter. Then combine with water and butter in a heavy saucepan. Turn heat high until the mixture comes to a boil, reduce heat, stir with a fork and cover. Simmer 12 to 14 minutes, or until all liquid is absorbed.

MUSHROOM RICE PILAF

1/2 lb mushrooms, sliced
1 clove garlic, minced
2 tablespoon olive oil
1 1/2 c chicken broth
1/2 teaspoon salt
1/4 teaspoon thyme leaves, crushed
1/8 teaspoon pepper
1 1/2 c instant rice
1/2 c sliced green onions with tops
1/4 c toasted pine nuts

Cook mushrooms and garlic in oil until tender, about 3 minutes. Add broth, salt, pepper and thyme; bring to boil. Cover and remove from heat. Let stand 5 minutes. Stir in onions and sprinkle with pine nuts.

BROWN RICE PILAF

2 c brown rice
3 c water or chicken stock
2 tablespoon butter
2 teaspoon salt
3 bay leaves
6 peppercorns
2 tablespoon cooking oil
1 onion, sliced
2 celery stalks, thinly sliced
2 tablespoon currants
1 tablespoon finely chopped ginger
1/2 teaspoon cumin
1 1/2 teaspoon ground coriander
pepper to taste
2 tablespoon soy sauce

In large pot place rice, water, butter, salt, bay leaves and peppercorns. Bring to a boil, cover and simmer for 25-35 minutes or until liquid has been absorbed by rice. Pour oil into skillet, add onion and saute three minutes. Add celery, currants, ginger, cumin, coriander, and pepper. Stir into cooked rice. Add soy sauce and mix well. Taste to correct seasoning. Makes 4-6 servings.

RICE CASSEROLE

1 c raw rice
1/2 c butter
1 can onion soup
1-2 cloves crushed garlic
1 can chicken consome
4 tablespoon Parmesan cheese

Melt butter in skillet. Brown rice in butter about 10 minutes. Add remaining ingredients with salt and pepper to taste. Pour into greased casserole, cover, and bake at 325 for 1 hour.

RICE, ZUCCHINI AND CHEESE

1 c cooked rice
1 can green chilies
3 zucchini
1 large tomato
1 lb Monterey Jack cheese
2 c sour cream
1 teaspoon garlic salt
1 tablespoon chopped green pepper
2 tablespoon chopped green onion
1 tablespoon parsley
1 teaspoon oregano
salt and pepper to taste
parsley

Cook rice until tender. Slice and parboil zucchini. Slice chilies in half and remove seeds. Cut cheese in narrow strips and insert into chilies. In a greased casserole place rice, then a layer of cheese filled chilies, then a layer of zucchini and tomato slices. Mix sour cream with spices, herbs, pepper and onions and pour over vegetables. Grate the remaining cheese over the mixture. Sprinkle with parsley and bake 30 minutes in 350 oven. Can be made ahead and refrigerated until 30 minutes before you are ready to eat.

WILD RICE CASSEROLE

1 lb pork sausage
1 lb fresh mushrooms
2 medium onions
8 oz wild rice
1/4 c flour
1/2 c heavy cream
2 1/2 c chicken broth
1 teaspoon salt
1 pinch oregano
1 pinch thyme
1 pinch marjoram
1/2 c toasted almonds

Pour water over rice to cover. Let stand until cold. Repeat two more times. Drain and set aside. Saute sausage; drain on paper towels. Reserve fat. Slice mushrooms and saute with onions in sausage fat. Mix flour with cream until smooth. Add chicken broth to flour. Cream mixture and cook until thickened. Season with herbs, salt and pepper. Combine with rice, sausage and vegetables. Stir in almonds. Pour in greased casserole and bake for 25-30 minutes at 350. Ready to serve when bubbly. Good with wild game birds, chicken or turkey.

ZESTY LEMON RICE

1 c uncooked long-grain rice
2 c chicken broth
6 drops chile pepper sauce
16 oz water chestnuts, drained and chopped
2 scallions, chopped
2 tablespoon grated lemon peel.
Combine rice, broth and pepper sauce. Bring to a boil, stir, then cover and lower heat to simmer. Simmer for 20 minutes or until rice is tender. Stir in water chestnuts, scallions and lemon peel. Remove from heat, replace cover and let stand 15 minutes to blend flavors. Makes 6 servings.

ENRAGED CHUNKY PASTA SAUCE

1/4 c oil
1 mild green chile such as Anaheim, seeded and chopped
1 hot green chile such as jalapeno, seeded and finely chopped
1 small red onion, coarsely chopped
1 large eggplant, cut into 1 inch cubes
4 cloves garlic, thinly sliced
1 (28 oz) can plum tomatoes, undrained
1/2 teaspoon salt
1/4 teaspoon pepper (black)
1/4 to 1/2 teaspoon crushed red pepper
1 (12 oz) pkg rigatoni or other tubular pasta
grated Parmesan cheese

Heat oil add chilies and onion; add eggplant and garlic; cook 8-10 minutes, stirring occasionally. Add tomatoes and liquid. Add salt, black and red peppers. Cover and cook 25 minutes, stirring occasionally, until thickened. Meanwhile, prepare pasta according to package directions. Drain pasta and return to pot. Add sauce and toss gently. Just before serving transfer to platter and sprinkle with Parmesan cheese. Makes 6 servings.

SPAGHETTI SAUCE

3 cloves garlic, minced
1/4 onion, minced
1/3 c red wine
3 1/2 c tomato puree (28 oz can)
1 1/2 c canned whole tomatoes, coarsely chopped (with juice)
1 tablespoon dried basil
2 teaspoon dried oregano
1/4 teaspoon dried rosemary
1 tablespoon minced fresh parsley
1 bay leaf
1 carrot peeled—leave whole
pinch of salt

Put garlic, onion, and celery in skillet with a little wine and saute for two or three minutes. Add rest of wine, cover and simmer for 10 minutes. For extra liquid use juice from tomatoes. Add rest of ingredients and simmer for 30 minutes longer. This tastes even better made the day before it is needed. Remove bay leaf and carrot before serving. Makes about 5 cups.

FRESH TOMATO SAUCE FOR PASTA

3 tablespoon olive oil
1/4 c finely chopped onion
1/2 teaspoon minced garlic
2 lb fresh ripe tomatoes (4-5 lg) peeled, cored, seeded and chopped
1 tablespoon minced fresh basil
1 tablespoon minced Italian parsley
1/2 teaspoon salt or to taste
pepper to taste

Heat oil, add onion and garlic. Reduce heat and saute until onion is tender. Stir tomatoes, basil and parsley into onion mixture. Reduce heat to very low; cook covered 30 minutes. Salt and pepper to taste. Sauce can be stored, tightly covered, in the refrigerator for a few days; for longer storage, freeze.

SPAGHETTI MEAT SAUCE

1 1/2 c ground beef
2 c finely chopped onion
2 cloves garlic, minced
2 tablespoon sugar
1 1/2 tablespoon salt
2 teaspoon dried basil leaves
1 teaspoon dried oregano leaves
1/8 teaspoon crushed red pepper
2 cans (large) Italian style tomatoes, undrained
1 can tomato paste
1 can tomato puree

Saute ground beef; drain fat. Add onions and garlic. Add other ingredients, breaking tomatoes apart with wooden spoon. Simmer, stirring until thickened, about 1 1/2 hours. Makes 3 quarts. Will keep one week in refrigerator. Freezes well.

VEGETABLE PASTA SAUCE

2 c chopped onion
1 c chopped carrot
1 c chopped green or yellow sweet pepper
4 cloves garlic, minced
1/4 c olive oil
8 lbs fully ripe tomatoes, peeled, cored and coarsely chopped (about 16 cups)
1 (12 oz) can tomato paste
1 c dry red wine or beef broth
2 teaspoon sugar
2 teaspoon dried basil, crushed
1 teaspoon dried thyme, crushed
1/2 teaspoon celery seed
2 teaspoon salt
1/2 teaspoon pepper
4 medium zucchini, chopped

Cook onion, carrot, green peppers and garlic in oil 5-7 minutes, stir occasionally. Add tomatoes, tomato paste, wine, sugar, basil, thyme, celery seed, salt and pepper. Bring to a boil. Reduce heat and simmer, uncovered, 60-75 minutes, or until thick; stir occasionally. Add zucchini. Simmer covered 5-7 minutes more. Transfer to freezer containers or in sterilized jars and seal. May be frozen or canned. If canned, process in boiling water bath 25 minutes. Makes 7 to 8 pints.

CLASSIC SAFFRON RICE

1 c long-grain white rice
2 c water or chicken broth
1 tablespoon butter
1 tablespoon finely minced onion
1/2 teaspoon salt
1 small pinch saffron, crumbled (about 20 threads)

Place butter and minced onion in a heavy quart saucepan. Saute until onion is transparent. Add rice, water, or broth, saffron, and salt. Bring to a full boil. Cover and reduce heat to simmer and cook until rice is tender and liquid is absorbed (about 18 minutes).

Note: Saffron is the red stigma of the fall flowering crocus. It gives a golden color and rich flavor to many traditional Indian, Spanish and European dishes and is becoming very popular in our country. Saffron is a very labor intensive crop to produce. The 3 saffron threads in each blossom have to be picked by hand. To produce one pound, about one acre of plants are needed (about 70,000 crocuses) and must be harvested, all by hand. These many hours of hand labor make saffron very expensive, but it is very potent so only a tiny amount is used each time you cook. A pinch will give a beautiful golden color and wonderful flavor to 4 servings of rice. The saffron crocus requires the same type of care given to the regular crocus that blooms in the spring in most of out gardens, so you could raise your own but considering how many it takes and the labor involved in raising it, it is much easier to buy. When buying saffron it is best to buy the whole threads as the powdered loses flavor quickly and has probably been cut with tumeric or calendula.

Above: Mandy Arrick's 21st birthday party at Frazure's in Lucasville, Ohio. Orville and Helen Shultz's family, February 1999. Mandy is their oldest grandchild.

Family Reunion at Shultz's, 1984.

Entrees

BEEF BURGUNDY

1/2 c all-purpose flour
3/4 teaspoon salt
1/4 teaspoon pepper
1 1/2 lb round steak, cut in 1 inch pieces
5 tablespoon oil, divided
1 1/2 c water
1 c Burgundy wine
1 medium onion, thinly sliced
1/2 c snipped fresh parsley
2 cloves garlic, halved
2 bay leaves
1 1/2 teaspoon instant beef bouillon granules
1 teaspoon dried thyme leaves
8 oz fresh mushrooms, sliced
1/4 c sliced almonds
hot cooked rice or noodles

Mix flour, salt and pepper in a bag. Add beef and shake to coat. Heat 4 tablespoon oil. Add beef and remaining flour mixture. Brown. Stir in water, wine, onion, parsley, garlic, bay leaves, bouillon and thyme. Cover, reduce heat. Simmer 1 1/2-2 hours, stirring occasionally. Stir in mushrooms, cover and simmer 20-30 minutes. Remove and discard garlic cloves and bay leaves. Heat remaining 1 tablespoon oil, add almonds cook and stir until almonds are lightly browned. Stir into beef mixture just before serving. Serve with rice or noodles. Makes 4-6 servings.

POT ROAST WITH HORSERADISH

5 lb boneless pot roast, rolled and tied
1 (8 1/2 oz) jar horseradish

Put oil and butter in pan. Put in pot roast. On top side, put 1/2 of jar of horseradish. Brown well; turn over and put the other 1/2 of horseradish on other side. Brown well. Add water and simmer slowly about 2 hours. Add potatoes, carrots and onions until cooked. Thicken slightly. You need no other spices. Number of people this serves depends on the size of the roast. Delicious!

POT ROAST WITH POTATOES

salad oil
6 medium potatoes (2 lbs) each cut into quarters
1 beef chuck arm pot roast, cut 2 inches thick (about 4 lb)
1 clove garlic, minced
1 1/2 c cooking or dry red wine
1 teaspoon rosemary, crumbled
2 beef-flavored bouillon cubes
1/3 c water
3 tablespoon all-purpose flour
salt
1 tablespoon chopped fresh parsley

Brown potatoes in 2 tablespoon hot oil. Remove potatoes and set aside. In same pan in 2 tablespoon more hot oil, brown roast on all sides. Add garlic, wine, rosemary and bouillon cubes to roast and heat to boiling. Reduce heat to low; cover; simmer 2 1/2 hours, basting roast occasionally with pan liquid. Add potatoes; heat to boiling. Reduce heat to low; cover and simmer about 30 minutes, until potatoes are done. Place meat and potatoes on platter. Stir water and flour until blended and stir into liquid in pan; cook, stirring constantly, until thickened. Add salt to gravy if needed. Sprinkle parsley over meat. Makes 12-14 servings.

MAKE-AHEAD COMPANY ROAST

3 lbs beef round roast
1 tablespoon oil
2 large onions, sliced
2 large carrots, sliced
2 large ribs celery, sliced
2 cloves garlic, crushed
2 cans (10 1/2 oz) condensed beef broth, undiluted
4 whole cloves
2 bay leaves
1 teaspoon thyme
1/4 teaspoon cayenne pepper
1 envelope unflavored gelatin
2 tablespoon dry sherry
6 carrots, peeled, cut diagonally in 1-1 1/2 inch pieces, cooked and drained

Brown meat on all sides in hot oil. Add onions. sliced carrots, celery and garlic. Saute until lightly browned. Add broth, cloves, bay leaves, thyme and cayenne. Cover, simmer 2-2 1/2 hours or until meat is tender. Remove meat from liquid, wrap airtight in foil and refrigerate several hours or overnight. Strain liquid (discard vegetables); refrigerate liquid several hours or overnight. Discard fat from liquid. Place 1/2 cup liquid in saucepan. Sprinkle with gelatin. Stir over low heat until gelatin dissolves. Stir into remaining liquid with sherry. Chill until mixture mounds slightly when dropped from spoon. Slice beef thin and overlap on platter with carrot pieces around it. Spoon liquid mixture over all. Chill. Makes 8 servings.

SAVORY POT ROAST

6 tablespoon all-purpose flour, divided
1 teaspoon celery salt
1 teaspoon dried marjoram leaves
1/2 teaspoon dried savory leaves
1/8 teaspoon pepper
3 1/2-4 lb beef chuck roast
1/4 c oil
1 medium onion, thinly sliced
1/2 c water
1 can (8 oz) tomato sauce
2 teaspoon beef bouillon granules
4 medium carrots, cut in 3 inch pieces
4 medium potatoes, quartered
3/4 c cold water

Mix spices with 4 tablespoon flour. Coat roast evenly with mixture. Heat oil in Dutch oven. Add roast and any remaining flour mixture. Brown over medium heat. Add onion, 1/2 cup water, tomato sauce, and bouillon. Cover, reduce heat and simmer about 2 hours. Add vegetables and simmer another hour or until vegetables are tender. Remove roast and vegetables from pot, reserving cooking liquid. Mix 1/4 cup cold water with remaining 2 tablespoon flour. Stir into reserved cooking liquid, stirring constantly until thickened.

MUSTARD AND HERB BROILED STEAK

1/4 c Dijon mustard
1 garlic clove, minced
1 green onion, minced
1/2 teaspoon basil
2 uncooked steaks, cut 1 1/2 inches thick

Combine mustard, garlic, green onion and basil. Spread on both sides of steaks. Broil 4 inches from heat until browned, about 3 minutes on each side. Turn oven to 375 and continue cooking, turning often until desired degree of doneness is reached. Sprinkle with salt and pepper.

LEMON-ROSEMARY T-BONE STEAKS

1 c olive oil
1/3 c fresh lemon juice
1/3 c chopped fresh rosemary or 1 1/2 tablespoon dried
6 (12-14 oz) T-bone steaks, 3/4 to 1 inch thick

Combine oil, lemon juice, rosemary and a generous amount of pepper in large glass baking dish. Add steaks and turn to coat. Cover and refrigerate 4-6 hours. Prepare barbecue. Remove steaks from marinade and sprinkle with salt. Place on grill and cook to desired doneness.

Note: Rosemary is a perennial in warm climates but must be wintered over indoors farther north. It is a very attractive plant and makes a nice container plant which can be moved indoors during the winter season. Rosemary is highly aromatic with a somewhat resinous scent and camphoric flavor. Rosemary helps in digesting rich and starchy foods. It gives a delicious, savory tang to all meats and poultry. It goes well with most vegetables and is a tasty addition to pasta sauces. A spring of rosemary tucked under the skin of a lamb roast or in the cavity of a roasting chicken makes a wonderful dish. Rosemary is easily dried for winter use and is one of the few herbs that is as flavorful dried or fresh.

ANISE OR FENNEL BEEF KABOBS

4-8 inch skewers
2 teaspoon olive oil
1 teaspoon anise seeds or crushed fennel seeds
1/2 teaspoon salt
pinch of crushed red pepper
1/4 teaspoon coarsely ground black pepper
1 lb top sirloin beef tip steak, 1 inch thick cut into 1 1/4 inch chunks

Combine olive oil, seeds, salt, and peppers. Add steak chunks, toss to coat and let stand about 10 minutes. Thread meat on skewers and place over medium heat on grill. Cook 6-10 minutes to desired doneness, turning occasionally.

Note: Anise is an annual herb with a sweet licorice flavor. The seeds are the most useful part though the leaves can be used in cooking. The seeds are easily dried and store well in a tightly covered container. Use a few seeds in soups or mix them with a soft cheese to serve with crackers. Anise seed can be added to any basic cake, cookie or bread recipe for an interesting variation. The leaves add an aromatic flavor to salads.

STEAK KEBOBS

2 tablespoon soy sauce
2 tablespoon honey
1 tablespoon grated fresh ginger or 1 teaspoon ground ginger
1 clove garlic, crushed
1 teaspoon grated lemon peel
1/4 teaspoon crushed hot red pepper
12 oz boneless sirloin steak, trimmed and cut into 1 inch cubes
8 cherry tomatoes
4 large mushrooms, cut in half
1 green bell pepper, seeded and cut in 8 pieces

Mix soy sauce, honey, ginger, garlic, lemon peel, and red pepper. Mix well. Add beef, stir to coat. Cover and refrigerate for 1 to 2 hours. Preheat broiler. Remove beef from marinade. Thread alternately, on skewers, beef, tomatoes, mushrooms and bell pepper and place on broiler pan. Broil 2-3 inch from heat, turning 2 or 3 times until meat is medium-rare and vegetables are done, about 10 minutes. Serve immediately. Serves 4.

MARINATED CHUCK STEAK

1 8 to 9 lb chuck steak, boned, rolled and tied
2 lbs onions, thinly sliced
2 c dark beer or ale
1/2 c oil
1/4 c cider vinegar
2 large cloves garlic, minced
3 bay leaves
1 tablespoon dry mustard
1 1/4 teaspoon basil
1 tablespoon pepper
1 teaspoon thyme
1/2 teaspoon oregano
1/2 teaspoon marjoram

Place meat in container. Combine remaining ingredients and pour over meat. Cover and refrigerate 2 days, turning meat often. Drain meat, reserving marinade. Remove onions from marinade and spread in pan around meat. Place in preheated 425 oven and brown meat. Reduce heat to 350 and cook 2-3 hours, until done, basting with marinade every 20 minutes.

PEPPER STEAK

1 tablespoon coarsely cracked black pepper
1/2 teaspoon dried rosemary
2 ribeye steaks, 1 inch thick
1 tablespoon butter
1 tablespoon vegetable oil
1/4 c brandy or dry red wine

Combine pepper and rosemary, coat both sides of steaks with mixture. Heat butter in skillet until hot; add steak, cook over medium heat 5-7 minutes per side or to desired degree of doneness. Remove steaks, sprinkle lightly with salt, cover to keep warm. Add brandy to skillet; bring to boil and scrap particles from bottom of skillet. Boil about 1 minute. Spoon sauce over steaks. Makes 2 servings.

STEAK AND VEGETABLES ON THE GRILL

4 (10 in) skewers
2 tablespoon fresh rosemary leaves, chopped
2 teaspoon salt
3/4 teaspoon coarsely ground black pepper
1 beef flank steak (about 1 1/2 lbs)
5 tablespoon olive oil
3 medium tomatoes-each cut in half
2 jumbo onions (about 1 lb each) cut in 1/4 inch slices
1 small eggplant (about 1 lb) cut in 1/2 inch thick crosswise slices
1 tablespoon balsamic vinegar
fresh rosemary sprigs for garnish

Mix chopped rosemary, salt, and pepper. Rub steak with 4 teaspoon of mixture; mix remaining herb mixture with oil and reserve for brushing on vegetables. Place onions on skewers and brush with oil; place on grill over medium heat. Cook 25-30 minutes until tender turning skewers occasionally. At the same time place tomato halves and eggplant slices on grill; brush with oil. Cook 12-15 minutes, until lightly browned, turning occasionally. Place on platter and keep warm. Place steak on grill with onions and cook steak 15-20 minutes or until desired doneness. Thinly slice steak; sprinkle with balsamic vinegar. Serve with grilled vegetables; garnish with rosemary sprigs if desired. Makes 6 servings.

FAVORITE POT ROAST WITH VEGETABLES

2 tablespoon salad oil
1 (4 lb) beef roast
1 bay leaf
2 teaspoon salt
1/2 teaspoon pepper
1/2 teaspoon thyme leaves
water
8 medium potatoes, peeled

8 large carrots
1 lb small white onions, peeled
1/4 c all-purpose flour

Brown roast on all sides in hot oil. Stir in bay leaf, pepper, thyme leaves and 3 cups water. Cover and simmer 2 hours and 15 minutes. Add potatoes, carrots, and onions. Cover and simmer 45 minutes or until fork tender. In a small bowl stir flour and 1/2 c water until well blended. Gradually stir into liquid from roast and cook until thickened for gravy. Makes 8 servings.

COUNTRY MEAT LOAF

2 lbs ground beef chuck
1/2 lb sausage meat
1 1/2 c herbed stuffing
4 hot dogs, chopped into small pieces
1 teaspoon sage
2 tablespoon chopped parsley or 1 tablespoon parsley flakes
1 egg
2 medium onions, chopped
1 teaspoon salt

Mix ingredients lightly but thoroughly. Bake in 9 x 5 x 3 inch loaf pan 1 hour at 350. Serve hot or cold.

MEAT LOAF WITH HERBS & FETA CHEESE

1 lb ground beef
1 lb ground lamb
2 large eggs
1 c fresh bread crumbs
1 c green onions, minced
1/2 c finely crumbled feta cheese
1/4 c minced fresh parsley
1 tablespoon dried oregano
2 tablespoon olive oil
1 tablespoon red wine vinegar

2 cloves garlic, minced
1/2 teaspoon salt
1/4 teaspoon pepper

Saute vegetables in olive oil until tender. Cool slightly. Mix with other ingredients until well combined (do not over mix). Bake in 375 oven for 1 hour and 15 minutes. Let stand 10-15 minutes before slicing. Makes 8 servings.

BAKED LIVER AND ONIONS

6 slices beef liver
2 large onions, sliced 1/2 inch thick
margarine
1/2 c dry red wine or water
salt and pepper to taste
1 bay leaf
1 teaspoon thyme
1/2 c chopped parsley
1/2 flour

Arrange onions in greased baking dish and dot with margarine. Add wine or water, season with salt and pepper, bay leaf, thyme and parsley. Cover and bake at 350 for 30 minutes. Dredge liver in flour and place on top of onion slices, cover and bake 30 more minutes, basting occasionally. Remove cover and bake 15 minutes longer. Serves 6.

VEAL CHOPS WITH TARRAGON

4 1/2 inch thick veal chops
4 teaspoon dried tarragon
1 teaspoon salt
black pepper
all purpose flour
2 tablespoon margarine
1 c chicken broth
2 tablespoon lemon juice

Dredge chops in mixture of flour, salt and pepper. Melt margarine in heavy skillet and brown chops about 4 minutes on each side. Remove chops to platter. Add broth, lemon juice and tarragon to skillet. Cook until juices are syrupy, stirring to scrape up browned bits. Return chops to skillet and cook until done.

> *Note:* Tarragon is a perennial herb which has a unique tart anise like flavor. It is commonly used in vinegar as a basis for salad dressings. It is an excellent herb to use with poultry, veal, fish and eggs. It makes a delicious addition to green vegetables. When buying tarragon plants be sure you purchase the French tarragon. Russian tarragon is easier to grow but is not as aromatic and has a bitter flavor when used in cooking.

VEAL SHOULDER ROAST

4 1/2-5 lb boned and rolled veal shoulder
1 tablespoon flour
1 teaspoon salt
1/2 teaspoon pepper
2 tablespoon olive oil
1 tablespoon minced fresh parsley
1 teaspoon dried rosemary
3 cloves garlic, minced
1 c water

Rub roast with flour, salt, and pepper mixed. Brown on all sides in olive oil. Put meat on rack in kettle. Add remaining ingredients. Cover and simmer 3 hours or until tender. Makes 8 servings.

LAMB WITH ALMONDS

1 tablespoon salad oil
1/2 c slivered almonds
1 lb ground lamb
1 1/2 c onions, chopped
1 beef bouillon cube
1/2 teaspoon salt
1/2 teaspoon garlic salt
1/4 teaspoon pepper
1 tablespoon lime or lemon juice
1 tablespoon chopped fresh mint
spinach leaves
   1 medium tomato, cut into wedges

Heat oil, cook almonds, stirring, until browned. Remove almonds and set aside. In same skillet cook lamb, onions, bouillon, salt, garlic salt and pepper, stirring frequently until meat in browned and onions are tender. Stir in almonds, lime juice and mint. Line platter with spinach leaves; with slotted spoon, spoon mixture onto leaves; top with tomato wedges. Makes 4 servings.

LAMB WITH WHITE BEANS & TOMATOES

1 lb boneless lamb chops, cut in 1 1/2 inch cubes
1 tablespoon butter
1 1/2 teaspoon chopped garlic
1 1/2 teaspoon dry white wine
1 teaspoon dried rosemary
1 c drained white kidney beans or other white beans
1 (14 1/2 oz) can stewed tomatoes

Season lamb with salt and pepper on all sides. Melt butter in skillet, add lamb and cook until brown on all sides, stirring frequently. Add garlic, wine and rosemary and cooka bout 3 minutes. Stir in beans and tomatoes with juice, breaking up tomato with back of spoon. Reduce heat and simmer until lamb is done and sauce slightly thickens, about 10 minutes. Makes 2 servings, but can be doubled.

CANTERBURY LAMB WITH HONEY

2 c beef stock or broth
6 tablespoon all-purpose flour
1/2 teaspoon salt
1/4 teaspoon pepper
4 lbs leg of lamb, trimmed and cut in 1 1/2 inch cubes
4 tablespoon butter
2 cloves garlic, finely minced
1 c coarsely chopped onion
2 c sliced (1/4 in) pared carrots
1 1/2 teaspoon chopped fine, pared fresh gingerroot
3 tablespoon mild honey
1 c chopped, seeded, peeled tomatoes, fresh or canned, drained

Combine flour, salt and pepper on waxed paper. Dredge lamb cubes in flour mixture, shaking off excess. Melt 2 tablespoon butter. Brown lamb pieces, a few at a time, remove and place on platter; reserve. Melt remaining 2 tablespoon butter. Saute garlic and onion, stirring often until onion is soft but not browned. Return lamb to skillet; add carrot and ginger. Drizzle honey over top; stir meat and vegetables to coat. Stir in tomatoes, along with enough beef stock to cover meat. Pour in casserole and place, covered, in 350 oven. Cook until lamb is tender, about 1 hour and 15 minutes. Remove from oven; skim fat from surface, if desired. Before serving, taste for seasoning. Add salt and pepper to taste. Makes 8 servings.

LEG OF LAMB WITH MINT SAUCE

thyme, sage and marjoram
1/2 c jelly (any kind)
garlic
leg of lamb

Place leg of lamb on rack in broiler pan. Cut small gashes on the surface. Tuck small cloves of garlic in the gashes. Mix thyme, sage and marjoram together and rub on the surface of the lamb. Bake at 325, 35 minutes per pound. About 1/2 hour before lamb is done, mix jelly with 1/2 cup hot water. Brush over surface. Return to oven and finish baking. Very good with or without mint sauce. We use this recipe for a large leg of lamb for our family reunion. There's never any left.

MINT SAUCE

1/2 c vinegar
1-1 1/2 c water
1/2 c fresh mint leaves
1/4 c lemon juice
2 tablespoon granulated sugar
1/4 teaspoon salt

Simmer vinegar, 1 cup water and 1/4 cup of the mint until mixture is reduced one half. Strain and add remaining ingredients except mint. Chill, then add the remaining 1/4 cup mint. Serve with lamb or fish. Makes about 1 cup sauce.

BREAST OF LAMB WITH POTATOES AND ONIONS

3 lb. breast of lamb
4 potatoes
8 onions
2 teaspoon salt
1/4 teaspoon pepper
1/2 teaspoon marjoram
1/4 c boiling water

Trim excessive fat from meat and cut lamb in serving size pieces. Put meat in a 3 quart casserole; sear in very hot oven, 475 for 30 minutes. Pour off fat; cover and bake 30 minutes. Add potatoes, onions, salt and pepper; cover and bake 1 hour. Pour off fat; add marjoram, water. Cover; bake about 20 minutes. Serves 4.

CROWN ROAST OF LAMB

lemon juice
1 (7-8 lb) crown roast of lamb, fat removed
salt and pepper
1/2 c Dijon mustard
2 tablespoon soy sauce
2 garlic cloves, minced
1 teaspoon dried rosemary leaves, crumbled
1/4 teaspoon ground marjoram
freshly cooked rice

Moisten paper towel with lemon juice and rub lamb. Place on rack in roasting pan and sprinkle with salt and pepper. Cover tips of bones with foil to prevent burning; crumple additional foil and place in center of roast to help retain shape. Bake at 325 until desired doneness is reached. Combine mustard, soy sauce, garlic, rosemary and marjoram. Remove foil from center and paint inside of roast generously with mustard mixture for last half hour of baking. Before serving fill center of roast with freshly cooked rice. Makes 8 servings.

ROAST LOIN OF LAMB

1 tablespoon peanut oil
1 tablespoon butter
1/4 c coarsely chopped onion
1 clove garlic, crushed
1/2 c diced (1/4 in) pared sweet potato
1 slice white bread, crusts removed, cut into 1/4 inch dice
1/2 teaspoon minced fresh rosemary or 1/4 teaspoon dried, crumbled
1/4 teaspoon salt or to taste
pepper
2 lb trimmed boned loin of lamb, in one piece
fresh rosemary sprigs, optional

Heat peanut oil and butter. Add onion and half the garlic; saute until soft. Stir in sweet potato, reduce heat, stirring until sweet potato is tender. Stir in bread, minced rosemary, salt and pepper. Increase heat, stirring, until everything is blended. Remove from heat. Place lamb loin, opened, with fat side down, long side facing you, on work surface. Sprinkle lightly with salt and a pinch of rosemary. Spoon sweet potato mixture along center of lamb in straight line. Roll up lamb and tie securely. Rub outside of lamb with remaining crushed garlic, salt and pepper to taste and a pinch of rosemary. Place in 425 oven in roasting pan. Roast to desired doneness, about 30 minutes. Garnish with rosemary sprigs, if desired. Makes 4 servings.

BAKED PORK CHOPS WITH ONION RINGS

6 pork chops
1 can cream of mushroom soup
1 can French-fried onion rings
1/2 teaspoon ginger
1/2 teaspoon rosemary
1/2 c sour cream

Combine soup, ginger, rosemary, sour cream, and

half of onion rings; pour over chops. Bake, covered at 350 for 45 minutes. Uncover; sprinkle with remaining onion rings and continue to bake, uncovered, for 10-15 minutes, until lightly browned.

LAMB WITH PLUMS

1/2 c blanched slivered almonds
1/2 c boiling water
1/4 c butter
3 lbs lean lamb, trimmed and cut into 1 inch pieces
3 medium onions, thinly sliced
1/4 c thinly sliced green chilies (either mild or hot)
1 tablespoon minced garlic
2 teaspoon Garam Masala (see following recipe or readymix in supermarkets)
1/2 teaspoon minced fresh ginger
1 to 1 1/2 c meat stock or water
1/4 teaspoon salt
1/2 c raisins
6 underripe plums (preferably green), pitted and cut into sixths

Combine almonds and water and let stand 10-20 minutes then puree. Heat butter in saucepan. Add half the lamb and brown on all sides. Repeat with remaining lamb and set lamb aside. Add onion to same pan and cook until golden. Add chilies, garlic, Garam Masala and ginger. Cook about 5 minutes. Return lamb to pan. Blend in almond puree, 1 cup stock or water and salt. Cover and simmer until lamb is tender, about 1 to 1 1/4 hours, adding stock as necessary. Stir in raisins and cook 15 minutes. Add plums and cook just until heated through. Serves 6-8. Serve with steamed rice, sliced cucumber and fresh mint salad. Delicious!

GARAM MASALA

1 tablespoon whole cumin
1 tablespoon whole coriander (cilantro)
8 whole cloves
2 teaspoon whole cardamom seed
1 1/2 teaspoon peppercorns
4 dried red chilies or 1/4 c pure ground chili
1 teaspoon ground tumeric

In preheated 300 oven roast cumin, coriander, cloves, cardamom and peppercorns for 5 minutes in shallow pan. Add chilies and roast 2 more minutes. Remove from heat. Seed and devein chilies. Put all in blender and process to powder. Seal tightly and freeze. Can be frozen up to six months. Delicious rubbed into meats or poultry before cooking. Gives sparkle to cream based sauces.

BARBECUED PORK CHOPS

8-12 thinly sliced pork chops
1 lemon, thinly sliced
1 large onion, thinly sliced
2 c water
1 c catsup
3 tablespoon Worcestershire sauce
1 teaspoon chili powder
1 teaspoon salt
2 dashes hot pepper sauce

Preheat oven to 450. Arrange chops in a single layer in a shallow baking dish. Cover each with a slice of lemon and a slice of onion. Bake for 15 minutes. Combine remaining ingredients in a saucepan and bring to a boil over medium high heat. Pour over pork chops. Reduce oven temperature to 350. Continue baking, basting once or twice, about 30 minutes.

PORK CHOPS IN AN ONION-MUSTARD SAUCE

1/3 c flour
salt and pepper to taste
1/4 teaspoon dry mustard
6 thick pork chops
3 tablespoon oil
2 c thinly sliced onions
2 tablespoon wine vinegar
3/4 c sour cream
1 tablespoon Dijon mustard
lemon juice
minced sweet marjoram or chives

In a paper bag place the flour, salt and pepper (to taste) and the dry mustard. Shake the bag, add the pork chops, shake again until chops are coated with flour. Set aside. Heat the oil and brown the chops. Place in casserole, in single layer. In same oil cook onions until limp. Remove pan from heat add the vinegar and pour vinegar and pan drippings over chops. Cover and bake at 325 for 30 minutes or until cooked. Remove chops from pan to serving dish. Skim off any fat from casserole. Add the sour cream and cook, stirring, long enough to mix sour cream and pan juices. Add mustard and lemon juice to taste and pour over pork chops. Sprinkle with marjoram or chives. Makes 4-6 servings.

MARINATED LAMB SHISH KABOBS

marinade
1 c olive oil
2 tablespoon lemon juice
2 tablespoon chopped parsley
1 tablespoon salt
2 teaspoon oregano
1 teaspoon pepper
4 cloves garlic, finely chopped
3 bay leaves
3 lb boned leg of lamb, cubed
1 onion quartered
3 green peppers, quartered and seeded
2 tablespoon olive oil
12 slices onion
2 tomatoes, quartered, or use cherry tomatoes
fresh mushrooms

Marinate lamb overnight. Saute green pepper in 2 tablespoon olive oil for 5 minutes; cool. On 6 12" metal skewers, thread lamb cubes, alternating with the vegetables. Brush the kabobs with a mixture of lemon juice and olive oil and broil 3" from heat turning once until brown on both sides and tender.

PARSLEY HAM

1 envelope unflavored gelatin
1 c chicken broth or bouillon
1 c dry white wine
1/4 c chopped onion
5 peppercorns
1/2 teaspoon thyme
1/2 c minced parsley
1 cooked or canned boneless ham (2-3 lbs) chilled
cucumber slices, optional

Sprinkle gelatin over 1/2 cup chicken broth. Stir over low heat until gelatin dissolves. Add remaining 1/2 cup broth, the wine, onion, peppercorns and thyme. Bring to boil. Cover and let barely simmer for 10 minutes. Strain through cheese cloth or fine sieve. Stir in parsley and chill until consistency of unbeaten egg whites. Place ham on rack in shallow pan. Spoon chilled gelatin over top and sides to coat lightly. Smooth with spatula and chill well. Continue spooning and chilling layers of gelatin over ham until gelatin is 1/4 inch thick. Carefully remove ham to serving platter or board. Refrigerate. Chill any remaining gelatin mixture. To serve, chop gelatin and place around thin-sliced ham. Garnish with cucumber. Makes 8-12 servings.

SPICED FRESH HAM

1 fresh ham (about 5 lbs)
1 1/2 c water
1 teaspoon each salt, dried thyme, sage, whole cloves
1 1/2 teaspoon whole allspice
1 bay leaf, crumbled
1 tablespoon slivered lemon rind
2 tablespoon lemon juice
1 onion, chopped
1 large carrot, diced

Brown meat in heavy kettle. Pour off fat, and put a rack under meat in kettle. Add remaining ingredients; cover and simmer 4 hours or until meat is tender, basting occasionally with liquid in kettle and adding more water if necessary. Thicken liquid, if desired. Makes 8 servings.

EASY BREADED CHILI PORK CHOPS

8 pork chops, 3/4 inch-1 inch thick, lightly scored on both sides
red wine vinegar or water
2 teaspoon chili powder
1 teaspoon garlic salt or to taste
ground cumin
cayenne pepper
3/4 c fine dry bread crumbs
3 tablespoon butter or margarine, melted
sour cream at room temperature

Brush chops lightly with vinegar; rub both sides with chili powder and garlic salt. Rub lightly with cumin and very lightly with cayenne. Let stand at room tem-perature for 20-30 minutes. Mix crumbs and butter; coat both side of chops. Place on rack in the large foil lined pan. Bake at 425 for 40-45 minutes or until chops are tender. Chill. Eat as finger food or remove bones and slice thin. Serve sliced pork with sour cream. Good with pepper strips and avocado slices on a bed of shredded lettuce. Makes 4-8 servings.

PORK MEAT BALLS IN TOMATO SAUCE

To 1 can (29 oz) tomatoes, add 1/4 cup instant minced onion, 2 teaspoon salt, 1 teaspoon sugar, 1/4 teaspoon each garlic salt, pepper and hot sauce, and 1 teaspoon each chili powder and oregano. Bring to a boil, cover, and simmer 30 minutes. Add browned meat balls (see below) and simmer, covered, 45 minutes. Serve on rice. Make 6-8 servings.

CHILI-PORK MEAT BALLS

Mix 1 lb. lean ground pork, 1/2 lb ground beef, 1 tablespoon instant minced onion, 1/4 teaspoon each pepper, garlic salt, 2 tablespoon chili powder, 1 tablespoon dried parsley, 1 teaspoon salt, 1/2 teaspoon oregano, 1 1/2 cup fine dry bread crumbs, 3/4 cup grated sharp cheddar, and 2 beaten eggs. Shape in 1 1/2 inch balls. Brown in fat.

HERB-ROASTED PORK LOIN

2 tablespoon dried rosemary
2 tablespoon all-purpose flour
1 tablespoon minced garlic
1 tablespoon each dried thyme and sage
1 teaspoon each salt and pepper
one 5-6 pound bone-in pork loin roast

Heat oven to 375. Have ready a large roasting pan with rack. Mix all ingredients (except pork) and rub all over pork, including cracks in bone between chops. Place meat, fat side up on rack. Roast uncovered for 1 hour and 15 minutes to 1 hour and 30 minutes or until desired doneness. Remove to cutting board and let stand 15 minutes. Slice meat between bones. Arrange chops on platter. To make slicing easier, have your butcher saw or crack the chine (back) bone almost through between each chop. Makes 4 servings with leftovers.

PORK LOIN WITH SAGE AND ONIONS

4 lb pork loin
4 large onions, chopped
salt and pepper
1 1/2 teaspoon dried sage

Roast meat on rack uncovered at 325 about 2 hours. Cook onions in small amount of boiling water until tender. Add 1 teaspoon salt and 1/4 teaspoon pepper and sage to the onions. Remove roast and rack from pan and pour off drippings. Reserve drippings for gravy. Arrange onions in center of pan and place roast on top. Season with additional salt and pepper. Roast at 325 for about 1 hour longer.

SPICY PORK ROAST

4 scallions, finely chopped
3 cloves garlic, finely chopped
2 jalapeno peppers, finely chopped
salt and pepper
1 fresh pork roast, 4-5 lbs, washed and dried

Mix scallions, garlic, jalapeno peppers and 1/4 teaspoon each salt and pepper. Cut 1/2 inch wide and 1/2 inch deep slits in roast. Stuff each slit with mixed seasonings. Rub outside roast with salt and pepper. Wrap roast in foil and freeze. Place frozen roast in 350 oven; cook for 2 1/2-3 hours or 30-45 minutes per pound. About 30 minutes before roast is done open foil and let roast brown. Makes 10-12 servings.

Note: Be sure to buy fresh pork, not smoked or cured ham. Boned pork roasts take longer to cook than those with bones.

HERBED STUFFED PORK

1 fresh pork shoulder, weighing about 5 lb, boned
2 tablespoon chopped onion
2 tablespoon chopped celery
2 tablespoon butter or margarine
2 c fresh bread crumbs (4 slices)
1/2 teaspoon salt
1/2 teaspoon leaf rosemary, crumbled
1/2 teaspoon leaf thyme, crumbled
1/4 c finely chopped parsley
1/4 c flour

Trim skin and excess fat from pork. Saute onion and celery in butter until soft. Combine bread crumbs, salt, rosemary, thyme and parsley; pour onion mixture over top; toss until evenly moist. Stuff mixture into pocket in pork, packing it well to give meat a rounded shape. Tie roast to hold in stuffing. Place, fat side up, on rack in roasting pan.  Do not add water or cover. Roast in slow oven (325) 3 hours or until pork is tender. Remove to serving platter. Pour pan drippings into 2 c measure; let stand until fat rises to top; then skim off. Measure 1/4 cup and return to pan. Add water to drippings to make 2 cups.

Blend flour into fat in pan. Cook, stirring constantly until bubbly. Stir in the 2 cups dripping mixture; continue cooking and stirring until gravy thickens and boil 1 minute. Slice roast 1/4 inch thick; serve gravy separately to spoon over roast. Makes 6 or 7 servings.

BARBECUED RIBS

3-4 lbs ribs, cut into serving pieces
1 lemon sliced
1 large onion, sliced
1 c catsup
3 tablespoon Worcestershire sauce
1 teaspoon chili powder
1 teaspoon salt
2 dashes hot sauce, more if desired
1 c water

Heat oven hot (450). Place ribs in baking pan, meaty side up. On each piece place a slice of lemon and onion. Roast for 30 minutes. Combine the remaining ingredients and pour over ribs. Reduce heat to 350 and bake for 1 1/2 hours more. Baste 2 or 3 times. Serves 4.

ZIPPY SPARERIBS

8 lbs pork spareribs, cut into 2-rib portions
2/3 c light molasses
2 tablespoon balsamic vinegar
3 tablespoon prepared mustard
2 tablespoon hot pepper sauce

Heat ribs in enough water to cover to boiling, cover, reduce heat and simmer 45 minutes or until ribs are tender. Drain. Meanwhile, combine molasses, vinegar, mustard and hot sauce. Place ribs on rack in broiling pan; brush with some of the sauce. Roast ribs 15 minutes about 7-9 inches from heat under broiler. Turn ribs occasionally and brush often with sauce. Makes about 8 servings.

PORK AND SAUERKRAUT CASSEROLE

2 lb pork shoulder, cubed
2 tablespoon salad oil
1 c sliced carrots
1 large onion, chopped
1 tablespoon salt
1 bay leaf
1/4 teaspoon pepper
4 c kraut, well drained
2 apples, cut in 1 1/2 inch pieces
1/2 c apple juice
2 tablespoon chopped parsley
1 tablespoon light brown sugar

Brown pork in Dutch oven, add 1 cup water, carrots and seasoning. Cover and reduce heat to simmer for about 1 1/2 hours or until meat is tender. Add kraut, apples, apple juice, parsley and brown sugar and cook covered for an additional 15-20 minutes.

RABBIT STEW

2 1/2-3 lb rabbit, cut in serving pieces
1 1/2 c red wine vinegar
1 c thinly sliced onions
3 teaspoon salt
2 bay leaves
1 teaspoon hot pepper sauce
flour
shortening
1/4 teaspoon thyme
1 c marinade, add water if needed
2 teaspoon sugar

Combine vinegar, onions, 2 teaspoon salt, bay leaves and hot sauce, mix well. Place rabbit pieces in glass baking dish or plastic baggy. Refrigerate 24 hours. Drain rabbit, reserving marinade. Mix remaining teaspoon salt with flour and coat rabbit pieces. Heat shortening in skillet and brown rabbit on all sides. Drain excess fat from skillet, add reserved marinade, thyme and water. Cover and cook on simmer 45-50 minutes, stirring occasionally. Add sugar and mix well before serving.

VENISON STEAKS WITH CRANBERRY-PORT SAUCE

4 venison steaks, 1/2 inch thick
pepper
1/2 Spanish onion, thinly sliced
2 tablespoon juniper berries, bruised
1 sprig fresh rosemary or 1/2 teaspoon dried
1 sprig fresh thyme or 1/2 teaspoon dried
1 bay leaf, crumbled
2 c red Burgundy
3 c ruby port
2 c cranberry sauce, canned or homemade
1/2 c fresh lemon juice
2-3 tablespoon butter

Wipe steaks dry with paper towels and sprinkle both sides with salt and pepper. Put steaks in container and distribute onion, juniper berries, rosemary, thyme and bay leaf evenly over steaks; add Burgundy and 2 cup of the port. Cover container tightly and refrigerate 36-48 hours, turning steaks at least once. Abut 25 minutes before serving steaks heat cranberry sauce, remaining cup of port and the lemon juice to boiling, stirring often. Boil sauce until thickened, about 20 minutes. Heat butter in a large heavy skillet. Remove steaks from marinade and pat dry. Brown steaks in hot butter, about 3 minutes per side. Remove to serving platter and cover with sauce. Makes 4 servings.

BARBECUED VENISON STEAKS

6 venison rib steaks
1/2 teaspoon pepper
1 medium onion, thinly sliced
1 lemon thinly sliced
1 c catsup
1 c water
1 teaspoon salt
1/3 c worchestershire sauce
1/4 c red wine vinegar
1 tablespoon Tabasco sauce

Place steaks in baking dish in a single layer. Season with pepper, place onion rings over steaks, top with lemon slices. Bake at 400 for 15 minutes. Meanwhile mix remaining ingredients in a saucepan and bring to a boil. Pour over venison steaks. Return steaks to oven and bake at 350 for another hour, basting often. If sauce becomes too dry, add a little water.

CROCK POT VENISON

3 1/2-4 lb venison roast
1/2 c red wine vinegar
2 tablespoon salt
4 cloves garlic, minced
1 large yellow onion, sliced
3 tablespoon brown sugar
1 1/2 teaspoon dry mustard
3 tablespoon flour
3 tablespoon Worcestershire sauce
2 c chopped canned tomatoes
1 tablespoon hot pepper sauce

Make marinade of red wine vinegar, salt and garlic. Place roast in glass dish and pour marinade over, adding additional water to cover roast. Refrigerate over night. Remove roast from marinade, reserving 1/3 cup. Coat roast with flour and brown on all sides in hot skillet. Put roast in crock pot, add remaining ingredients and cook on low about 9-10 hours or until meat is fork tender.

Poultry

CHICKEN LIVERS ROSEMARY

1 lb chicken livers
2 tablespoon shortening
1/3 c chopped onion
1/4 c chopped green pepper
1/2 teaspoon salt
3/4 c sour cream
2 hard cooked eggs, diced
1/2 teaspoon rosemary
1 tablespoon flour
2 tablespoon water

Saute livers in hot shortening until firm. Add onion, green pepper and salt; saute until onions are golden and livers are done. Reduce heat and add sour cream and rosemary. Make a paste of the flour and water and stir into livers, stirring until thick. Add diced eggs. Serve on toast.

ORIENTAL CORNISH HEN (MICROWAVE)

1/2 c soy sauce
1/2 c sherry
1/4 c honey
1 garlic clove, minced
1 teaspoon grated fresh vinegar
1 cornish hen split lengthwise
freshly cooked rice

Combine first 5 ingredients in baking dish. Cover and microwave on high 3 minutes. Arrange hen halves, breast side down and baste with sauce. Cover and cook on high 4 minutes. Turn halves over and baste with sauce. Cover and cook on high 4 minutes. Let stand until juices run clear when pricked with a fork, about 5-8 minutes. Serve with rice and sauce. Makes 2 servings.

CORNISH HENS WITH MUSHROOM STUFFING

Stuffing for each game hen
1/8 c minced onion
1/4 c chopped celery-stalks and leaves
3 tablespoon butter or margarine
3/4 c soft bread crumbs
1/4 teaspoon salt
1/4 teaspoon crushed sage leaves
1/8 teaspoon thyme leaves
dash of pepper
dash of rosemary
1/4 c sliced mushrooms

Baste for each hen
1/4 c butter or margarine
1/4 teaspoon marjoram
1/4 teaspoon oregano
1/4 teaspoon pepper
1/4 teaspoon salt
1/8 teaspoon ginger
1/4 c chablis wine

Stuffing: In skillet cook onion and celery in butter until tender. Stir in 1/4 to 1/3 of bread cubes. Pour into bowl; add remaining ingredients and toss until all cubes are coated. Stuff hens just before roasting.

Baste: Melt butter in saucepan; add all ingredients. Heat to simmer. Keep warm. After stuffing hens tie legs together to hold in stuffing; place hens, breast side up, on rack in shallow pan. Roast 325-350 for 60-70 minutes. Brush hens 3 or 4 times with baste.

STUFFED CORNISH HENS

4 cornish hens
1 can (8 oz) pineapple tidbits, packed in juice
1 jar (12 oz) red pepper jelly
1 tablespoon butter or margarine
1 c chopped onions
4 c cooked brown rice
3/4 c currants
3/4 c macadamia nuts
1/2 c chicken broth
1-2 tablespoon diced crystallized ginger

Remove giblets and rinse hens with cold water. Drain and set aside. Drain pineapple. Place pineapple juice in saucepan with the jelly. Heat, low heat, until jelly melts. Cook onions in butter until tender. Add rice, pineapple, currants, nuts, broth and ginger; heat thoroughly. Spoon about 2/3 cup mixture into cavity of each hen. Place hens, breast side up, in roasting pan on rack coated with cooking spray. Baste with jelly mixture. Roast at 400 for 10 minutes; reduce heat to 350 and roast for 1 hour, basting often with jelly mixture. Cover remaining stuffing and bake last 30 minutes. Cut hens in half and serve with remaining rice.

ROAST GOOSE

Wash and dry goose. Stuff with dressing made of bread crumbs, sage, onion, salt and pepper, butter and water. Cook onion in butter before adding. Truss goose so that legs and wings lie close. Baste often while cooking. Bake at 325 for 4-5 hours or until done. Cook and chop giblets and thicken for gravy. Tart jelly in very good with goose.

ROAST DUCK WITH POTATOES, TURNIPS AND OLIVES

2 (5 lb) ducks
fresh or dried thyme
2 large onions sliced
4 potatoes, quartered lengthwise, cut crosswise into 1/2 inch thick slices
5 turnips, peeled and cut same as potatoes
1 c Nicoise olives
1 1/2 c canned beef broth
1/2 c dry white wine

Remove fat pieces from inside cavities and pat ducks dry. Season cavities with thyme, salt and pepper. Place a few onion slices in cavity of each duck. Tie legs together. Place each duck in a separate roasting pan. Pierce all over with fork. Rub outside of ducks with generous amount of thyme, salt and pepper. Place remaining onions around ducks. Roast at 450 for 15 minutes. Remove from oven and add potatoes and turnips. Sprinkle vegetables with thyme, salt and pepper. Stir vegetables to coat with pan drippings. Return to oven and roast 15 minutes longer. Reduce heat to 375 continue roasting until vegetables and ducks are done.

SAUSAGE MUSHROOM STUFFING

4 c soft bread crumbs
1/2 lb bulk sausage meat
butter if needed
1 lb fresh mushrooms, thinly sliced
1/2 c onion, chopped
1/2 c celery, chopped
1/4 teaspoon thyme
1/2 teaspoon marjoram
broth to moisten

Cook sausage, stirring and breaking it apart until it is brown and crumbly. Remove sausage and measure fat in skillet, and if there is not 1/2 cup add butter to make up the difference. Return fat to skillet and saute the onion, celery and mushrooms for 4-5 minutes. Mix in sausage, bread crumbs and seasonings. Moisten with broth. Fill birds cavity about 3/4 full, dressing expands in cooking. Dressing may be made ahead and refrigerated. Makes 6-7 cups.

BAKED ROSEMARY CHICKEN

2 medium onions, sliced thin
4 large tomatoes, cut into large dice
1/4 c flour
1- 4 pound chicken, skinless and cut into serving pieces
1 tablespoon cooking oil
1 teaspoon minced garlic
1 teaspoon fresh rosemary, fine chopped
1 c chicken broth

Dredge chicken pieces in flour and set aside. In oven proof skillet, heat oil over medium heat. Add onions and saute until translucent. Add garlic and rosemary and cook about 2 minutes longer. Make a single layer of chicken around skillet and brown for 5 minutes on each side. Add chicken broth and tomatoes. Increase heat and bring liquid to a boil. Cover skillet and place in 400 oven. Bake for 30 minutes. Serve chicken and sauce over rice.

CHICKEN WITH PASTA AND VEGETABLES

3/4 lb thin strips chicken breast
1 tablespoon oil
1 tablespoon chopped fresh cilantro
1 pkg Pasta Accents (Green Giant) garlic seasoning vegetables and pasta
3/4 c salsa (hot)

Brown chicken in oil. Add vegetables and pasta and salsa. Cover and simmer 8-10 minutes, until vegetables are crisp tender, stirring occasionally. Stir in cilantro. Good for a quick meal. Serves 4.

HOT GRILLED CHICKEN BREASTS

6 chicken breasts
4 tablespoon fresh lime juice
1/4 c olive oil
1/2 teaspoon chili powder
1/4 teaspoon pepper
hot salsa
1 tablespoon finely chopped cilantro

Mix together lime juice, olive oil, chili powder and pepper. Add chicken, turn to coat. Cover and marinate in refrigerator for two hours. Place chicken on grill, skin side down and grill about 8 minutes. Turn chicken and grill 8 minutes on other side or until juices run clear. Place chicken on platter and cover with hot salsa. Sprinkle with cilantro.

CHICKEN DRUMSTICKS AND POTATOES

1/4 c chicken bouillon
3/4 teaspoon salt
12 drumsticks
1 clove garlic, minced
1 large sliced onion
6 large potatoes, cut into 1/4
1 tablespoon fresh chopped dill
2 tablespoon margarine
2 tablespoon cooking oil
1/2 teaspoon grated pepper

Season drumsticks with salt and pepper. Brown in margarine and oil until golden brown. Add onion, garlic and potatoes. Add 1/4 cup hot chicken bouillon. Cover tightly and cook on top of stove for 45 to 60 minutes. Add dill. Serves 4 to 6. Potatoes are good with a little sour cream spread on them.

SMOTHERED CHICKEN AND CORN

1 chicken, cut up
6 to 8 ears fresh corn
2 medium tomatoes
1 medium onion, chopped
1/2 c flour
1/4 c cooking oil
2 tablespoon butter
salt and pepper to taste
hot sauce to taste

Cut the tops of the kernels off the corn; then bring the knife across the cob so that the pulp and juice is squeezed out. Set aside. Cut up chicken and salt and pepper to taste. Dredge chicken in flour and brown in oil. Remove chicken and pour out oil. Put butter in skillet and saute onion. Add chicken, corn pulp, and tomatoes, peeled and diced. Season with salt, pepper and hot sauce. Cover and simmer slowly until chicken is tender. If it appears too dry add a little milk.

OVEN BAKED CHICKEN

1 c dry bread crumbs
1 (2 1/2-3 lb) chicken, cut up
2/3 c grated Parmesan cheese
2 teaspoon salt
dash of pepper
1/4 c chopped fresh parsley
1 garlic clove, crushed
1/2 c margarine or butter, melted

Combine all ingredients except chicken and butter. Dip chicken in butter. Roll in crumbs. Place pieces, skin side up in pan, pieces not touching. Sprinkle with remaining butter. Bake 45 minutes at 375. Not necessary to turn. Serves 4.

GRILLED CHICKEN WITH HERBS

1 teaspoon parsley
1/2 teaspoon basil
1/2 teaspoon thyme
1/2 teaspoon oregano
1/8 teaspoon garlic salt
6 boneless, skinless chicken breast halves
1 tablespoon oil
juice of 1 lemon
cooking spray

Combine parsley, basil, thyme, oregano and garlic salt. Place each chicken breast half between wax paper and flatten to 1/4 inch thickness using a meat mallet or rolling pin. Brush chicken with oil and sprinkle with herbs and lemon juice. Coat grill with cooking spray. Grill chicken until tender, turning once. Makes 6 servings.

CRISPY OVENBAKED CHICKEN

4 chicken breast halves, bone in, skin removed
1/2 c buttermilk
2 tablespoon Dijon mustard
1/2-1 teaspoon red hot pepper sauce
1/3 c plain dry bread crumbs
1/2 c cornmeal

Heat oven to 425. Spray baking sheet with cooking spray. Sprinkle chicken with salt. Place buttermilk, mustard, pepper sauce and chicken in large plastic bag, seal and shake well. Combine bread crumbs and meal. Dip chicken in crumb mixture to coat. Place chicken on baking sheet and spray with cooking spray. Bake 20 minutes. Remove chicken from oven and spray with cooking spray again. Do not turn. Bake 10-15 minutes longer or until juices run clear when chicken is pierced. Serves 4.

CHICKEN TOSTADOS

1 clove garlic, minced
2 tablespoon vegetable oil
3 c shredded cooked chicken breast
1 can (4 oz) diced green chilies, drained
1/2 c commercial sour cream
1 3/4 c vegetable oil
6 (6 in) flour tortillas
1/2 small head lettuce, thinly sliced
1 c shredded Cheddar cheese
2 tomatoes, chopped
Avocado Dressing, recipe follows

Saute garlic in 2 tablespoon oil until tender. Stir in chicken, chilies, and sour cream. Cook until heated and keep warm. Heat 1 3/4 oil. Fry tortillas, one at a time, 30 seconds on each side. Drain. Arrange lettuce on each tortillas; top with chicken mixture. Sprinkle with cheese and tomato, and top with Avocado Dressing. Makes 6 servings.

AVOCADO DRESSING

3 tablespoon vegetable oil
2 tablespoon cider vinegar
2 teaspoon minced jalapeno pepper
1/2 teaspoon sugar
1/2 teaspoon salt
1 avocado, peeled and chopped
1 tomato, chopped

Combine all ingredients. Mix. Cover and chill. Makes 2 cups.

HERBED OVEN-FRIED CHICKEN

8 meaty pieces of chicken
2 envelopes chicken broth seasoning
1 teaspoon dried basil
1/2 c water
1/3 c lemon juice
3/4 c flour
1 teaspoon salt
1/4 teaspoon pepper
oil

Rub chicken with a mixture of broth, seasoning and basil. Place in a bowl with water and lemon juice. Turn to coat chicken well; cover and refrigerate several hours or overnight. Drain chicken, reserving marinade. Mix flour, salt and pepper and use to coat chicken. Brown in 1/2 inch hot oil in skillet. Place chicken in baking dish and pour reserved marinade over it. Bake in 375 oven for 45 minutes or until tender. Makes 4 servings.

CHICKEN WITH BLACK EYED PEAS

2 slices bacon
1 frying chicken, cut in parts
1/2 teaspoon salt
1/8 teaspoon pepper
3/4 c uncooked medium grain rice
1/2 c chopped onion
1 tablespoon chicken bouillon
2 c hot water
1/4 teaspoon hot red pepper sauce
1-15 oz can black-eyed peas, drained
1/4 c chopped parsley
1/2 teaspoon thyme leaves, crushed

In large skillet, cook bacon until crisp, drain, crumble and reserve. Drain all but 2 tablespoon drippings from skillet. In same skillet, brown chicken until brown on all sides. Sprinkle with salt and pepper. Turn heat to low and cover and simmer chicken for about 15 minutes; add rice and onion to skillet. Dissolve bouillon in hot water, add hot sauce and stir. Pour over chicken. In medium bowl mix black-eyed peas, parsley and thyme. Stir into chicken. Cover and cook until chicken is tender, about 25 minutes. Sprinkle with reserved bacon.

HERBED CHICKEN AND DUMPLINGS

2 (4 lb) chicken, cut up
1 teaspoon salt
1 teaspoon pepper
1 bay leaf
2 sprigs thyme or 1/2 teaspoon dried
2 sprigs marjoram or 1/2 teaspoon dried
1/4 teaspoon paprika
1 tablespoon minced parsley
1/2 small clove garlic, minced
2 tablespoon flour, dissolved in 1/3 c cold water
1 large onion, sliced in 1/4 inch thick rings
1 carrot, cut into 3/4 inch dice
1 large potato, peeled, cut into 3/4 inch dice

Cook first 9 ingredients together until almost tender, add vegetables, cook until tender. Thicken broth with paste made of flour and water.

DUMPLINGS

2 c self-rising flour
1/2 c water
1/2 egg (1 3/4 tablespoon of beaten egg)
3/4 teaspoon salt
pinch of paprika, thyme and marjoram
1/2 teaspoon minced parsley
1 1/2 teaspoon butter, melted
1/2 teaspoon pepper

Mix all ingredients and drop by spoon full in chicken mixture.

MEXICAN CHICKEN

1 (3 lb) frying chicken, cut up
1 teaspoon salt
1/4 c oil
8 small boiling onions
1/4 teaspoon crushed garlic
1 tablespoon flour
1 (1 lb) can tomatoes
1 bay leaf
1/2 teaspoon oregano
2 tablespoon chopped green chilies
1 c canned pitted ripe olives, drained
1/2 lemon, thinly sliced

Sprinkle chicken with 1/2 teaspoon salt. Heat oil and brown chicken slowly. Cover onions with water and boil 5 minutes; drain. Place browned chicken pieces in baking dish. Discard all oil except 1 tablespoon from skillet in which chicken was browned. Add garlic and flour to remaining oil. Stir in tomatoes, bay leaf, oregano and remaining 1/2 teaspoon salt and heat to boiling. Add chilies, onions and olives. Pour over chicken. Top with lemon slices. Cover and bake 30 minutes in a 350 pre-heated oven. Uncover and bake 30 more minutes. Makes about 4 servings.

GRILLED BARBECUED CHICKEN

4 skinless, boneless chicken breast halves
sauce:
1/4 c ketchup
3 tablespoon vinegar
1 tablespoon horseradish
2 teaspoon packed brown sugar
1 clove garlic, minced
1/8 teaspoon dried thyme
1/4 teaspoon black pepper

For sauce—Combine ketchup, vinegar, horseradish, brown sugar, garlic and thyme. Mix well. Bring to a boil and cook about 5 minutes. Remove from heat and stir in pepper. Brush tops of chicken pieces with sauce. Place chicken on foil lined broiler pan, sauce side down or on grill rack. Brush other side lightly with sauce. Broil or grill 3 inches from heat, basting with remaining sauce and turning until no longer pink in center, about 5-7 minutes on each side. Let chicken stand for 5 minutes before serving. Serves 4.

HONEY LEMON HERB CHICKEN

1/3 c honey
1/4 c lemon juice
1 teaspoon dried rosemary leaves, crushed
1/4 teaspoon crushed red pepper
2 lbs chicken pieces

Combine first 4 ingredients. Brush 1/2 the sauce on chicken. Bake at 350 for one hour or until thoroughly cooked, brushing on remaining sauce halfway through baking time.

TARRAGON CHICKEN

1/2 c lemon juice
1/2 c orange juice
6 cloves garlic, finely chopped
2 teaspoon vegetable oil
1 teaspoon ground ginger
1 teaspoon tarragon leaves
salt and pepper to taste
6 boneless, skinless chicken breasts

Combine all ingredients except chicken; pour over chicken. Cover; marinate in refrigerator two hours. Drain chicken and discard marinade. Grill or broil chicken as desired until fully cooked. Serves 6.

CHICKEN WITH MINT AND ORANGE

5 sprigs mint
1-3 to 3 1/2 lb chicken
1/4 c butter
salt and pepper
2 tablespoon Grand Marnier
1/4 c orange juice
1/2 c chicken stock or broth
1/4 c cold butter, cubed
2 tablespoon fresh, chopped mint leaves
1 teaspoon grated orange rind

Place mint sprigs in cavity of chicken and truss so cavity is closed. Rub skin with softened butter and season with salt and pepper. Place chicken on a rack in roasting pan in a preheated 450 oven and immediately reduce heat to 350. Roast for 1 to 1 1/4 hours basting every 15 minutes. Place chicken on warm platter and remove mint sprigs. Mix pan juices and Grand Marnier. Add orange juice and chicken stock and bring to a boil. Cook until reduced to one half over high heat. Remove from heat and add butter, whisking in one pat at a time. Add chopped mint and grated orange rind. Serve separately with chicken. Makes 4 servings.

ZUCCHINI-CORN-BREAD STUFFING

1 1/2 c chopped onion
1 c chopped celery
1 clove garlic, minced
1/2 c butter or margarine
1 1/2 c ground cooked ham
1/2 c finely chopped giblets
12 c coarsely crumbled cornbread
2 c shredded zucchini, well drained
2 teaspoon ground sage
1 1/2 teaspoon crushed dried basil
1/4 teaspoon pepper
2 beaten eggs
1 1/2 c chicken broth

In skillet cook onion, celery and garlic in butter or margarine until tender. Add the ham and giblets and cook until giblets are lightly browned. Combine the ham mixture with the other ingredients and toss lightly to mix. Enough stuffing for a 12 lb turkey with enough left over to bake in 1 1/2 quart casserole.

CHICKEN BREASTS IN HERB & TOMATO SAUCE

12 chicken breast halves, skinned and boned
salt and pepper
3 tablespoon all-purpose flour
1/4 c olive oil
3 tablespoon minced garlic
2 tablespoon paprika
1 c rich veal stock, preferably homemade
1 c pearl onions, peeled and parboiled
1/2 c dry white vermouth
1 tablespoon dried basil, crumbled
1 teaspoon dried thyme, crumbled
1 teaspoon dried oregano, crumbled
1 c diced tomato (about 2)
1/2 c sliced green onion

Pat chicken dry. Season with salt and pepper. Dredge in flour, shaking off excess. Heat oil and brown chicken on both sides. Remove from skillet. Reduce heat to low, add garlic and paprika and cook 3 minutes. Add stock, onions, vermouth, basil, thyme and oregano. Bring to a boil. Reduce heat and simmer until onions are tender, about 10 minutes. Blend in tomato and return chicken to skillet. Cover and simmer until chicken is tender. Transfer chicken to platter, cover to keep warm. Stir green onions into sauce and cook 5 minutes. Pour sauce over chicken and serve. Serves 6 or more.

FENNEL RUBBED TURKEY

Spice Rub:
2 tablespoon Fennel seed
2 tablespoon Kosher salt (no substitute)
2 tablespoon imported sweet Hungarian sweet paprika
1 tablespoon freshly ground black pepper
2 tablespoon garlic powder
1/2 teaspoon cayenne pepper
Olive oil
1 13-14 lb. fresh (not frozen) whole turkey with pop-up doneness indicator

Combine all ingredients for spice rub in food processor or mortar and pestle (preferred), until fennel is crushed. Remove giblets from turkey and reserve for another use. Rub turkey with olive oil (about 3-4 tablespoon). Apply spice rub inside and out, evenly, reserving about 1 tablespoon.

Lay turkey breast side down on a rack in a roasting pan. Add about 1 cup of water. Place turkey in a 375 degree oven for one hour, turning it over, and then sprinkling with reserved rub. Turn oven down to 350 degrees. Check in another 1-1 1/2 hours for doneness, and every 15 minutes thereafter. Keep water under rack at all times. When turkey is well browned and timer pops up, remove from oven and let stand 15 minutes before carving.

Note: This was submitted by Katrina Refett.

Fish & Seafood

CRABMEAT PIE

1 lb crabmeat
3 eggs, beaten
1/2 c butter or margarine
1/2 c Worcestershire sauce
1/2 teaspoon pepper
1 teaspoon salt
1 c evaporated milk
1/2 c salad dressing
1/4 c green pepper, minced
1 tablespoon onion, chopped
hot sauce to taste
1/4 c buttered crumbs

Combine all ingredients except crumbs. Place in greased casserole; sprinkle crumbs on top and bake 350 for 30 minutes or until browned. Makes 8 servings.

HOMEMADE CRAB CAKES

1 lb fresh or frozen crabmeat (if frozen, thawed and blotted dry with paper toweling)
1/4 c mayonnaise
1 medium onion, coarsely grated
1 egg, lightly beaten
1 teaspoon prepared mustard
1 teaspoon Worcestershire sauce
dash of hot pepper sauce
pinch of salt
pinch of pepper
1 c fresh white bread crumbs or more as needed
vegetable oil

Combine all ingredients except oil. Mix until well blended. If mixture does not stick together add more crumbs. Shape mixture into 3 inch patties using 1/4 cup of mixture for each patty. Heat 1/4 inch oil in skillet. Fry cakes, turning once, until golden brown on both sides. Drain on paper towels. Serve immediately. Makes 12 cakes.

CRAWFISH ETOUFFE

Etouffe (smothered) is a popular dish with a number of variations across the state of Louisiana. This one is not made with a roux.

3/4 c butter
2 c chopped onion
1/2 c chopped bell pepper
2 cloves garlic, mashed
1/2 c minced scallions (5 or 6)
2 lb shelled crawfish tails
6 drops hot sauce or to taste
1 teaspoon salt
1/4 teaspoon pepper
1 c chicken stock
1/2 c minced parsley

Melt butter, saute onion, bell pepper and garlic until softened but not browned, about 15 minutes. Add scallions, crawfish tails, hot sauce, salt, pepper and chicken stock. Simmer, covered, stirring often until crawfish is cooked, about 15-20 minutes. Stir in parsley and cook 5 more minutes. Serve over rice. Makes 6-8 servings.

BROILED FISH WITH THYME BUTTER

thyme butter:
1/2 c unsalted butter, melted
4-5 sprigs fresh thyme
1 tablespoon white wine vinegar
mix ingredients together and set aside:
6 fillets of fish
sprigs of fresh thyme
coarse black pepper
lemon wedges

Brush broiler rack and fish with thyme butter and place fish on rack. Brush again when turning once or twice. Fish should be ready in 6-8 minutes. Serve at once with pepper and lemon wedges. Use fresh sprigs of thyme as garnish.

CRISPY FRIED FISH

salad oil
2 tablespoon minced onion
6 medium tomatoes, cut into wedges
2 tablespoon red wine vinegar
1 teaspoon basil
1/4 teaspoon pepper
2 lbs frozen cod fillets, partially thawed
1 egg
2 1/2 c fresh bread crumbs
1 teaspoon salt

Cook onions in 2 tablespoon oil until tender. Add tomatoes, vinegar, basil and pepper; cover and cook 10 minutes. Keep warm. Cut each package of fish crosswise into 4 pieces. Beat egg. Combine bread crumbs and salt. Dip fish in egg, then coat with bread crumb mixture. Heat 1/3 cup oil in skillet, cook fish in oil 10 minutes, turning once. To serve, spoon tomato sauce onto deep platter and arrange fish in sauce. Makes 8 servings.

BAKED CATFISH WITH VEGETABLES

2 tablespoon butter, cut in pieces
4 catfish fillets (about 6 oz each)
1 leek and 1 large carrot, cut into 2 x 1/8 inch strips
12 cherry tomatoes, halved
1/3 c Spanish olives, sliced
1/3 c dry white wine
1/2 teaspoon dried thyme
1/4 teaspoon salt
1/8 teaspoon pepper
1/3 c fresh basil leaves, sliced

In center of each of four 12 x 12 inch pieces of foil, place butter. Place fish, leek, carrot, tomatoes and olives on butter. Mix thyme, salt, pepper, basil with wine and sprinkle over fish. Fold foil to seal; place on baking sheet. Bake in 350 oven for 35 minutes or until fish is opaque. Serves 4.

FISH CASSEROLE

2 lb cod or haddock fillets
4 potatoes, sliced
3 onions, peeled and sliced
few celery tops
1 bay leaf
1 clove garlic
1/4 teaspoon dried dill seed
1/4 teaspoon white pepper
2 1/2 teaspoon salt
1/4 lb butter or margarine
1/2 c dry white wine
2 c boiling water
2 c light cream
chopped parsley

Put all ingredients, except last 2, in a 3 quart casserole. Cover; bake in 375 oven for 1 hour. Add scalded cream. Top with parsley. Serves 6.

FISH CREOLE

1 lb fresh of frozen fish fillets, in 1 inch pieces
1/2 c chopped onion
1/2 c chopped green peppers
1 clove garlic, minced
1/4 c butter or margarine
1-16 oz can tomatoes, cut up
1 tablespoon dried parsley flakes
1 tablespoon chicken bouillon granules
1/4 teaspoon hot pepper sauce
1 tablespoon cornstarch
1 tablespoon cold water
hot cooked rice

Cook onion, green peppers and garlic in butter until tender but not brown. Add undrained tomatoes, parsley, bouillon granules and hot pepper sauce. Simmer, covered, for 10 minutes. Make a paste of cornstarch and water, stir into tomato mixture. Cook, stirring, until thick and bubbly. Add fish to tomato mixture, stirring to coat. Return to boiling then reduce heat and simmer, covered, for about 7-10 minutes or until fish flakes easily with a fork. Serve over hot rice.

SALMON CHEESE PUFF WITH PARSLEY SAUCE

1-1lb can salmon, drained
3 eggs, separated
3/4 c milk
1 c soft bread crumbs
1 c shredded cheddar cheese
1 teaspoon instant minced onion
1/2 teaspoon salt
1/8 teaspoon pepper
2 teaspoon lemon juice

Remove bones and flake salmon. Beat egg yolks and add milk. Add salmon and other ingredients except egg whites; mix. Beat egg whites until stiff and fold into salmon mixture. Turn into 1 quart baking dish and bake 30-35 minutes in 350 oven until knife inserted in center comes out clean. Makes 6 servings. Serve with parsley sauce.

PARSLEY SAUCE

3 tablespoon butter
3 tablespoon flour
3/4 teaspoon salt
1 1/2 c milk
1 tablespoon lemon juice
1 1/2 tablespoon chopped parsley

Melt butter; stir in flour and salt. Gradually add milk and cook until thickened, stirring constantly. Add lemon juice and parsley before serving over salmon.

SALMON BAKE

4 eggs, beaten
1 can cream of mushroom soup, undiluted
1 tablespoon finely chopped fresh dill or 1 teaspoon dill weed
1/4 teaspoon pepper
1 can salmon, drained and flaked
1 pkg (10 oz) green peas, thawed
2 c shredded sharp cheddar cheese, divided
1/2 c chopped red bell pepper
1/2 c chopped onion
1/4 c dry bread crumbs

Mix eggs, soup, dill and pepper. Add salmon, peas, 1 cup cheese, red pepper, onion and bread crumbs. Pour into greased baking dish. Bake 45 minutes. Sprinkle with remaining cheese and bake 2 or 3 minutes until cheese starts to melt. Let stand 10 minutes before serving. Cut into squares. Makes 8 servings.

SALMON STEAKS WITH CUCUMBER DILL SAUCE

4 c water
1/2 c lemon juice
1 small onion quartered and sliced lengthwise
1 teaspoon salt
10 whole peppercorns
four 6 oz salmon steaks
cucumber dill sauce, recipe follows

Add water, lemon juice, onion, salt and peppercorns to a large skillet. Bring to a boil and add salmon steaks. Poaching liquid must cover steaks, if it does not, add more water. Bring back to a boil and simmer, covered, until salmon flakes easily with a fork. Remove steaks and drain. Serve hot or cold with cucumber dill sauce. Serves 4.

CUCUMBER DILL SAUCE

Peel cucumber, cut in half lengthwise and scoop out seeds. Slice thinly and sprinkle with 1 teaspoon salt. Mix well and set aside for 15 minutes. Drain liquid from cucumbers. Stir cucumbers into 1 cup plain yogurt or sour cream, 1 teaspoon grated lemon rind, 1/2 teaspoon lemon juice, finely chopped fresh dill and salt and pepper to taste. Makes about 2 cups.

SHRIMP WITH HOT CAJUN BUTTER

1/2 c butter, room temperature
1/4 c chopped fresh chives or green onions
4 teaspoon crab broil, ground in spice grinder or in mortar with pestle
1 1/2 teaspoon hot sauce
1 c sliced red onion
1 red or green bell pepper, sliced
1 lb uncooked large shrimp, peeled, deveined
1/3 c dry vermouth

Mix first 4 ingredients. Can be prepared 4 or 5 days ahead, just cover and refrigerate. Melt 2 tablespoon of Cajun butter, add onion, and bell pepper and cook until almost tender. Push vegetables to side of skillet and melt another 2 tablespoon cajun butter; add shrimp and saute just until cooked through, about 3 minutes. Mix shrimp and vegetables together. Season with salt. Divide among 4 plates. Add vermouth to skillet; boil one minute. Gradually add remaining cajun butter, whisking until just melted. Pour sauce over shrimp. Serve this over grits that have been cooked and seasoned, sauted garlic and chopped green onions. Makes 4 servings.

SHRIMP AND GRITS

1 lb fresh peeled shrimp
6 slices bacon
2 c sliced mushrooms
1 c sliced scallions
1 large clove garlic, minced
4 teaspoon lemon juice
hot sauce
chopped fresh parsley
salt and pepper

CHEESE GRITS

4 c water
1 c old fashioned grits
1/2 teaspoon salt
4 tablespoon butter
1 c grated, sharp cheddar cheese
1/2 c grated, fresh Parmesan
pinch each white pepper, cayenne and nutmeg

Wash shrimp and pat dry. Dice bacon and cook until crisp. Drain and reserve. Add enough oil to bacon fat to make a thin layer. Heat and add shrimp. When shrimp turns pink add mushrooms. Add scallions and garlic. Season to taste with lemon, hot sauce, parsley, salt and pepper. Cook grits as usual. Stir cheese and seasonings into grits and divide among four plates. Spoon shrimp mixture over grits and serve.

SHRIMP AND OKRA

2-3 tablespoon bacon fat or vegetable oil
2 ribs celery, chopped
2 cloves garlic, chopped
1 medium bell pepper, chopped
1 lb okra, fresh or frozen, sliced in 1/2 inch pieces
1 (16 oz) can stewed tomatoes, undrained
2 bay leaves
salt and pepper
1 lb shrimp, shelled and deveined

Heat bacon fat or oil and saute celery, onion, garlic, bell pepper and okra for 15-20 minutes. The okra "rope" (its gelatinous stringy quality) should almost disappear if cooked that long. Add tomatoes and bay leaves. Simmer for 20 minutes. Season to taste with salt and pepper. Five to ten minutes before serving stir in shrimp and cook gently until they turn pink. The cooking time depends on the size of the shrimp. Serve by itself or over rice. Make 6 servings.

THAI SHRIMP CURRY

3/4 c chopped shallots
3 tablespoon chopped garlic
2 jalapeno chilies, seeded and chopped
2 tablespoon minced peeled fresh ginger
1 1/2 tablespoon ground cumin
4 teaspoon sugar
1 tablespoon minced lemon peel
1 teaspoon tumeric
1 c canned unsweetened coconut milk (sold in Southeast Asian and Latin American markets and many supermarkets)
1/2 c bottled clam juice

12 oz uncooked large shrimp, peeled and deveined
hot cooked rice

Puree first 9 ingredients until they form a paste. This paste can be prepared ahead as much as a week and refrigerated. Boil clam juice, coconut milk and 1/4 cup paste until slightly thickened, stirring frequently, about 6 minutes. Reduce heat and add shrimp. Cook until shrimp is hot through, about 3 minutes. Spoon rice onto plates, cover with curry and serve. Makes 2 servings.

GRILLED SWORDFISH WITH PASTA

3 medium ripe tomatoes, cut into 1/2 inch chunks
1/4 c chopped fresh mint
1 tablespoon red wine vinegar
1 small clove garlic, minced
3 tablespoon olive oil
1 teaspoon salt
1/2 teaspoon coarsely ground black pepper
1 lb penne or bow-tie pasta
1 teaspoon grated orange peel
1 swordfish steak, 1 inch thick (about 1 lb)

Combine tomatoes, mint, vinegar, garlic, 2 tablespoon olive oil, 1/4 teaspoon salt and 1/4 teaspoon pepper. Cover and let stand 30 minutes. Combine orange peel, 1 tablespoon olive oil, 1/4 teaspoon salt, and 1/4 teaspoon pepper; brush on both sides of swordfish. Place swordfish on grill over medium heat; cook 8-10 minutes until just opaque, turning once. Remove to cutting board and cut into 1/4 inch pieces. Prepare pasta as package directs; drain. Add swordfish and pasta to tomato mixture; toss. Makes 6 servings.

TROUT, ANCHOVY SAUCE

4 trout
seasoned flour
olive oil
3 tablespoon butter or margarine
4 anchovy fillets, cut fine
1/2 c white wine
1 teaspoon fresh or dried mint, chopped
1 tablespoon chopped parsley
juice of 1 lemon

Roll fish in seasoned flour. Heat enough oil to cover bottom of skillet. Pan fry fish about 5 minutes on each side. Meanwhile, melt butter, add anchovies and heat 5 minutes. Add wine, mint and parsley and simmer 3 minutes. Add lemon juice. Put fish on hot platter and pour sauce over all. Serves 4.

DILLED TUNA, CABBAGE, AND ONION BAKED IN PASTRY

1 pkg hot roll mix
4 c finely chopped cabbage
1 onion, chopped
1/4 c butter
2 cans tuna
2 tablespoon dill weed
1 egg
1 tablespoon water

Prepare hot-roll mix according to package directions. Cook cabbage and onion in butter until wilted. Add tuna, flaked, and dill weed. Season to taste. After dough has risen, divide in half, and roll each half into a rectangle about 9 x 11 inches. Put one in shallow baking pan, and spread with tuna-cabbage mixture. Moisten edges of dough and top with second rectangle, seal. Brush top with beaten egg mixed with water. Bake in 400 oven about 20 minutes. Cut in squares. Serves 12.

TUNA CASSEROLE

2 cans (6 1/2 oz each) chunk-style tuna
6 oz (3 c) uncooked egg noodles
1/2 c chopped celery
1/2 c sliced green onions
1/2-2/3 c dairy sour cream
2 teaspoon mustard
1/2 c mayonnaise
1/2 teaspoon dried thyme leaves
1/4-1/2 teaspoon salt
1 small zucchini, sliced
1 c shredded Monterey Jack cheese
1 medium tomato, chopped

Drain and flake tuna. Cook noodles according to package directions. Drain and rinse in hot water. Combine noodles, tuna, celery and green onions. Mix sour cream, mustard, mayonnaise, thyme and salt and blend into tuna mixture. Spoon half the mixture into casserole and top with half the zucchini. Repeat layers. Top with cheese. Bake in 350 oven for about 30 minutes, until bubbly. Sprinkle with chopped tomato. Makes 4-6 servings.

FRESH TUNA TARRAGON

Marinate 2 lbs tuna steaks in white wine to cover (about 1 1/2 c) two hours. Drain. To marinade, add 1 tablespoon dried tarragon, and let soak. Dry steaks, dust lightly with flour, sprinkle with salt and brown on both sides in 1/4 c butter or oil. Add wine and tarragon mixture, and cook at high heat until wine is reduced one half. Remove fish to hot platter, pour over wine and tarragon sauce, and serve. Makes 4 to 6 servings.

Breads

ANISE SEED BREAD

2 c rye flour
about 4 c all-purpose flour
2 pkg active dry yeast
1/4 c sugar
1 tablespoon salt
2 c milk
2 tablespoon molasses
2 tablespoon butter or margarine
2 teaspoon anise seed
1 egg white

Combine rye flour and 3 1/2 cups all-purpose flour. Combine yeast, sugar, salt and 1 1/2 cups flour mixture. Stir milk, butter, molasses and anise seed in a saucepan. Heat but do not boil. Beat liquid into flour mixture. Beat in enough flour to make a soft dough. Knead dough on floured surface for 10 minutes; shape dough into a ball; grease top, turn dough and grease other side. Let stand, covered, until doubled in bulk. Punch dough down, turn out on lightly floured board and cut in half. Cover with towel and let rest fifteen minutes. Shape dough into two ovals and place on greased cookie sheet. Cover with towel and let rise until doubled in bulk. Brush with egg white. Bake at 375 about 35 minutes or until done. Cool on wire rack. Makes 2 loaves.

BLUE CORNBREAD

2 tablespoon vegetable oil
2 c blue cornmeal
2 tablespoon all purpose flour
4 teaspoon baking powder
1 1/2 teaspoon salt
2 c buttermilk
1 egg
2-3 large jalepeno peppers, seeded and finely chopped

Combine dry ingredients in large mixing bowl. Add eggs, milk and peppers, mix well. Heat the oil in an 8 inch baking pan in 450 oven, then add corn bread mixture to hot pan and bake at 450 about 20 to 25 minutes.

Note: Blue cornmeal is made from a variety of corn which has blue kernels. It is grown primarily in New Mexico and is important to the Pueblo Indians as a food staple and in their religious ceremonies. Blue corn has a lower starch content than the white or yellow corn and it has a nutty flavor. The type of liquid, fat or sweetener used with it will influence the color of the food prepared with it. Color can vary from dark to light blue, slate gray, lavender or a bluish green. Many restaurants in New Mexico feature recipes using blue corn. Blue corn meal is difficult to find outside New Mexico. Two sources we use are:

> The Baker's Catalog
> PO Box 876,
> Norwich, Vermont 05055,
>
> Mo-Hotta Mo Betta,
> PO Box 4136,
> San Luis Obispo, California 93403

These catalogs also offer a wide variety of foods difficult to find such as flours, herbs and spices.

BLUE CORN MUFFINS

1 egg, lightly beaten
1 c milk
2 tablespoon vegetable oil
1/2 c blue cornmeal
3/4 c flour
1/4 c sugar
1 1/2 teaspoon baking powder
1/2 teaspoon salt
1 can chopped green chilies, drained

Butter 12 muffin forms or line with paper liners. Preheat oven to 400. In a medium bowl, combine egg, milk, oil and blue cornmeal. Mix well. Let stand 8-10 minutes to soften cornmeal. Mix dry ingredients in another bowl. After corn meal mixture has rested, stir well to remix and add to flour mixture. Add green chilies and mix well. Fill each muffin cup two-thirds full with batter. Bake about 15 minutes or until lightly browned.

SERRANO CHILE BLUE CORNBREAD

1 1/4 c blue cornmeal
1 c all-purpose flour
1 tablespoon baking powder
1 teaspoon salt
1/8 teaspoon baking soda
2 tablespoon sugar
2 tablespoon margarine
3 to 4 serrano chilies, unseeded and finely chopped
3 cloves garlic, minced
1 sweet red pepper, finely chopped
2 large eggs, slightly beaten
1 c buttermilk
1/3 c butter or margarine, melted
1/3 c shortening, melted
2 tablespoon plain low-fat yogurt
1 (11 oz can) Shoepeg or white corn, drained
3 tablespoon chopped fresh cilantro

Combine first 6 ingredients; make a well in center of mixture. Set aside. Melt butter; add serrano chilies and next 3 ingredients and cook until vegetables are tender. Set aside. Combine eggs and next 5 ingredients; add to dry ingredients, stirring just enough to moisten. Stir in vegetable mixture and cilantro. Place a 10 inch well greased cast-iron skillet in a 450 oven until hot. Remove from oven; spoon batter in skillet. Bake 450 for 25 minutes or until lightly browned. Serves 8-10.

CHEESE BISCUITS

1 egg, beaten
1/2 c milk
1 teaspoon Worcestershire sauce
1 teaspoon instant minced onion
hot pepper sauce to taste
2 c biscuit mix
1 1/2 c shredded cheddar cheese

Mix first 5 ingredients and add to biscuit mix. Mix well. Stir in cheese. Roll dough on floured board and cut into biscuits. Bake at 425 until golden brown. Makes about 20. Very good with tart jelly.

CHEESE BISCUIT WEDGES

1/2 c chopped onion
1 tablespoon margarine
2 c Bisquick
1/2 c milk
1 egg, slightly beaten
1 c finely shredded cheddar cheese
1 tablespoon minced parsley
2 slices crisp bacon, crumbled

Saute onion in margarine about 5 minutes, until tender. In a bowl combine baking mix, milk, egg, onion, 1/2 cup cheese and parsley. Spread in 8 or 9 inch pan. Top with remaining 1/2 cup cheese and bacon. Bake in preheated 400 oven for 20 to 25 minutes, until browned. Cut in wedges, serve warm.

Saturday April 29, 2006
Lexington Center
Admission is Free!

Lexington Herald-Leader

www.bluegrassfestivalofbooks.com

Bluegrass FESTIVAL OF BOOKS

The world of literature in the heart of Kentucky

Joseph-Beth Booksellers

Local & National Authors

Ticketed Breakfast featuring
Kim Yorio & Caitlin Friedman,
authors of *The Girls Guide to Being the Boss
(Without Being a Bitch)*

Ticketed Lunch featuring
Sue Grafton and Jane Fonda

Writers' Workshop

American Girl teas

Children's Activities throughout the day

Author Panels/Special Events

Author Readings

Music & More!

For a complete list of attending authors
and special events
visit:
www.bluegrassfestivalofbooks.com

Ticketed Events

Breakfast with Kim Yorio & Caitlin Friedman, authors of *The Girls Guide to Being the Boss (Without Being a Bitch)**

Lunch with Sue Grafton & Jane Fonda*

Writers' Workshop*

American Girl teas*

Author Panels/Special Events

Travel Talk featuring Arthur Frommer, founder of Frommer Travel Guides

Small Space Gardening with Jon Carloftis

How to Throw a Party with CBS's *Wickedly Perfect* winner, Kimberly Kennedy

Racing Panel featuring Dorothy Ours, Joe Drape & John Eisenberg

Women's Fiction Panel featuring Ann B. Ross, Karen Robards, Ronda Rich & Emyl Jenkins

Many More Panels
For a full list of special events, visit www.bluegrassfestivalofbooks.com

Raffle for a Library of Books

Receive a signed book from every author at the Festival!*

*Reservation, ticket, and/or purchase required

Brought to you by

UNIVERSITY OF KENTUCKY

CHEESE BREAD

1 loaf French bread
1/2 c butter or margarine, softened
1 teaspoon dried dill weed
1 c grated cheddar or mozzarella cheese
1 garlic clove, crushed or 1/2 teaspoon bottled garlic

Slice bread in half lengthwise. Combine remaining ingredients and spread on one half of the loaf. Put the bread halves together. Wrap bread in aluminum foil and heat in 350 oven for 20 minutes or just until cheese melts. This makes a great appetizer or very good with hamburgers.

COTTAGE CHEESE BREAD

1 pkg dry yeast
1/4 c warm water
2 teaspoon green onion tops, minced
1 tablespoon butter, softened
1 teaspoon salt
1 teaspoon oregano leaves, chopped
1 c small curd cottage cheese, at room temperature
2 tablespoon sugar
1/4 teaspoon baking powder
1 egg
2 to 2 1/2 c sifted flour

Soften yeast in warm water. Mix all other ingredients, except flour. Add yeast mixture and beat well. Gradually add enough flour to make a firm dough. Cover and let rise 1 hour or until doubled in bulk. Punch down and place in well buttered 1 1/2 quart casserole. Let rise 30 minutes or until light. Bake 40 minutes at 350. Remove from casserole and brush with butter.

CORN-CHEESE BREAD

Delicious with soup or toasted & served with chili

2 pkgs active dry yeast
1 c yellow cornmeal
1/2 teaspoon baking soda
1/2 c oil
1 c buttermilk
1 tablespoon each salt and sugar
2 eggs
1 c canned cream-style corn
1 onion, minced
1 (4 oz) can green chili peppers, minced (or hot jalapeno)
1 1/2 c shredded sharp cheddar cheese
4 1/2-5 1/2 c all purpose flour
2 tablespoon butter

Place yeast, cornmeal and baking soda in mixing bowl. Heat oil, butter, salt and sugar and add to yeast mixture. Add eggs, corn, onion, peppers, cheese and about 4 cup of flour. Mix and add enough flour to make a stiff dough. Knead on floured board. Return to bowl. Cover and let rise until doubled. Divide dough in half. Shape into 2 loaves or 16 rolls. Place in greased pans or on baking sheets. Let rise about 1 hour or until doubled. Bake at 400, 30 minutes for loaves or 20 minutes for rolls. Cool completely on rack before slicing, storing or freezing.

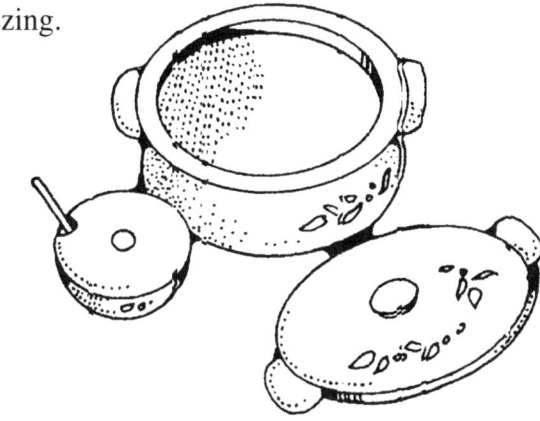

DILL BREAD I

1/4 c warm water
2 pkgs dry yeast
1 tablespoon honey
4 c small curd cottage cheese
2 1/4 c warm water
3/4 c honey
1/4 c dill seed
6 eggs
6 tablespoon oil
6 tablespoon instant onion
2 tablespoon salt
1 1/2 teaspoon baking soda
18 c flour
oil

Grease 6 (9 x 5) loaf pans and set aside. Stir honey into 1/4 cup water; then stir in yeast. Let stand until mixture bubbles. In large bowl mix all other ingredients except flour and oil. Add yeast mixture after it has bubbled. Add flour, two cups at a time until dough forms a ball but is still tacky. Place in bowl, turn to coat all surfaces with oil. Cover and let rise until double in size. Punch dough down, divide into six and place in loaf pans. Let rise again. Bake at 350 for 45-60 minutes, until brown and sounds hollow when thumped on side or bottom. Cool on rack. Makes 6 regular loaves.

DILL BREAD II

1 c creamed cottage cheese
2 tablespoon sugar
1 tablespoon minced onion
1 tablespoon butter
2 teaspoon dill weed
1 teaspoon salt
1/4 teaspoon soda
1 egg
1 pkg dry yeast
1/4 c warm water
2-2 1/4 c flour

Heat cottage cheese until lukewarm and add the next 7 ingredients. Mix yeast and warm water; add to mixture. Add flour to make a stiff dough. Let rise in a round casserole or two loaf pans until double. Bake at 350 for about 45 minutes. Brush with butter and cool on rack.

FENNEL RYE BREAD

1 pkg dry yeast
1 tablespoon dark molasses
1 c warm water
2 c bread flour
2/3 c rye flour
1/4 c dry milk powder
1 1/2 teaspoon salt
1 teaspoon fennel seeds
1 tablespoon cornmeal

Combine yeast and molasses with warm water and let stand until foamy, about 10 minutes. Combine 1 3/4 cups bread flour, rye flour, powdered milk, salt and fennel seeds. Add yeast mixture and mix well. If dough is too wet add the rest of the bread flour. Place dough in oiled bowl, cover and let stand until doubled in bulk. Punch dough down and divide in half. Knead each half on a floured board and place each in a greased baking pan or on a baking sheet. Brush with a glaze made by beating an egg with 1/2 teaspoon salt. Cover and let rise until doubled in bulk. Bake at 375 until dark brown and sounds hollow when tapped. Cool on wire rack.

> *Note:* Fennel is a tall perennial which makes a very attractive addition to the back of a flower border. Fennel has a sweet anise-like flavor and can be used whenever this flavoring is desired. It is called the "fish herb" as it helps to counter the oily, strong fish taste. The leaves can be added raw to green salads and to raw or cooked vegetables. The seeds are used whole or ground in sweet pickles, breads and soups. Fennel seed is an important seasoning in Hot or Sweet Italian sausage.

GARDEN PEPPER BREAD

2 tablespoon butter or margarine
1/2 c chopped onion
1/3 c chopped red bell pepper
1/3 c chopped green bell pepper
7-8 c all-purpose or unbleached flour
1/2 c sugar
1/2-1 teaspoon salt
1/8 teaspoon pepper
2 pkgs dry yeast
1 c milk
3/4 c water
1/3 c margarine or butter
6 egg whites or 3 whole eggs

Cook onion and peppers in 2 tablespoon margarine until tender. Set aside. Combine 2 cup flour, sugar, salt, pepper and yeast. Heat milk, water and 1/3 cup margarine until very warm and add to flour mixture. Beat about 3 minutes. Add eggs, cooked vegetables and one cup flour. Beat for about 3 minutes. By hand, stir in additional flour to make a stiff dough. Knead on floured surface until smooth and elastic. Place in greased bowl, cover and let rise until double in size. Punch down dough and divide in half. Place in 2 greased loaf pans, cover and let rise until double in size. Bake at 375 for 30-40 minutes or until golden. Remove from pans and cool on wire rack.

For a zippier bread hot peppers may replace part or all of the bell peppers

CRUSTY GARLIC BREAD
(Serve hot with pasta)

2 small loaves (4 oz each) Italian or French bread
2 cloves garlic, minced
2 teaspoon olive oil
2 tablespoon chopped fresh parsley
2 tablespoon chopped fresh thyme or 2 teaspoon dried thyme
2 teaspoon chopped fresh marjoram or 1/4 teaspoon dried
1/2 teaspoon paprika
2 tablespoon grated Parmesan cheese

Preheat oven to 350. Combine garlic and oil, mix well. In another bowl mix parsley, thyme, marjoram and paprika; add Parmesan, mix well. Cut each loaf crosswise into diagonal slices without cutting through bottom crust. Brush cut side of slices with garlic oil and sprinkle with herb mixture between slices. Wrap each loaf in foil; place on baking sheet. Bake about 10-15 minutes until heated through. Serve immediately. Makes 10 slices.

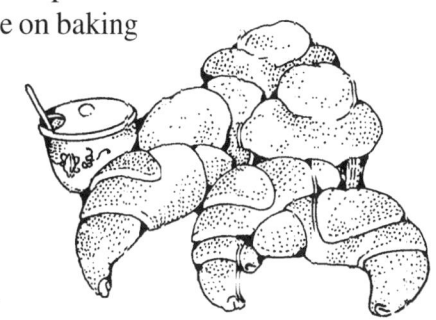

HERB AND ONION BREAD

1 1/2 c finely chopped Spanish onions
2 tablespoon butter or margarine
3 c biscuit baking mix
1 egg
1 c milk
1 teaspoon dried basil
1 teaspoon dried dillweed

Saute the onions in butter until tender. Combine all remaining ingredients; add onion and mix just until blended. Pour in loaf pan and bake 1 hour or until golden brown. Cool in pan.

HERB-PARMESAN BREAD

2 pkgs dry yeast
2 c warm water (105-115 degree)
1/2 c grated Parmesan cheese
2 tablespoon sugar
2 tablespoon butter or margarine
1 tablespoon + 1 1/2 teaspoon dried whole oregano
2 teaspoon salt
4 1/2 c flour
1 tablespoon grated Parmesan cheese

Dissolve yeast in warm water in a large mixing bowl; let stand 5 minutes. Add 1/2 cup Parmesan cheese, sugar, butter, oregano, salt and 3 cups flour; beat for 2 minutes with mixer. Gradually stir in rest of the flour. Place dough in well greased bowl, grease top of dough, cover and let rise until double in bulk. Punch down and divide into two loaf pans or place all of dough in a lightly greased 2 quart dish. Sprinkle 1 tablespoon Parmesan cheese over dough. Bake at 375 until golden brown, about 45 minutes. Remove from pans and cool on wire rack.

HERBED TOMATO BREAD

2 tablespoon brown sugar
2 teaspoon salt
2 pkg active dry yeast
about 5 1/2 c all-purpose flour
1 c milk
butter or margarine
1 c peeled, seeded, minced tomatoes (about 2)
2 eggs
3/4 teaspoon thyme leaves
1/2 teaspoon basil

Combine sugar, salt, yeast and 1 cup flour. In saucepan, over low heat, heat milk and 3 tablespoon butter or margarine until very warm (butter does not need to melt completely). With mixer blend liquid into dry ingredients. Beat in tomatoes, eggs, thyme, basil and 1 1/2 cup flour. Beat at medium speed for about 3 minutes. By hand, stir in enough additional flour to make a stiff dough. Knead on a floured board until dough is smooth and elastic. Place in a greased bowl, cover and let rise until doubled in size. Punch down dough and divide in half. Place in two greased loaf pans. Cover and let rise until double in size. Bake at 375 in preheated oven for 30-40 minutes until golden. Remove from pans and cool on racks.

SKILLET HERB BREAD

1 1/2 c all-purpose flour
2 tablespoon sugar
4 teaspoon baking powder
1 1/2 teaspoon salt
1 teaspoon rubbed sage
1 teaspoon dried thyme
1 1/2 c yellow cornmeal
1 1/2 c chopped celery
1 c chopped onion
1 jar (2 oz) chopped pimento, drained
3 eggs, beaten
1 1/2 c milk
1/3 c vegetable oil

Combine flour, sugar, baking powder, salt, sage and thyme. Combine cornmeal, celery onion and pimentos; add to dry ingredients and mix well. Add eggs milk and oil; stir just until softened. Pour into a 10 or 11 inch iron skillet. Bake at 400 until done, about 35-45 minutes. Makes 10 servings.

JALEPENO CORN BREAD I

1 c yellow cornmeal
1/2 c flour
2 teaspoon baking powder
1/2 teaspoon baking soda
1/2 teaspoon salt
1 c (4 oz) cheddar cheese, shredded
2 fresh jalapenos, seeded and minced
2 large eggs
1 c buttermilk
1/4 c corn oil

Preheat oven to 350. Grease a 8-inch square baking pan. In a medium bowl, combine cornmeal, flour, baking powder, baking soda and salt. Stir to mix very well. Stir in cheese and jalapenos, tossing to mix thoroughly. In another bowl, beat eggs until well blended. Beat in buttermilk and oil. Add egg mixture to corn meal mixture and stir to combine. Pour into prepared pan. Bake 25 to 30 minutes or until corn bread is golden brown. Serve hot.

JALAPENO CORNBREAD II

1 1/2 self-rising cornmeal
1-8 oz carton sour cream
1/2 c melted shortening
3 beaten eggs
1 can whole kernel corn, undrained
at least 3 jalapeno peppers, chopped (I use about 6 or 7)

Combine all ingredients. Pour into a well greased iron skillet or pan. Bake at 425 for 20 minutes or until nice and brown. Yield: about 8 servings.

JALAPENO HUSHPUPPIES

2 c cornmeal
1/2 c flour
1 teaspoon sugar
1 teaspoon salt
2 teaspoon baking powder
1/2 teaspoon baking soda
1 c chopped onion
1 bell pepper, chopped finely
3 chopped Jalapenos, seeds removed
1/2 c buttermilk
3/4 c water
1/2 c melted butter

Mix dry ingredients. Blend in remaining ingredients. Drop by spoon in 375 hot fat.

KENTUCKY JALAPENO CORNBREAD

1 c all-purpose flour
1 c yellow cornmeal
1 tablespoon baking powder
1 tablespoon sugar
1 teaspoon salt
1 egg, well beaten
1 c milk
1/4 c solid white shortening, melted
4 oz cheddar cheese, grated
1 (4 oz) can mild green chilies, drained and chopped
1 jalapeno, halved, seeded and minced
1/2 c cooked corn kernels
1/2 c chopped onion

Sift flour with cornmeal, baking powder, sugar and salt. Combine egg, milk and shortening. Combine both mixtures and mix well. Stir in cheese, chilies, jalapeno, corn and onion. Bake at 425 oven for 25-35 minutes or until brown.

MEXICAN CORNBREAD I

1 c cream-style corn
1 c cornmeal
1 c chopped hot peppers
1 1/2 c grated sharp cheddar cheese
2 eggs beaten
3/4 c sweet milk
1/2 c salad oil
1/2 teaspoon salt

Mix all ingredients. Bake in greased 9 x 13 inch pan. Serve hot with or without butter.

MEXICAN CORN BREAD II

1 1/4 c yellow cornmeal
1/2 c all purpose flour
1 tablespoon baking powder
1 teaspoon salt
2 eggs, beaten
1 1/4 c milk
3/4 c shredded sharp cheddar cheese
1/2 c vegetable oil
1/2 can, canned cream-style corn
1 medium onion, minced
3 strips crisply cooked bacon, crumbled
2 tablespoon finely chopped jalapeno peppers or more if desired

Lightly grease iron skillet and place in oven until hot. Mix cornmeal, flour, baking powder and salt. Mix remaining ingredients in another container. Stir in dry ingredients just until blended. Spoon into hot skillet, bake at 350 until golden, about 30 minutes. Serve hot.

MEXICAN CORNBREAD III

1 c yellow cornmeal
1 c all-purpose flour
1 tablespoon + 1 teaspoon baking powder
1/2 teaspoon salt
1/2 c instant nonfat dry milk powder
2 tablespoon sugar
2 eggs
1 c water
1/3 c vegetable oil
1 c shredded cheddar cheese
chopped hot peppers to taste

Combine first 6 ingredients. Make a well in center of mixture. Beat eggs, add water and oil, mixing well. Add egg mixture to cornmeal mixture. Stir in cheese and hot peppers. Melt butter in 8 inch square baking pan. Pour batter into pan and bake at 375 for 30-35 minutes or until cornbread is golden brown. Makes 8 servings.

ONION-PARSLEY BUTTERFINGERS

2 c buttermilk baking mix
1 egg
1/3 c milk
1/2 c butter or margarine
2 tablespoon onion flakes mixed with 2 tablespoon minced parsley

Combine mix, egg and milk and beat. Turn out on floured board and knead lightly. Roll to 12 x 8 inch rectangle and cut with knife into 4 x 1 inch fingers. Melt butter in jelly roll pan in 450 oven. Lay fingers in butter; turn to coat both sides. Sprinkle with onion-parsley mixture and bake in preheated oven about 8 minutes or until golden brown. Serve warm. Make 2 dozen.

OVERNIGHT BREAD

2 c all-purpose flour
2 tablespoon sugar
2 teaspoon baking powder
3/4 teaspoon dried sage, crushed
1/4 teaspoon baking soda
1/4 teaspoon salt
2 eggs
1 c buttermilk
3 tablespoon olive oil
1/2 c shredded cheddar cheese
1/2 c pitted ripe olives, drained and sliced

Mix flour, sugar, baking powder, sage, baking soda and salt. In another bowl combine eggs, buttermilk, and olive oil; mix well. Add egg mixture to flour mixture and mix until moistened; fold in cheese and olives. Pour in loaf pan. Bake at 350 for about 45 minutes or until done. Cool on wire rack. Wrap and chill overnight before slicing. Slice thick and serve with cream cheese, honey, jam or any favorite spread.

ROMAN BREAD

1 1/2 c warm water
1 tablespoon sugar
1 pkg yeast
4 c all-purpose flour
1/2 c finely chopped onion
2 teaspoon salt
dried rosemary, crumbled
1 teaspoon coarse salt

Combine water and sugar in mixing bowl. Crumble yeast over and stir well. Let stand about 5 minutes, until foamy. Stir in 2 cups flour, onion and 2 teas. salt. Add two more cups flour. Place on floured board and knead until smooth, adding more flour if necessary to prevent sticking. Place in bowl and grease all sides, cover and let rise until doubled.

Place dough on greased baking sheet. Shape into round loaf 1 inch thick. Brush top lightly with oil. Let rise until doubled, about 30 minutes. Sprinkle top with coarse salt and rosemary. Bake at 400 until top is browned, about 20-25 minutes. Serve warm. Makes 1(8 in) round loaf.

SAGE BREAD

2 1/2 c all-purpose flour
1 tablespoon sugar
2 teaspoon dried sage, crumbled
1 teaspoon salt
1/4 teaspoon baking soda
1 pkg yeast
1/4 c warm water
1 c small curd cottage cheese
1 egg
1 tablespoon butter

Combine first 5 ingredients and blend well. Combine yeast and water and let stand until foamy, about 10 minutes. Combine cottage cheese and egg in blender and heat until smooth. Transfer to large bowl add butter and yeast and beat well. Add flour, a small amount at a time, beating after each addition (dough will be stiff). Cover and let stand until doubled about 1 hour. Punch down. Turn out on work surface and knead about 1 minute. Transfer to generously greased 2 quart round baking dish. Cover and let rise until doubled, about 40 minutes. Bake in 350 oven. Bake loaf until top is browned and bread sounds hollow when tapped, about 35-40 minutes. Cool on rack. Makes 1 loaf.

SAFFRON BRAID

1 1/3 c dried currants
1/4 c sweet sherry
1 tablespoon saffron threads
1/3 c water
1 pkg yeast
1 tablespoon sugar
1 c very warm milk
1/2 c unsalted butter, softened
1 egg
1 teaspoon salt
1 teaspoon nutmeg
1 teaspoon caraway seeds (optional)
1/2 teaspoon cinnamon
1/2 teaspoon mace
1/4 teaspoon cloves
4-4 1/2 c all-purpose flour
1 egg yolk
1 tablespoon milk

Toss currants in sherry, let stand at room temperature, covered, 5 hours or overnight. Drain, pat dry. Heat saffron and water to barely simmering, simmer 15 minutes and cool to room temperature. Dissolve yeast and sugar in milk; let stand until bubbly. Whisk in saffron and water, butter, egg, salt, nutmeg, caraway, cinnamon, mace and cloves. Whisk in 2 cups of the flour. Slowly add enough flour to make a stiff dough. Knead dough, shape into ball, place in greased bowl and let rise until double in bulk. Punch dough down, roll into a circle on floured surface, sprinkle with currants. Work currants into dough; let rest, covered about 8 minutes. Divide dough into three parts; make a rope of each part about 14 inches long. Place side by side on greased baking sheet. Braid dough without stretching. Pinch ends together, tuck under. Let rise, covered, until doubled. Heat oven to 400. Whisking egg yolk and milk together; brush braid with mixture. Bake 10 minutes, reduce heat to 375, bake until bottom sounds hollow when tapped, about 20 minutes. Cool on rack. Serve fresh with coffee, sherry; or toast for breakfast.

SAUERKRAUT RYE BREAD

2 pkg dry yeast
1/4 c warm water
3 or 4 medium potatoes
water to boil potatoes
1 c warm milk
1 (27 oz) can sauerkraut (hot or plain) thoroughly drained
1/2 c melted shortening
3 eggs, slightly beaten
1/2 c sugar
1 1/2 tablespoon salt
2 tablespoon caraway seeds
4 or 5 c rye flour
8 c white flour or 1/2 white and 1/2 whole wheat (we find white flour works better)

Peel and boil potaotes in water. Put potatoes (and water they are boiled in) in blender. You need 3 cups of potatoes and water. Dissolve yeast in warm water. Add warm milk to potato in blender. Remove half milk-potato mixture from blender and add sauerkraut to blender. Chop kraut. Pour all the potato, milk and kraut mixture into a large bowl. Add shortening, eggs, milk and salt. Stir in yeast and let stand about 5 minutes. Stir in caraway seeds and rye flour. Add enough other flour to make a soft dough. Turn out on floured board and knead until smooth and elastic. Place in greased bowl; cover and let rise until doubled in bulk; punch down and let rise again. Form into four loaves and place in four pans. Cover and let rise until double. Bake at 375 for about 40 minutes. Makes 4 large delicious loaves of breads.

SPICY HOT CORNBREAD

2 pkg (8 1/2 oz) corn muffin mix
2 tablespoon vegetable oil
jalapeno peppers, chopped (4 or more)
1/2 c canned or frozen corn

1/4 c sour cream
2 tablespoon honey

Prepare corn muffin mix according to package directions. Add remaining ingredients to mix. Bake in 9" x 13" greased baking dish at 400 about 20 minutes or until golden.

BASIC SPOONBREAD

6 tablespoon unsalted butter
3 c milk, use whole milk, not skim
1 c white or yellow cornmeal
1 1/2 teaspoon salt
1/2 teaspoon pepper
4 large eggs room temperature, separated
pinch of salt

Melt 1 tablespoon butter in a 2 quart casserole, iron skillet or spoonbread pan. Brush sides and bottom with butter. Set aside. Pour milk into saucepan and bring almost to a boil. Gradually stir in cornmeal with wooden spoon or whisk. Continue stirring over reduced heat until thick. Add remaining butter, salt and pepper and cook 2 minutes longer. Remove from heat and add beaten egg yolks. Beat egg whites until stiff with a pinch of salt. Fold egg whites into meal mixture. Pour bat-ter into buttered casserole, spreading evenly. Bake, uncovered, for 30 to 40 minutes until puffed and browned. Serve at once with butter, fresh tomato sauce (recipe follows) or a green chile sauce. Makes 4 servings as an entree; 6 servings as a side dish.

FRESH TOMATO SAUCE

2 medium onion, diced
2 tablespoon olive oil
12 medium tomatoes (about 3 1/2 lb); chopped
3 cloves garlic, crushed
2 teaspoon fresh, chopped parsley
2 teaspoon mixed dried basil, marjoram, and thyme or 2 tablespoon chopped fresh
2 tablespoon sugar
salt and pepper

Saute onions in oil until tender, about 5-7 minutes. Add tomatoes, garlic, parsley and mixed basil, marjoram, thyme, and sugar. Simmer for 40-50 minutes or until tomatoes have reduced to a thick pulp. Season with salt and pepper to taste. Makes 4 cups.

RED PEPPER-GARLIC SPOONBREAD

5-6 sweet red peppers
3 cloves garlic, minced
6 tablespoon butter
2 1/2 c milk
1 c white or yellow cornmeal
1 1/2 teaspoon salt
1/2 teaspoon pepper
3 large eggs, room temperature, separated
pinch salt

Roast red peppers by placing in a pan under broiler, broiling on all sides until skins have charred. Remove skins and run peppers under cold water. Remove stems and seeds and process to a rough puree in blender. Saute garlic in 1 tablespoon butter about 3-5 minutes. Melt 1 tablespoon margarine 2-3 minutes in a 350 preheated oven. Brush bottom and sides of casserole with melted butter and set aside. Bring milk almost to a boil, add pepper puree, garlic with butter from cooking garlic. Gradually stir in meal and cook until thick. Add remaining butter, salt and pepper and mix well. Cook 2 more minutes. Remove from heat and add lightly beaten eggs. Beat egg whites with a pinch of salt until stiff and fold into yolk-meal mixture. Pour into buttered casserole and bake, uncovered, 30-40 minutes until puffed and browned. Makes 4 servings as an entree; 6-8 servings as a side dish.

CHEDDAR SPOONBREAD

5 tablespoon butter
2 1/2 c milk
1 c white or yellow cornmeal
1 teaspoon salt
1/4 teaspoon nutmeg
1/4 teaspoon cayenne pepper
generous dash hot sauce
1 c grated, sharp, white cheddar cheese
4 large eggs, at room temperature, separated
pinch salt

Place 1 tablespoon butter in casserole and melt in 350 oven. Brush sides and bottom of casserole with melted butter. Set aside. Bring milk almost to a boil, gradually stir in cornmeal. Stir and cook until thick. Add remaining butter, salt, nutmeg, pepper, hot sauce and cheese. Mix well and cook 2 more minutes. Remove from heat and add lightly beaten egg yolks. Beat egg whites with a pinch of salt until stiff. Fold egg whites into yolk, meal mixture. Pour batter into buttered casserole, smoothing top with spatula. Bake, uncovered, 30-40 minutes until puffed and browned. Makes 4 servings as an entree; 6-8 as a side dish.

> *Note:* Often called batter breads, spoonbreads are not "real" bread but a baked mixture of cornmeal, eggs, butter and milk. They should be served piping hot, directly from the baking dish. Use whole milk, not skim milk, in spoon-bread. For richer flavor, substitute medium cream or half and half for part of the milk.

ZUCCHINI SPOONBREAD

1 1/2 c grated zucchini (about 2 medium)
5 tablespoon butter
3 c milk
1 c white or yellow cornmeal
1 teaspoon salt
1/4 teaspoon pepper
1 1/2 teaspoon fresh, minced oregano or 1/2 teaspoon dried
1/2 c freshly grated Parmesan cheese
3 eggs at room temperature, separated
pinch of salt

Place zucchini in a colander and drain well for at least an hour. In a 350 oven melt 1 tablespoon butter in a casserole 2 or 3 minutes. Brush sides and bottom of dish with melted butter. Set aside. Bring milk to a boil, add drained zucchini. Gradually stir in cornmeal. Cook, stirring constantly until thick. Add remaining butter, salt, pepper, oregano and Parmesan cheese. Cook for 2 more minutes. Remove from heat and add lightly beaten egg yolks. Beat egg whites with pinch of salt until stiff. Fold into yolk-meal mixture. Bake, uncovered, 35 to 40 minutes, until puffed and browned. Serve hot. Makes 4 servings as entree; 6-8 servings as a side dish.

100% WHOLE WHEAT BREAD

1 pkg active dry yeast
1/4 c warm water
1 tablespoon + 1 teaspoon honey
1/2 c water
1/2 c milk
1 1/4 teaspoon salt
2 tablespoon butter
3 c stone ground 100 percent whole wheat flour divided into 1 c portions
1 egg
2 tablespoon fresh rosemary, sage, or basil, or 2 teaspoon dried

Sprinkle yeast into 1/4 c warm water. Add 1/2 teaspoon honey. Let stand 5-8 minutes until bubbly. Heat 1/2 c milk, remaining tablespoon honey, salt and butter. Cook until butter is nearly melted; cool to lukewarm. In a mixing bowl place 1 cup flour and the egg. Add the yeast mixture and milk mixture. Mix. Add remaining flour to make a stiff dough. Add herbs and knead dough on a floured board until smooth and elastic. Place in a greased bowl and turn to grease all sides. Cover until double in bulk. Punch dough down and roll into a 8 x 12 inch rectangle. Roll from short side as you would a jelly roll. Pinch ends to seal and place, seamside down, in greased 8 x 4 inch loaf pan. Let rise 40-45 minutes. Bake in 375 oven for about 40 minutes or until brown and sounds hollow when tapped. Let cool on rack completely before slicing. Makes 1 loaf.

WHOLE WHEAT PESTO BREAD

1 recipe 100 percent whole wheat bread, preceding
4 tablespoon fresh minced basil or 1 1/2 tablespoon dried
1/4 c coarsely chopped pine nuts, toasted and combined with 2 teaspoon stone-ground whole wheat flour
1 tablespoon butter
2 tablespoon olive oil
2 cloves garlic, crushed
1/3 c grated Parmesan cheese

Mix ingredients for preceding recipe for 100 percent whole wheat bread, eliminating herbs and kneading in basil and pine nuts. Let rise until doubled in bulk. Heat butter and oil and add garlic. Saute but do not let brown. Cool. Roll out bread as directed in previous recipe. Brush rolled out dough with butter-oil mixture, reserving 2 teaspoon for top of loaf. Sprinkle dough with grated cheese. Let rise and bake as in previous recipe. Makes 1 loaf.

Note: You may substitute 4 tablespoon fresh dill weed for the basil in 1 tablespoon butter, saute 1 tablespoon chives and 1/8 teaspoon cayenne to replace butter, oil and garlic. Use 1/2 cup gruyere cheese instead of Parmesan.

ROSEMARY FLAT BREAD

1 recipe for 100 precent whole wheat bread, preceding
2 tablespoon fresh rosemary or 2 teaspoon dried
1 tablespoon melted butter

Mix 100 percent whole wheat bread, eliminating the herbs, begin to knead. Knead in rosemary. Let rise until doubled in bulk. Roll dough as in preceding recipe to a 12 inch circle and place on greased baking sheet. Make about ten 1/4 inch indentions in dough with your fingertips. Brush with melted butter and let rise about 10 minutes. Bake about 30 minutes in 375 preheated oven. Slide onto a rack and serve warm. Makes 1 round loaf.

HERBED WAFFLES

1 3/4 c flour
2 teaspoon baking powder
3/4 teaspoon salt
1 tablespoon sugar
2 eggs, lightly beaten
1 3/4 c milk
5 tablespoon butter, melted
2 tablespoon each chopped fresh parsley and dill or 2 teaspoon each, dried
oil for waffle iron

Sift dry ingredients together and make a well in center. In another bowl mix eggs, milk, melted butter and herbs together and pour into well. Stir to a smooth batter. Heat waffle iron and brush with oil. Pour about 2/3 cup batter onto waffle iron and cook according to manufacture's directions. Keep warm, uncovered. Repeat cooking for 4 or 5 waffles. Makes 4-5 eight inch waffles.

Condiments

FLAVORED VINEGARS

Flavored vinegars have become very popular over the past few years but they are not new. 19th century recipe books have notes on making vinegars with herbs, fruits and flowers. Flavored vinegars can be used in all the ways you would use plain vinegar, just be sure to pair up flavors that complement each other the same way you do when using herbs.

Preparing herbal vinegars is a simple process. It consists of putting fresh herbs or dried herbs in a glass container and filling the container with the vinegar of your choice, place it in a warm place out of direct sunlight and letting it stand for awhile until the flavor has developed. The same procedure is used to make seed and hot pepper vinegars.

The following recipes call for a specific vinegar, but we have made them using plain white or cider vinegar and they are just as good. Generally white vinegar is better with milder herbs and the cider vinegar goes best with strong herbs like sage.

A good place to start when deciding which herbs to include in a vinegar, is to consider which herbs you use regularly. Some interesting combinations to try are; parsley, garlic and oregano; basil, thyme, chives and summer savory; basil, dill and sage. You can also make tasty vinegars with coriander seed and peppercorns.

BASIC HERBED VINEGAR

1 quart vinegar
1 c fresh herbs or 1/2 c dried herbs

Combine ingredients in glass bottle or jar. Cover with a non-reactive lid. Let stand in a warm area for about 10 days. Check to see if it is the right flavor at this time. If it is too strong just add a little more vinegar and if its not strong enough, recap and let infuse a few more days. Strain the herbs from the vinegar and rebottle. A nice touch at this time is to add a sprig of whatever fresh herb you have used to the bottle. Be sure to label the vinegar

TARRAGON OR DILL VINEGAR

1 c long sprigs of fresh tarragon or dill
1 quart white wine vinegar, room temperature
(use the same procedure as in the basic vinegar recipe)

The tarragon vinegar is nice with fish and in mayonnaise. The dill vinegar can be used with cucumbers, green salads and with seafoods.

FRESH BASIL VINEGAR

1 c fresh basil sprigs
1 quart red wine vinegar (use the same procedure as in the basic vinegar recipe)

Good with tomatoes or tomato dishes.

ROSEMARY OR THYME VINEGAR

4 or 5 whole peppercorns
1 c fresh rosemary or thyme branches (or a combination)
1 quart red wine vinegar, room temperature
(use the same procedure as in the basic vinegar recipe)

Very pungent, mouth watering vinegar to use in marinades for lamb or in dressings for meat, salads and greens.

MUSTARD SEED VINEGAR

2 tablespoon whole mustard seed
1 quart white or cider vinegar

Gently bruise mustard seed. Place in center of 3-inch square of double-thickness cheesecloth and tie with a string. Place in tall 1 quart glass bottle. Bring vinegar to a simmer, then pour into bottle. Cover. Let stand in a cool, dark area for about 10 days. Remove cheesecloth bag. This is good for a marinade or rub for roast pork and in vinaigrette dressings.

HOT, HOT VINEGAR

Add horseradish, onion, pepper, and chili peppers, any or all, as much as you want to vinegar. Stand in a warm place until it suits your taste, then strain and bottle it up. It will "knock your socks off."

BASIC FRESH HERB VINEGAR

Infuse 10-14 days, 1 cup crushed or minced fresh herb leaves, 1 pint best quality white vinegar. Strain through cheesecloth and store in clean tightly capped bottles.

LEMON THYME VINEGAR

1 large bunch lemon thyme
1 quart good quality white wine or distilled vinegar

Place the lemon thyme in glass container, cover with vinegar and let stand for several weeks. Strain and place vinegar in a pretty bottle, add a fresh sprig of lemon thyme, and top with a cork. Makes 1 quart. You may follow the same method for other vinegars, substituting purple or green basil, tarragon, rosemary, dill, oregano for the lemon thyme.

TARRAGON VINEGAR

3 bunches fresh tarragon sprigs
3 quarts cider vinegar

Rinse tarragon under cold running water; drain on paper towels. Fill a one gallon jar with tarragon sprigs. Heat vinegar to lukewarm. Pour over tarragon. Seal tightly; store in a dark place for two weeks. Strain and bottle. Place a sprig of tarragon in each bottle. Seal tightly. Makes 3 quarts.

VINAIGRETTES

Vinegars flavored with herbs make good vinaigrettes. These vinegars are especially delicious on tomatoes, beets and carrots. The better the vinegar you start with, the more intense its flavor after its infused with herbs. The general method for herb vinegars is to bring vinegar to a boil. Pour over herbs in a jar, cover and let steep for 48 hours. Store in a cool dark place and use within a year.

BASIL-GARLIC VINEGAR

4 c white wine vinegar
6-8 sprigs fresh basil
4-6 big cloves garlic, peeled (place in jar with basil)

RED WINE-HERB VINEGARS

4 c red wine vinegar
2-3 sprigs of each of any three of the following herbs: basil, oregano, rosemary, thyme, marjoram, or savory

LEMON-DILL VINEGAR

4 c Japanese rice wine vinegar
6-8 sprigs fresh, leafy dill
zest of 1 lemon

Thread lemon zest on wooden skewer and remove skewer from jar after vinegar has steeped 48 hours.

FRESH DILL VINEGAR

2 c sugar
3 tablespoon salt
2 onions, quartered
2 whole banana peppers, cut up
3 garlic cloves
4 or 5 heads and sprigs fresh dill
white vinegar

In a quart jar mix everything but the vinegar. Fill the jar with vinegar, refrigerate for at least a week before using. Keep refrigerated and use as desired. To replenish, add more sugar, salt and vinegar as vinegar is used. To make a salad dressing, combine 1 part dill vinegar with 3 parts salad oil. Use this dressing over salad greens or fresh fruit.

VINAIGRETTE DRESSING

Good on vegetables or greens

To 3/4 cup French dressing add 1 chopped hard-cooked egg and 1 teaspoon chopped chives.

HERB FLAVORING

Take thyme, mint, sweet marjoram and rosemary. Pick these from the stalks, put them in a large jar, pour on strong vinegar, let stand 24 hours. Take out the herbs and add fresh ones, do this 3 times; then strain the liquid, put in a bottle, cork and seal tight. Do not let herbs stay in vinegar more than 24 hours or solution will be bitter. Refrigerate. Makes a delicious flavor in soups and stews.

To make your own pure ground chili powder, toast ripe chili peppers in 325 oven until they begin to darken, then rinse, dry and stem them. Process the pods a few at a time in a blender or food processor until finely ground. If you want a milder chili powder, remove some of the seeds before grinding.

MAKE YOUR OWN POULTRY SEASONING

1 c dried crumbled sage leaves
2 c dried parsley
1 teaspoon dried onion powder
2 tablespoon salt
1 teaspoon freshly ground black pepper
1/2 c ground rosemary leaves
1/2 c ground marjoram leaves

Combine ingredients in large container and allow to sit covered for several days to meld flavors. Package some in small amounts in jars, plastic bags or cheesecloth package to give to friends. Label with directions to add 1 tablespoon seasoning to 1/4 lb butter for rubbing over poultry before roasting or the same amount in stuffing called for in recipes.

MUSTARD

The mustard plant is a member of the cabbage family. It is easily grown and self sows readily if the seeds are not collected. The young leaves can be used as a salad green or cooked and served like spinach. The seeds are ready to be collected anywhere from 60 to 90 days depending on the variety grown. The seed heads should be pinched off just as they start to turn tan. Spread the pods on paper or a screen to air dry; this takes about 2 weeks. At this time the seeds are easily separated from the husks. Store in a tightly covered container until ready to use.

> *Note:* These mustards contain no added salt and are low in sodium. They should be refrigerated after preparing and used within six months.

THYME AND HONEY MUSTARD

1 tablespoon whole coriander seeds
6 tablespoon whole mustard seeds
1 tablespoon black peppercorns
1/4 teaspoon dried thyme
3/4 c cold water
2 teaspoon honey
1/4 c red wine vinegar

Place coriander seed in a flat dish and microwave on high about 4 minutes. Crush mustard seeds, peppercorns and coriander seeds in a mortar or blender until fine. Mix the crushed seeds, thyme and cold water in top of a stainless steel double boiler and let stand 3 hours. In bottom of double boiler heat water to boil, then reduce to simmer; place the upper pan containing the seed mixture on top. Stir in the honey and vinegar and cook about 10 minutes or until is as thick as you want. It will thicken a bit more as it stands. Put into a covered container and refrigerate.

JALAPENO MUSTARD

2 teaspoon whole coriander seeds
1/2 c whole mustard seeds
1/4 c dry powdered mustard
3/4 c cold water
3 cloves garlic, peeled and chopped
1 small onion, peeled and chopped
2 or 3 jalapeno peppers, seeded
1/4 c cider vinegar
1/2 c dry white wine

Place coriander seeds in a flat dish and microwave on high about 4 minutes. Crush the mustard and coriander seeds slightly in a mortar or blender, then mix them with the powdered mustard and cold water and let stand 3 hours. Mix the remaining ingredients and grind in a blender until smooth. Stir this mixture into the mustard.

In a non-reactive pan, bring the mixture to a boil, then lower the heat and simmer about 5 minutes, stirring occasionally. It will thicken as it cools. Store covered in refrigerator.

TARRAGON MUSTARD

1/2 c mustard seeds
1/4 c dry powdered mustard
3/4 c cold water
1/4 c dry white wine
1/4 c white wine vinegar
1 teaspoon dried tarragon
1/8 teaspoon ground allspice

Mix mustard seeds, powdered mustard and water in the upper part of a glass or stainless double boiler. Let stand 3 hours. In another non-reactive pan mix the wine, vinegar, tarragon and allspice, bring to a boil. Strain the liquid into the mustard mixtur, mix well. In the lower part of the double boiler, heat water to boiling then reduce to simmer. Place the upper pan containing the mustard mixture on top. Cook, stirring, until the mustard is as thick as you like it. Cover and refrigerate.

SWEET TARRAGON MUSTARD

3/4 c white wine vinegar
2/3 c dry mustard (2 oz)
1/4 c dry white wine
1/2 c butter or margarine
1/3 c sugar
1 teaspoon dried tarragon, crushed
1/2 teaspoon salt
4 egg yolks

In top of double boiler combine vinegar, mustard and wine. Cover and let stand at least 3 hours to mellow. Add butter, sugar, tarragon and salt. Cook and stir over boiling water until butter melts. Remove from heat, add egg yolk, one at a time, beating well after each. Return to heat and cook over boiling water until very thick, approximately 8 to 10 minutes. Pack in jars, cover, cool and refrigerate until needed.

HERB BUTTER

1 c butter or margarine, softened
2 tablespoon lemon juice
1 teaspoon salt
1/4 teaspoon pepper
1/4 c chopped fresh dill, thyme or parsley
1 teaspoon dried tarragon leaves
dash hot sauce

Beat butter with wooden spoon until fluffy. Beat in rest of ingredients until smooth and fluffy. Put in covered container and refrigerate. Makes 1 cup. This makes a nice gift.

> *Note:* These butters add a special touch to steak, and may also be served on hot bread, baked potatoes, broiled tomatoes and other vegetables.

GARLIC BUTTER

1 stick butter
1 tablespoon minced parsley
1 tablespoon shallow
1 teaspoon minced garlic (or more to taste)
1 teaspoon dry white wine
1/2 teaspoon lemon juice

Combine all ingredients and mix. Dollop on cooked steaks or serve separately. Makes about 1/2 cup.

SHALLOT-TARRAGON BUTTER

1 stick (1/2 c) butter at room temperature
3 shallots, minced
1-2 teaspoon dried, crumbled tarragon
salt and pepper

Combine all ingredients and mix. Dollop on cooked steaks or serve separately. Makes 1/2 cup.

BASIL BUTTER

1/2 c (1 stick) butter
1 tablespoon basil
1/2 teaspoon minced garlic
1 teaspoon tomato paste
salt and pepper

Mix all ingredients. Dollop on steaks or serve separately. Makes 1/2 cup.

ANCHOVY BUTTER

1/2 c (1 stick) butter, room temperature
4 anchovy fillets, rinsed, drained and chopped
1 teaspoon fresh lemon juice
hot sauce to taste

Combine all ingredients. Dollop on steaks or serve separately. Makes about 1/2 cup.

WHIPPED HERB BUTTER

In small bowl with mixer at high speed beat 1 cup softened butter or margarine, 1 teaspoon ground marjoram leaves, 1 teaspoon ground thyme leaves, 1 teaspoon ground rosemary, 1/8 teaspoon ground basil, 1/8 teaspoon ground sage and 1/8 teaspoon garlic powder until fluffy. Spoon into small container, cover and refrigerate. Use on corn on the cob, fish, poultry, steaks or vegetables.

HERB BUTTER

Basil and Garlic Butter:
1 clove garlic
2 tablespoon chopped basil
6 tablespoon butter
salt and pepper to taste

Mix in blender or food processor. Serve with grilled steaks, lamb or fish.

CHIVE BUTTER

6 tablespoon butter
3 tablespoon chopped chives
1 tablespoon lemon juice
salt and pepper to taste

Mix well. Serve with lamb or white fish.

MINT BUTTER

6 tablespoon butter
2 tablespoon chopped mint
1 tablespoon lemon juice
salt and pepper to taste

Mix well. Good with new potatoes, carrots, green peas, and lamb.

PARSLEY BUTTER

6 tablespoon butter
1 clove garlic, mashed
3 tablespoon chopped parsley
1 tablespoon lemon juice
salt and pepper to taste

Mix well. Serve with steaks or grilled fish.

SAGE BUTTER

6 tablespoon butter
12 sage leaves
2 teaspoon lemon juice
1 teaspoon onion juice
salt and pepper to taste

Mix in blender or food processor. Serve over lamb, veal or broiled tomatoes.

TARRAGON AND PARSLEY BUTTER

6 tablespoon butter
1 1/2 tablespoon tarragon
1 tablespoon parsley
1 tablespoon lemon juice
salt and pepper to taste

Mix in blender or food processor. Good served with broiled steaks, white fish or noodles.

MIXED HERB BUTTER

6 tablespoon butter
1/2 tablespoon tarragon
1/2 tablespoon chervil
1/2 tablespoon dill
1/2 tablespoon chives
1/2 tablespoon mint
1 tablespoon lemon juice

Mix in blender or food processor. Excellent on grilled meats, fish and noodles.

COMPOUND HERB BUTTER

1 medium green onion, finely chopped
1/2 c packed fresh basil or parsley leaves finely chopped
1 teaspoon fresh lemon juice
1/4 teaspoon salt
1/4 teaspoon white pepper
several drops hot pepper sauce
1/4 teaspoon, dry mustard
1 stick unsalted butter, softened

Mash green onion and herbs by hand or in a food processor. Add the lemon juice, salt, pepper, hot sauce, mustard and butter and mix thoroughly. Shape into a log and wrap in plastic wrap. Freeze until ready to slice and use. Keep on hand to dress up grilled meats, chicken, fish, to swirl into soups or stews or to serve on hot breads.

HERB BUTTER

1/2 c (1 stick) butter at room temperature
1 tablespoon lemon juice
3 tablespoon finely chopped fresh herb or use 1-3 teaspoon dried herb

Mix thoroughly by hand or in food processor. Store in a tightly covered container in the refrigerator. Use within a few days for a better flavor. This will also freeze well.

Herb flavored butters are very good as topping for bread, vegetables, meats and sea foods.

HERB SALTS

Thyme salt:
Crush 3 tablespoon thyme leave to a fine powder and mix with 1/2 cup salt.

Oregano salt:
substitute oregano for thyme

Tarragon salt:
substitute 2 tablespoon crushed tarragon for thyme

These are delicious on roast beef or pork, broiled steak, poultry, seafood, omelets and hot or cold vegetables. Can be stored in tightly covered container for up to a month.

HERB SALT

1 teaspoon garlic salt
4 teaspoon onion salt
2 teaspoon dried parsley
1 teaspoon dried basil
1 teaspoon dried marjoram
pinch of thyme

Combine all ingredients and grind with mortar and pestle, in coffee grinder or rub between fingers until fine and combined. Pack in a jar and seal or keep in a shaker.

SEASONED SALT

1 c coarse pickling salt
2 1/2 teaspoon paprika
2 teaspoon dry mustard
1 1/2 teaspoon dried oregano, crushed
1 1/2 teaspoon garlic powder
1 teaspoon dried thyme, crushed
1 teaspoon curry powder
1/2 teaspoon onion powder
1/4 teaspoon dried dillweed

Combine all ingredients, mix well. Pour into airtight container. Good to season egg, cheese, fish and meat dishes.

AN HERBAL SALT SUBSTITUTE

2 tablespoon dried dill leaf, crumbled
1 teaspoon dried oregano, crumbled
2 tablespoon onion powder
1 teaspoon celery seed
2 tablespoon toasted sesame seeds
1/2 teaspoon paprika
1/2 teaspoon garlic powder

Combine all ingredients. Place in shaker. Serve on vegetables, salads or wherever you would use salt.

SEASONED FLOUR

Mix 1-2 teaspoon dried herbs with
1/2 teaspoon salt
1/2 teaspoon black pepper
2 c flour

Seal tightly. Use in sauces, gravy, biscuits, pizza crust or dredging foods before frying.

Sweet Endings

THE SWEET HERBS

Anise Hyssop is a perennial plant that is very aromatic and makes a lovely addition to a flower border. It has an anise-like flavor which can be used in cookies and cakes. It makes a wonderfully fragrant tea.

Scented Basils have the basil aroma and flavor with the addition of the other flavor as described in their names. They are best used fresh as the aroma and taste is reduced by cooking. To name a few that are most common—anise, cinnamon, and lemon.

Cardaman has a very sweet, gingery taste. It is a tropical plant so must be purchased. It goes well in hot fruit punches, coffee cakes, fruitcakes and when mixed with honey it makes a wonderful sweetener for fruits.

Lemon Balm is a hardy perennial that makes a very attractive flower border plant. The leaves can be used in recipes as a lemon peel substitute. It has a citrus flavor which can be used generously in fruit drinks, vegetables or desserts.

Lemon Verbena is not winter hardy so should be kept in a container so it can be moved indoors during winter months. The leaves are very much like a lemon and can be used when you wish this flavor. A few leaves placed in the bottom of a cake pan before pouring in the batter transfers the lemon flavor to the cake during baking.

Pineapple sage is a member of the same family as garden sage and the bright red annual salvia you see in flower gardens. It needs to be protected during cold weather so should be grown in a container. It really has a pineapple aroma and taste and is good in fruit salads, punches and as a garnish for iced tea.

ANISE COOKIES

3 eggs
1 c sugar
2 c sifted flour
1 tablespoon ground aniseed
1/2 teaspoon baking powder

Beat eggs until they are light and pale yellow. Add the sugar and beat vigorously for about 3 minutes. Sift the flour together with the aniseed and baking powder; add to egg mixture. Continue beating 3 to 5 minutes. Drop batter by teaspoonful on a well-greased cookie sheet leaving about 1 inch space between cookies. Do not cover. Let stand in warm place overnight to dry. Preheat oven to 350 and bake about 8 minutes. Yield 3 dozen.

ANISE SEED WAFERS

1/3 c shortening
1 c sugar
3 eggs, separated
2 c flour
3 teaspoon anise seed
1/4 teaspoon nutmeg
1/2 teaspoon salt

Cream shortening and sugar, add egg yolks, one at a time, beating constantly. Beat egg white until stiff and add to shortening mixture alternating with 2 cups flour to which has been sifted with anise seed, nutmeg, and salt. Add just enough extra flour to dough to roll very thin. Shape with cutter and bake in a hot oven until golden.

APPLE CAKE

3 tablespoon butter or margarine, softened
1 c sugar
1 large egg, beaten
1 c all-purpose flour
1/2 teaspoon ground cinnamon
1/2 teaspoon ground nutmeg
1/2 teaspoon salt
1 teaspoon baking soda
3 c diced peeled apples
1/4 c chopped pecans
1/4 teaspoon hot sauce
1 teaspoon vanilla

Cream butter, sugar and egg. Sift together dry ingredients and add to creamed mixture. Batter will be very thick. Add vanilla and hot sauce. Stir in apples and nuts. Spread into greased 8 inch baking pan. Bake at 350 for 35-40 minutes until done. Yield: 8 servings. Delicious served hot with coffee or cold with whipped cream or ice cream.

APPLE PIE WITH FENNEL

Pastry for a 2-crust pie
1 c sugar
2 tablespoon flour
1 teaspoon ground cinnamon
1/4 teaspoon ground fennel seed
1/4 teaspoon salt
6 c sliced cooking apples
3 tablespoon butter or margarine

Combine sugar, flour, cinnamon, fennel and salt in a bowl. Arrange half the apples in crust lined pie plate. Sprinkle with half the sugar mixture. Repeat with remaining apples and sugar mixture. Dot with butter. Top with other crust, flute and cut slits in top. For a sparkly crust, brush lightly with milk and sprinkle with sugar. Bake at 425 about 40 to 45 minutes.

BASIL POUND CAKE

1/2 lb butter
2 c sugar
4 eggs
2 c flour
1/4 teaspoon salt
1/2 teaspoon dried basil leaves, ground to a powder

Cream butter and sugar together until light; beat in the eggs, one at a time. Sift flour and salt together, add basil, and beat into the butter mixture. Pour into a well-buttered loaf pan and bake at 300 for 1 1/2 hours.

CHEESE-APPLESAUCE PIE WITH CINNAMON CORN-FLAKE SHELL

1 c packaged corn-flake crumbs
2 tablespoon + 1/2 c sugar
1 teaspoon cinnamon
2 tablespoon butter, melted
2 c cottage cheese
1/8 teaspoon salt
1/2 c heavy cream
2 tablespoon flour
2 eggs
3 teaspoon grated lemon rind
3 tablespoon lemon juice
1 teaspoon hot sauce
1 jar (15 oz) applesauce
3/4 c chopped almonds

Mix crumbs, 2 tablespoon sugar, cinnamon and butter. Press firmly on bottom and sides of 9" pie pan. Press cheese through sieve. Add eggs, 1/2 cup sugar, salt, cream, flour, 1 teaspoon lemon rind and 1 tablespoon lemon juice. Beat until smooth, pour into pie shell. Bake in slow oven, 325, about 1 hour. Cool. Mix remaining rind, juice, applesauce, hot sauce and almonds. Spread over pie.

CARDAMON COOKIES

3 3/4 c flour
2 c butter or margarine, softened
1 c chopped california walnuts
1 1/2 teaspoon almond extract
1 teaspoon ground cardamon
1/8 teaspoon salt
1 1/2 c confectioners sugar

Measure ingredients into a large bowl. Knead together until well blended. Shape into 1 inch balls. Place 2 inches apart on cookie sheets. Bake at 350 for 20 minutes or until lightly browned. Remove from pan to rack; cool. If you like roll in additional confectioners sugar when cool.

COTTAGE CHEESE SNOW

1/2 c heavy cream
2 tablespoon sugar
1/2 teaspoon ground ginger
1 lb cream style cottage cheese
1 tablespoon finely snipped lemon balm leaves

Beat cream with sugar and ginger until stiff; fold into cottage cheese, add lemon balm and chill until serving. Perfect complement to fresh fruits.

MINTED CANTALOUPE AND BLUEBERRIES

1/2 c sugar
1 c water
1 tablespoon fresh mint, chopped
1 c fresh blueberries
2 c cantaloupe balls (about 1 1/2 cantaloupe)
fresh mint sprigs

Combine the sugar, water and mint in a saucepan. Bring to a boil and boil 3 minutes. Strain and chill. Add the blueberries and melon balls to the syrup and garnish with sprigs of fresh mint.

CHOCOLATE MINT PIE

1 (8 inch) graham cracker pie crust
2 squares of bittersweet chocolate
1 stick butter or margarine
2 eggs, well beaten
1 1/2 c confectioners sugar
1 teaspoon vanilla
1 teaspoon peppermint flavoring

Melt chocolate and butter over hot water. Beat eggs, add sugar, chocolate, butter and flavorings. Beat thoroughly for 15 minutes (use hand mixer). Pour into crust and top with whipped cream. Refrigerate. Very rich but very good.

CHOCOLATE MINT SILK PIE

crust:
1 1/2 c crushed chocolate sandwich cookies
1/4 c butter, melted

filling:
1 c sugar
3/4 c butter, softened
3 squares semi-sweet chocolate, melted and cooled
1/2 teaspoon peppermint extract
3 eggs
sweetened whipped cream

Mix crust ingredients together and press on sides and bottom of pie pan; refrigerate. Combine sugar, 3/4 cup butter and beat well. Add chocolate and peppermint extract. Add eggs and beat until light and fluffy. Spoon into crust and refrigerate at least 3 hours or until set. If desired, serve with whipped cream.

CHOCOLATE MINT MALLOW CUPS

1 c semi-sweet chocolate chips
1/2 c milk
24 large marshmallows
pinch of salt
1 teaspoon vanilla
pinch of peppermint extract
6 drops red food coloring
1 c whipping cream
1/3 c crushed peppermint candy (reserve 1 tablespoon)

Melt chocolate chips in double boiler. Place light paper liners in muffin pan. Coat inside of each liner with chocolate (brush on), bringing coating close to top, but not over. Refrigerate until firm. Combine milk and marshmallows; cook over low heat until marshmallows are melted. Remove from heat; stir in salt, vanilla, peppermint extract and red food coloring. Refrigerate until mixture mounds slightly when dropped from a spoon. Beat chilled whipping cream until stiff peaks form. Stir marshmallow mixture until smooth. Fold marshmallow mixture and candy into whipped cream. Spoon about 1/3 cup into each chocolate cup. Refrigerate at least 2 hours. Carefully remove paper liners from chocolate cups. To serve, sprinkle with reserved tablespoon crushed candy.

FRESH MINT CHOCOLATE CHIP COOKIES

1 1/3 c sugar
3/4 c butter or margarine, softened
1 tablespoon finely chopped mint leaves (1/4 teaspoon mint extract can be substituted)
1 egg
2 c all-purpose flour
1 teaspoon baking soda
1/2 teaspoon salt
1 pkg (10 oz) mint chocolate chips

Mix sugar, margarine, mint leaves and egg. Stir in flour, baking soda and salt. Stir in chocolate chips. Drop by rounded tablespoonfuls. About two inches apart onto ungreased cookie sheet. Bake 11 to 13 minutes or until golden brown. Cool slightly; remove from cookie sheet.

FRESH MINTED PINEAPPLE

1 whole fresh pineapple, sliced into 1 inch thick slices
1/2 c sugar
3/4 c coarsely chopped fresh mint leaves
6 maraschino cherries or strawberries
6 sprigs fresh mint

Sprinkle sugar evenly over tops of pineapple slices. Sprinkle mint evenly over sugar. Stack slices to reform the pineapple shape and place in a plastic bag. Set upright in a medium bowl and refrigerate 6 hours or overnight. To serve, scrape chopped mint from slices, place a slice on serving plate and garnish with the fruit and a sprig of mint.

GRASSHOPPER PIE

crust:
18 oreo cookies
1/2 stick margarine, melted

Crush Oreos and stir in melted margarine. Mix well. Press in bottom of pie pan and up the sides.

Pie Filling:
2 envelopes Dream whip
1 large jar marshmallow cream
1 small cool whip, thawed
1/4 c milk
5-6 drops oil of peppermint
green food coloring

Stir air out of the marshmallow cream. Add milk

and peppermint and stir until smooth. This can be done in the jar. Prepare Dream Whip according to package directions. Mix in marshmallow cream. Fold in cool whip and food coloring. Pour into pie crust. Freeze several hours.

HOT KRAUT FUDGE CAKE

2/3 c butter
1 1/2 c sugar
3 eggs
1 teaspoon vanilla
1/4 teaspoon salt
2/3 c chopped hot kraut
1/2 c cocoa
2 1/4 c sifted flour
1 teaspoon baking powder
1 teaspoon baking soda
1 c beer

Cream together butter and sugar; beat in eggs and vanilla. Add dry ingredients. Mix well and add kraut and beer. Be sure all ingredients are well mixed. Bake in two well greased and floured eight inch cake pans. Bake in 350 oven until done. Frost with fudge frosting.

Note: Our friend Doris Cooper gave us this recipe. It doesn't sound good. When we made it our tasters loved it.

QUICK FUDGE FROSTING

Sift 2 cups confectioners sugar and 1/4 cup cocoa. Add 1/2 teaspoon salt. Heat 1/4 cup undiulted evaporated milk and 2 tablespoon butter. Add to first mixture with 1 teaspoon vanilla. Beat until smooth.

LEMON BALM COOKIES

2 tablespoon minced lemon balm leaves
1 teaspoon vanilla
1 c butter, softened
2/3 c sugar
1 egg
2 1/3 c flour
1/4 teaspoon salt

Combine lemon balm and vanilla in a small bowl, pressing with back of spoon to blend. In large mixer bowl cream butter and sugar till light and fluffy. Beat in egg and lemon mixture. Gradually beat in flour and salt. Cover and refrigerate about 3 hours or until mixture is firm. Roll dough to 1/8" thickness and cut into rounds. Place on ungreased cookie sheet and bake in 350 oven about 8-10 minutes or until lightly browned.

LEMON BREAD

1/2 c liquid shortening
1/2 c softened butter
1 c sugar
2 eggs
1 1/2 c flour
  1/2 c milk
  1 teaspoon baking powder
  pinch of salt
  rind of 1 lemon, snipped into small bits
  1/2 teaspoon lemon thyme or lemon balm leaves, chopped

Mix shortening, butter and sugar. Add eggs one at a time. Combine lemon rind, thyme and dry ingredients. Add to butter mixture alternately with milk. Pour into greased and floured loaf pan and bake at 350 for 45 minutes. Before the bread cools and while it is still in the pan, punch holes in top and spoon the following mixture over: juice of 2 lemons, 1/2 teaspoon vanilla, and 1/2 c sugar. Better if stored 1 day before serving.

LEMON TEA BREAD

3/4 c milk
1 tablespoon finely chopped lemon balm
1 tablespoon finely chopped lemon thyme
2 c all purpose flour
1 1/2 teaspoon baking powder
1/4 teaspoon salt
6 tablespoon butter at room temperature
1 c sugar
2 eggs, beaten
1 tablespoon grated lemon zest (peel)

Butter a 9 x 5 inch pan. Preheat oven to 325. Heat the milk with the chopped herbs (DO NOT BOIL) and let set until cool. Mix flour, baking powder and salt together in a bowl. In another bowl cream the butter until fluffy then gradually beat in sugar until light and fluffy. Add eggs one at a time. Beat in the lemon zest. Add the flour mixture alternately with the herbed milk. Mix just until batter is blended. Pour into prepared pan and bake for about 50 minutes. Remove from the pan onto a wire rack over a sheet of waxed paper. Pour lemon glaze over the bread while still hot.

LEMON GLAZE

Juice of 2 lemons and confectioners sugar. Put lemon juice in bowl and add sugar stirring until thickened but is still pourable.

LEMON VERBENA MUFFINS

1 c softened butter
2 1/2 c sifted powdered sugar
4 eggs at room temperature
2 c flour
1 teaspoon grated lemon zest
1 tablespoon finely chopped lemon verbena leaves

Beat butter until fluffy, then gradually add sugar with mixer going. Add eggs one at a time beating well after each. Add flour and mix thoroughly. Stir in lemon zest and chopped leaves. Spoon into muffin cups and bake at 350 about 30 minutes.

LEMON TOPPING FOR GINGERBREAD

8 oz cream cheese softened
1/2 c confectioners sugar
1/4 c light cream
1 tablespoon finely snipped lemon verbena leaves
small amount lemon zest for garnish

Blend ingredients except lemon zest in small bowl. Chill slightly. Serve over warm gingerbread squares and garnish with lemon zest.

MILLION DOLLAR POUND CAKE

2 c butter softened (do not substitute)
3 c sugar
6 eggs
4 c all-purpose flour
3/4 c milk
1 teaspoon almond extract
1 teaspoon vanilla extract
2 teaspoon medium hot sauce

In a mixing bowl cream butter. Gradually add sugar; beat well. Add eggs, one at a time, beating well after each addition. Add flour alternately with milk. Stir in extracts and hot sauce. Pour batter into greased and floured 10 inch tube pan. Bake at 300 for about 1 hour and 40 minutes or until cake tests done.

CHILLED MELON BALLS WITH GRAPE JUICE AND MINT

1 ripe cantaloupe
1/2 ripe honeydew
1 c white grape juice (or 1 c semi dry white wine)
1 c seedless red grapes
3 tablespoon finely chopped fresh mint

Cut cantaloupe in half. Scrape out seeds. Scoop out balls with spoon or melon baller and place in large bowl. Add grape juice, grapes, and mint to melon balls. Toss, cover and refrigerate at least 2 hours.

MINTS

2 c sugar
1/2 c water
1/2 c white corn syrup
1/4 teaspoon cream of tartar
8 drops oil of peppermint or wintergreen food color

In saucepan bring first 4 ingredients to a boil. Boil to soft ball stage. Add 8 drops of preferred flavoring and coloring. Beat until it gets cloudy and thick. Drop on wax paper or in molds.

MINT CHIP ICE CREAM

1 can sweetened condensed milk
2 tablespoon water
1/4-1/2 teaspoon peppermint extract
3-4 drops green food coloring
2 c whipping cream, whipped
1 c (6 oz) semisweet chocolate chips

Combine milk, water, extract and food coloring. Fold in whipped cream and chocolate chips. Pour into foil-lined 9 x 5 x 2 inch loaf pan and freeze for 5-6 hours or until firm. Lift out of pan, remove foil and slice. Makes 8 servings.

FRESH MINTED FRUIT

1/2 c sugar
3/4 c water
2 tablespoon fresh lime juice
1 teaspoon chopped fresh mint
1/2 teaspoon aniseed
1/16 teaspoon salt
5 c fresh cantaloupe pieces
4 c fresh peach slices
2 c fresh blueberries

Combine sugar, water, lime juice, mint, aniseed and salt. Bring to a boil and boil 2 minutes. Cover and let steep 10 minutes. Cool; chill. Place fruit in a bowl; strain syrup over fruit. Cover; chill for at least 2 hours. Serve same day. Makes 10 servings.

MINT CREAM PIE

6 c miniature marshmallows
1/4 c milk
1/3 c green creme de menthe
1 teaspoon vanilla
3-4 drops green food color
1 (8 oz) container whipped topping
1 prepared chocolate-flavored 9 inch pie crust

Combine marshmallows and milk; cook over low heat, stirring until marshmallows melt. Remove from heat and cool. Stir every few minutes until partially set. Stir in liqueur, vanilla and food color. Fold in whipped topping and pour into pie shell. Freeze until firm. Before serving, let stand at room temperature for 10 minutes.

MINT SOUFFLE

butter for mold
sugar for mold
2 c milk
1 1/2 c fresh mint sprigs
5 eggs, separated
6 tablespoon sugar
4 tablespoon flour
pinch of salt
2 tablespoon chopped fresh mint
minted chocolate sauce, recipe follows

Lightly butter a 1 1/2 quart souffle mold and sprinkle with sugar. Scald milk with mint sprigs. Bruise mint by pressing it against the pan with wooden spoon. Remove from heat, cover and let stand for 30 minutes. Beat egg yolks with sugar; beat in flour. Strain scalded milk into egg yolk mixture, squeeze mint to get out all moisture. Discard mint and stir egg mixture to blend well. Return mixture to pan, stirring constantly, cook about 3 minutes. Strain into bowl and set aside to cool slightly. Beat egg whites with salt to soft peaks. Stir one-quarter of beaten whites into egg mixture to lighten, then carefully fold in remaining whites and chopped fresh mint. Spoon into prepared souffle mold and bake in 375 preheated oven for 20-25 minutes or until center is set but still soft. Serve immediately with minted chocolate sauce. Makes 6 servings.

MINTED CHOCOLATE SAUCE

1/2 c heavy cream
1/4 c fresh mint sprigs
3 oz bittersweet chocolate
1 oz sweet chocolate
2 tablespoon butter

Scald cream with mint, pressing mint to side of pan with wooden spoon to bruise. Remove from heat, cover and let stand for 20 minutes. Strain cream into a bowl and press all moisture out of mint. Discard mint. In top of double boiler, melt chocolate and butter, over hot, not simmering, water. Stir until smooth. Beat into cream until well blended and smooth. Serve warm. Makes about 3/4 cup.

PINEAPPLE MINT SHERBET

3 c water
2 c sugar
1 ripe pineapple, peeled, cored and cut into cubes
2 c firmly packed whole mint leaves
1 c finely chopped mint leaves
juice of 1 lemon

Heat water and sugar; simmer for 3 minutes. Remove from heat and cool slightly. In food processor puree pineapple with half the sugar syrup. In a bowl crush whole mint leaves with heavy blunt instrument. Pour remaining syrup over mint leaves, cover and set aside for 30 minutes. Strain mint leaves through a sieve and pour syrup into pineapple puree. Add lemon juice and freshly chopped mint leaves and stir to blend. Freeze in commercial ice cream freezer or pour into a large shallow dish. Cover and freeze for about an hour or until it is partially frozen. Remove from freezer and beat until frothy. Return to freezer, cover and refreeze for about 1/2 hour, or until mixture begins to harden again. Remove from freezer and beat again. Return to freezer and freeze completely before serving, at least 2 to 3 hours. Makes 2 quarts.

POPPY SEED CAKE

1 box yellow cake mix
3/4 c salad oil
1 c cooking sherry
Eggs as called for in cake mix
1-2 oz poppy seed
1 box instant butterscotch pudding

Mix in order given. Bake in greased, but not floured bundt pan for about 45 minutes or until done. Needs no frosting. Delicious!

HOT PUMPKIN PIE

crust for a 9 inch pie, unbaked
16 oz can pumpkin
12 oz can evaporated milk
2 large eggs
3/4 c packed brown sugar
2 teaspoon (or more) hot pepper sauce
1 1/2 teaspoon ground cinnamon
1/2 teaspoon ground nutmeg
1/2 teaspoon ground ginger
whipped cream
1/4 c chopped pecans

Combine pumpkin, evaporated milk, eggs, brown sugar, pepper sauce and spices. Beat until well mixed. Pour into pie shell. Bake at 400 until knife inserted 1 inch from edge comes out clean (about 40-45 minutes). Cool on wire rack. Serve each piece with a dollop of whipped cream and garnish with pecans. You might want to experiment with hot sauce. This pie is deliciously hot and spicy.

HOT PEPPER SAUCE COOKIES

2 1/4 c all-purpose flour
1/2 teaspoon baking soda
1/2 teaspoon salt
1 c granulated sugar
2/3 c butter or margarine, at room temperature
1 large egg
2 teaspoon hot pepper sauce
1 teaspoon vanilla

Combine flour, salt and soda. Cream sugar and butter. Add egg, hot sauce, vanilla and flour mixture. Beat until well blended. Divide dough in half. Shape each half into a log. Cover, and refrigerate until firm. Cut dough rolls into 1/4 inch slices. Dip each slice in granulated sugar. Place one inch apart on ungreased cookie sheet. Bake 10-12 minutes at 350 or until edges are brown. Cool on wire rack. Makes about 5 dozen cookies.

ROSE GERANIUM CAKE

Mix:
2 c flour
1/2 teaspoon salt
1 teaspoon baking powder

cream together:
1/2 c butter
1 c sugar
2/3 c water
4 egg whites, unbeaten
Rose Geranium leaves
Butter

Butter Rose Geranium leaves. Cream butter and sugar. Mix dry ingredients. Add the dry ingredients alternately with water to the creamed mixture. Lastly, add the unbeaten egg whites and beat for 3 minutes. Line a loaf pan with butter and rose geranium leaves. Pour in batter. Bake at 350 for 35 to 40 minutes or until cake is done. Remove the leaves from the cake.

ROSE GERANIUM SCONES

2 c flour
2 1/2 teaspoon baking powder
1/4 teaspoon baking soda
2 tablespoon sugar
1/2 teaspoon salt
1 teaspoon grated orange peel
4 rose geranium leaves, minced fine
1/4 c butter
1 egg, slightly beaten
2/3 c buttermilk

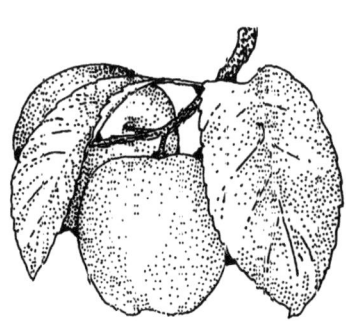

Combine dry ingredients, orange peel and geranium leaves in a large bowl. Cut in the butter until the mixture resembles corn meal. Stir in the egg and buttermilk just until combined. Turn out on a floured board and knead briefly. Divide dough in half and pat out into a 3/4 inch thick round. Cut each round into 6 wedges and place on ungreased baking sheet. Bake at 400 for 20 minutes.

SEED CAKE

1 c butter or margarine
4 eggs
2 teaspoon caraway seed
2 c flour
1 teaspoon baking powder
1/4 teaspoon salt
1 c sugar
1 teaspoon vanilla

Have butter and eggs at room temperature. Crush caraway seeds and set aside. In bowl combine flour, baking powder and salt. Cream butter until light and fluffy, gradually add sugar. Beat about 6 minutes. Add vanilla. Add eggs 1 at a time beating about 1 minute after each addition. Gradually add in dry ingredients. Beat until well combined. Stir in caraway seed. Pour batter into greased and floured 9 x 5 x 3 inch loaf pan. Bake at 325 for 60-70 minutes. Cool on rack about 10 minutes before removing from pan. Sesame seed or poppy seed may be substituted.

TOMATO SPICE CAKE

6 medium tomatoes (about 2 lbs) peeled and seeded
4 c all-purpose flour
2 1/2 c sugar
1/2 c vegetable oil
2 1/2 teaspoon baking soda
2 1/2 teaspoon cinnamon
2 teaspoon vanilla
1 1/2 teaspoon salt
1 teaspoon nutmeg
1 teaspoon cloves
1 tablespoon hot sauce
1/2 c chopped walnuts

Puree tomatoes (need 2 1/2 cups). Mix tomatoes and all other ingredients, except walnuts. Pour into 9 inch tube pan. Sprinkle with walnuts. Bake 65 to 70 minutes or until done at 350. Makes 12 servings. If you do not have fresh tomatoes try one of the following cakes using tomato soup.

TOMATO SOUP CAKE

1/2 c vegetable shortening
1/4 c light brown sugar
2 large eggs
1-10 3/4 oz can tomato soup, undiluted
2 c sifted all purpose flour
2 teaspoon baking powder
1/2 teaspoon baking soda

1/4 teaspoon ground cloves
1/2 teaspoon ground nutmeg
1 teaspoon ground cinnamon
1/2 c dark seedless raisins

1. Heat oven to 350. Grease and flour 9 inch square pan.

2. Beat shortening and brown sugar together until light and fluffy. Add eggs one at a time beating after each addition.

3. Add tomato soup, flour, baking powder, baking soda, spices and stir until well combined. Fold in raisins.

4. Pour into prepared pan and bake about 50 or 60 minutes until center springs back when gently touched.

Serve warm or cool. If desired, sift some powdered sugar over the top.

SPICY TOMATO CAKE

1/4 c butter
1/4 c vegetable shortening
1 1/4 c sugar
3 eggs
2 c flour
1 teaspoon baking powder
1 teaspoon baking soda
1/2 teaspoon nutmeg
dash salt
1/4 teaspoon cinnamon
1 teaspoon ground ginger
1/4 teaspoon ground lemon rind
1 c tomato soup, undiluted

Beat butter and shortening until smooth; add sugar and beat until well mixed. Add eggs and beat until light and fluffy. Combine dry ingredients and add to creamed mixture alternately with soup, beating well after each addition. Spoon batter into greased 8 or 9 inch tube pan and bake at 350 for 50 minutes.

Canning & Preserving

DILLY BEANS

3 1/2 c water
3 1/2 c white vinegar
6 tablespoon pickling salt
4 lbs green beans, washed and cut in 1 inch pieces
18-21 black peppercorns, 1 1/2 teaspoon crushed red pepper flakes or 6-7 small dried hot red peppers
1 tablespoon dill seed or fresh dill
1 tablespoon mustard seed

Combine water, vinegar and salt and bring to a boil. Pack beans into hot sterilized jars (pint) and divide remaining ingredients among jars. Pour boiling liquid over. Seal according to manufacturer's directions. Process 20 minutes in boiling water bath.

PICKLED BROCCOLI WITH TARRAGON

2 quarts water
1/2 c pickling salt
3 lbs broccoli, whole florets and peeled stalks
6 c white vinegar
2 c water
5 tablespoon mixed pickling spice
1/4 c pickling salt
1 bunch fresh tarragon or 2 tablespoon dried
1 tablespoon black peppercorns

Combine water and salt, add broccoli and let set overnight. Drain, rinse and pack into hot sterilized jars. Combine remaining ingredients and bring to a boil. Boil 10 minutes. Pour over broccoli and seal according to manufacturer's directions. Process 20 minutes in boiling water bath. Makes 5 pints.

PICKLED BEETS

8 small beets (2 lbs)
1 c cider vinegar
1 teaspoon salt
1/4 c sugar
5 peppercorns
1 teaspoon pickling spice
1 bay leaf
fresh dill, optional

Can be put in 1 quart canning jar and refrigerated or be "put up" (canned) in 4 half-pint canning jars.

Scrub beets; trim, leaving 1 inch of the tops and the roots attached. Cook, covered in boiling salt water until barely tender. Drain, reserving 1 cup of liquid. Rinse beets in cold water and slip off skins, tops and roots. Fill the jars with quartered or sliced beets. Combine the reserved cooking liquid with vinegar, salt, sugar, peppercorns, pickling spices and bay leaf. Bring to boiling; pour over beets to 1/4 inch from top of jars. If using 1 quart jar, seal and refrigerate. If using half-pints to "put up" beets seal the jars and process for 10 minutes in boiling water bath. Beets should be refrigerated for 10 days before using.

PICKLED MUSHROOMS

2 (12 oz) pkgs fresh mushrooms, stems removed
2/3 c tarragon vinegar
1/2 c vegetable oil
2 garlic cloves, crushed
1 tablespoon sugar
1 1/2 teaspoon salt
2 tablespoon water
dash hot pepper sauce
1 small onion, chopped
1 tablespoon chopped fresh parsley
1 tablespoon dried tarragon

Combine all ingredients except mushrooms. Add mushrooms. Marinate overnight in refrigerator, turning occasionally. May be stored in tightly covered container for as long as two days. Serve with toothpicks. Serves 8-10 people.

HOT SAUCE

8 c cored and chopped ripe tomatoes
2 1/4 c seeded and chopped hot peppers
1 1/2 c chopped onions
3 c cider vinegar
1/2 c sugar
1 tablespoon mixed pickling spice, tied in bag
2 1/2 teaspoon pickling salt

Combine tomatoes, peppers, onions and 2 cup of the vinegar. Bring to a boil and cook until vegetables are soft, about 15 minutes. Put through food mill or sieve. Return to pan and add remaining vinegar, sugar, pickling spice and salt. Bring to a boil, stirring often and simmer until the consistency of barbecue sauce, about 25 minutes. Fill jars. Seal. Process in boiling water bath 15 minutes. Makes 7 half pints.

KETCHUP

10 lb ripe tomatoes
3 medium onions, chopped
2 medium red bell peppers, chopped
1 large clove garlic, minced
1 1/4 c sugar
1 1/4 c cider vinegar
1 tablespoon pickling salt
1 tablespoon paprika
1 tablespoon celery seed, crushed
1/2 teaspoon ground allspice
1/2 teaspoon black pepper
1 teaspoon hot pepper sauce

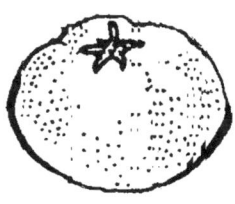

Cut stem ends off tomatoes and cut into chunks. Put tomatoes, onion, peppers and garlic in a large heavy saucepan and bring to a boil. Continue to cook over medium heat, stirring occasionally until vegetables are tender. Remove from heat and run through a sieve or food mill. Add remaining ingredients. Return to heat and bring to a boil. Simmer over low heat until it is reduced to half, stir occasionally to prevent scorching. When ketchup is ready, ladle into hot sterilized jars. Seal with sterilized lids. Process in boiling water bath for 10 minutes. Makes 6 1/2 pints.

DILL PICKLED OKRA

2 lbs young tender okra, washed
12-14 sprigs celery leaves
6-7 cloves garlic
6-7 sprigs dill
6-7 hot red peppers
3 c water
3 c white vinegar
3 tablespoon pickling spice

Pack okra into jars. Divide celery leaves, garlic, dill and hot peppers among jars. Bring water, vinegar and salt to a boil and pour over okra. Seal according to manufacturer's directions. Process 5 minutes in boiling water bath. Makes 6-7 pints.

OKRA PICKLES

2 lb okra
3 c water
1 c white vinegar
1/4 c pickling salt
2 teaspoon dill seed
1/2 teaspoon crushed red pepper

Thoroughly wash okra, drain well. Pack into hot, sterilized jars leaving 1/2 inch head space. In saucepan combine water, vinegar, salt, dill weed and red pepper; bring to boil then pour over okra. Wipe rims put on lids. Process in boiling water bath for 10 minutes.

PICKLED OKRA

4 c vinegar
2 c water
1/2 c salt
heads of dill
cloves garlic
hot peppers
pickling spice

Use small tender pods of okra, leaving a little stem on pod. Pack okra straight up in jars. Into each jar put 2 heads of dill, 1 clove garlic, 1 small hot pepper and 2 teaspoon pickling spice. Mix vinegar, water and salt together; bring to a boil. Pour hot vinegar solution over okra and seal. Enough liquid for 4-5 pints.

HOT SWEET AND SOUR SAUCE

4 lbs plums, pitted and quartered
1/2 lb hot peppers, seeded and chopped
1 medium onion, quartered
3 cloves garlic, peeled and chopped
3 1/2 c sugar
3 c cider vinegar
1 tablespoon ground ginger
1 tablespoon dry mustard
1/2 teaspoon ground cloves
2 teaspoon pickling salt

Puree plums, peppers, onions and garlic in food processor or blender. Combine with other ingredients and pour in saucepan. Bring to a boil, reduce heat and simmer for 2 hours, stirring often. Pour into sterilized jars, seal and process in boiling water for 10 minutes. Makes 8 half-pints or 4 pints.

PICKLED ONIONS

1 quart tiny pickling onions
1/4 c pickling salt
water
1/2 c sugar
2 c white wine vinegar
2 small dried hot red peppers
2 small bay leaves

Cover onions with boiling water and let stand 2 minutes, drain. Rinse with cold water and peel onions. Return to bowl, add salt and cover with cold water. Stir to dissolve salt. Let stand in cool place about 12 hours. Drain onions and rinse with cold water. In a medium saucepan, heat sugar, vinegar, peppers and bay leaves to boiling. Simmer 15 minutes then strain out peppers and bay leaves. Pack onions into hot sterilized jars, pour boiling vinegar over to 1/4 inch from top of jar. Seal with hot sterilized lids. Process in boiling hot water bath for 10 minutes. Makes 2 pints.

CANNED PEPPERS

4 quarts peppers
1 1/2 c salt
1/4 c sugar
2 cloves garlic
2 tablespoon horseradish
10 c vinegar
2 c water

If peppers are hot wear rubber gloves. Cut 2 small slits in each pepper. Dissolve salt in 4 quarts water and pour over peppers; let stand 12-18 hours in a cool place. Drain, rinse, drain. Combine remaining ingredients and heat. Pack peppers in jars. Remove garlic from liquid and pour, boiling hot, over peppers. Seal. For extra crisp peppers, add 1/2 teaspoon alum to each jar before sealing. We use this recipe for hot bananas, whole or sliced, jalapenos (for stuffing and other uses) or any kind of pepper to be canned.

HOT BANANA PEPPERS STUFFED WITH WIENERS

4 quarts peppers
1 1/2 c pickling salt
1/4 c sugar
2 clove garlic
2 tablespoon horseradish
10 c vinegar
2 water

Wear rubber gloves. Cut off stem ends and remove seeds. Stuff peppers with wieners and place in jars. Mix all other ingredients and pour over peppers. Process 10 minutes at 5 lbs pressure. These can be served whole or sliced crosswise and served on toothpicks as appetizers. Makes great gifts for people who like hot food. Makes 12 pints.

PICKLED BANANA PEPPER RINGS

3 lbs banana or Anaheim chili peppers
2 c distilled white vinegar
1 c water
2 tablespoon granulated sugar
1 tablespoon pickling salt
4 cloves garlic

Wash peppers and cut in 1/4 inch thick rings. Remove core and seeds. Combine all other ingredients, except pepper rings and garlic. Bring to a boil. Add peppers, bring back to a boil and remove from heat. Place 1 clove garlic in each pint jar. Place pepper slices in jars; cover with hot vinegar. Seal and process in boiling water for 5 minutes. Makes 4 pints.

PICKLED BANANA PEPPERS

6 c vinegar
5 c water
2 c sugar
canning salt

Enough sliced hot banana peppers for 12 pints. Remove seeds and stems from peppers and slice into rings. Pack in hot sterilized jars. Add 1/2 teaspoon salt to each jar. Bring vinegar, water and sugar to a hard boil, pour over peppers leaving 1/4 inch head space. Wipe jar rims apply lids and seal. Process 5-10 minutes in hot water bath to seal.

HOT PEPPER RELISH I

1 lb green hot peppers, seeded
1 lb green bell peppers, seeded
1 lb onions, peeled and quartered
3 c white vinegar
1 c sugar
1 tablespoon pickling salt

Finely chop peppers and onions. In saucepan combine all ingredients. Boil 5 minutes, stirring constantly. Immediately fill sterilized pint jars. Seal. Process in boiling water bath 10 minutes. Yields 4 pints.

HOT PEPPER RELISH II

2 dozen hot banana peppers
7 medium onions
2 tablespoon mustard seed
2 tablespoon salt
3 c vinegar
3 c water

Grind peppers and onions (do not drain). Combine all ingredients. Boil 30 minutes. Pack into jars and seal. Process in boiling water bath 5 minutes. If a hotter relish is desired add one Scottish Bonnet or a few jalapenos to each batch. Makes 4 or 5 pints.

HOT SWEET RELISH

1 peck green tomatoes
1/2 c pickling salt
1 quart hot banana peppers
8 large sweet green or red peppers (or mixed)
2 1/2 lb onions
3 c sugar
4 1/2 c vinegar
1/2 box mixed pickling spice (tied in cheese cloth)

Grind tomatoes and sprinkle with pickling salt. Let stand while grinding peppers and onions. Then drain well. Mix all ingredients. Cook slowly about 30 minutes, stirring occasionally. Put in sterilized jars and seal.

PICCALILLI

1 lb green tomatoes
1 large red pepper, seeded and chopped
1 large green pepper, seeded and chopped
1-2 finely chopped hot peppers or more
2 large onion peeled and chopped
1 small head cabbage, cored and chopped
1 tablespoon pickling salt
1 c sugar
1 tablespoon mustard seed
1 tablespoon celery seed
1 c light corn syrup
2 c cider vinegar

Core tomatoes and chop coarsely. Combine with rest of the ingredients. Bring to a boil, lower heat and cook about 30 minutes or until vegetables are tender. Ladle into half-pint jars. Seal. Process in boiling water 10 minutes. Makes 6 half-pint jars.

SAUERKRAUT STUFFED HOT PEPPERS

peppers
sauerkraut
sprig of dill or 1 teaspoon dill seed
coarse salt
brine of: 1/2 part white vinegar and 1/2 part water

Wash peppers, cut off tops and remove seeds, wash again. Drain sauerkraut, then stuff into each pepper. Pack in jars, add sprig of dill and 1 tablespoon salt to each jar. Then make brine of vinegar and water. Bring to a boil. Pour boiling hot over peppers and seal. Process in hot water bath for 5 minutes. May be served whole or sliced crosswise.

TACO SAUCE

3 c chopped, peeled tomatoes
4 jalapeno peppers, seeded and chopped
3/4 c onion, chopped
3 cloves garlic, minced
1/2 c vinegar

Combine all ingredients and bring to a boil. Cover and simmer 5 minutes. Pour into hot sterilized jars. Use all liquid, dividing it equally among the jars. Adjust lids and process in boiling water bath 20 minutes. Makes 2 pints.

DILLED WHOLE CHERRY TOMATOES

green cherry tomatoes
celery
sweet green peppers
garlic
2 quarts water
1 quart vinegar
1 c salt
fresh dill

Pack tomatoes in jars. To each jar add a clove garlic, a small stalk of celery, 2 strips of pepper and a sprig of dill. Make a brine of water, vinegar and salt and boil 5 minutes. Pour hot brine over tomatoes and seal. These will be ready to use in 4-6 weeks. This amount of liquid makes about 6 quarts or 12 pints.

GREEN TOMATO PICKLES (SLICED)

5 lbs green tomatoes, cored, cut in 1/4 inch slices
3 large onions, cut in 1/4 inch slices
4 teaspoon coarse salt
6 whole allspice
3 large cloves garlic, bruised
3 sprigs celery leaves
3 small whole dried hot red chili peppers
4 c distilled vinegar
1 c sugar

Layer tomatoes and onions in colander. Sprinkle each layer with salt. Top with plate small enough to fit into colander. Weight down and let stand at room temperature 1 1/2 hours. Sterilize three quart jars. Place 2 allspice, 1 garlic clove, 1 sprig celery leaves and 1 dried hot red chili in each jar. Layer tomatoes and onions until almost filled to top. Heat vinegar and sugar, stirring until sugar is dissolved, to a boil. Fill jars to within 1/2 inch of top with liquid. Seal. Makes 3 quarts. If using pint jars double amounts of allspice, garlic, celery leaves and chili peppers. Place same amount of these ingredients in each pint as you would in a quart jar.

HOT TOMATO KRAUT

hot peppers—we use hot banana
pickling salt
equal parts of green tomatoes and cabbage

Chop cabbage and tomatoes. Add chopped hot peppers, depending on hotness desired. Mix all thoroughly. Pack canning jar half full. Add 1 heaping tablespoon salt to a quart jar or 2 teaspoon to a pint. Finish filling jar with chopped vegetables. Fill jar with hot water, running a knife between vegetables and jar to remove air pockets. Seal and store in a coal place. If kraut is left on the cellar floor it will be whiter than if stored on a shelf, so my good friend Phyllis Salyers discovered.

TOMATO CHUTNEY

15 medium firm tomatoes, peeled and seeded
3 c packed brown sugar
1 c cider vinegar

2 (4 oz) can mild green chilies, drained and chopped
1 (6 inch) piece ginger root, peeled and minced
4 garlic cloves minced
2 1/2 teaspoon salt
about 8 (1/2 pint) canning jars

Mix all ingredients and heat to boiling. Reduce heat to low and simmer, uncovered, until very thick, about 1 1/2 hours, stirring occasionally. Meanwhile, prepare jars; spoon mixture into jars while hot to within 1/4 inch of top. Seal and process in boiling water bath 10 minutes. Store in a cool place. Will keep for a year or more. Makes eight one-half pints.

TOMATO JUICE COCKTAIL

5 quarts chopped tomatoes
1/4 c chopped celery
2 tablespoon chopped onions
1/2 small bay leaf
2 sprigs parsley
1 tablespoon sugar
1 tablespoon Worcestershire sauce
4 tablespoon lemon juice
salt and Tabasco sauce to taste

Wash, core, chop and measure tomatoes. Add all other ingredients except lemon juice, salt and Tabasco sauce. Cook slowly until tomatoes are soft. Press through a sieve. Add lemon juice. Add salt and Tabasco sauce to suit your taste. Reheat. Fill jars and seal. Process in boiling water bath 15 minutes.

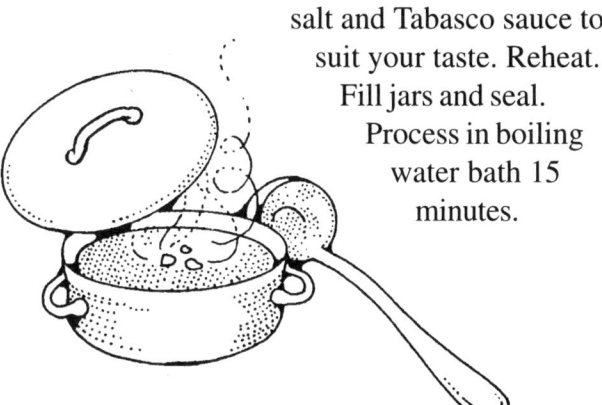

PICKLED VEGETABLES

2 lbs carrots
3 sweet peppers
2 hot peppers
1-3lb cauliflower
1 bunch celery
1 3/4 lb white boiling onions
2 quarts white vinegar
4 quarts water
1 1/2 c honey
1/3 c mustard seeds
1 tablespoon fennel seeds
1 tablespoon celery seeds
1 tablespoon peppercorns
4 cloves garlic

Peel and halve the carrots lengthwise, and cut them into 2 inch long pieces. Seed all the peppers and cut them into 1 1/2 inch pieces. Divide the cauliflower in 1 1/2 inch florets. String the celery, then slice it lengthwise and cut into 2 inch long pieces. Peel the onions and cut across on base of each onion. Place the vinegar, water, honey, mustard seed, fennel seeds, celery seeds and peppercorns in a 10 quart enameled or stainless steel pot. Bring to boil, boil until honey dissolves, about 5 minutes. Skim off any foam on the surface. Add the onions and cook for 3 minutes. Stir in the carrots, celery and cauliflower. Cook 5 minutes. Add peppers and cook 3 minutes longer. Spoon vegetables into 21 gallon jars, add 2 cloves garlic to each jar. Cover with hot vinegar. Seal and store in refrigerator. Let marinate 1 week before serving.

APPLE-MINT JELLY

3 lbs tart red apples to make 4 c juice
3 c sugar
1 c chopped mint leaves and stems
green food color

Wash apples. Cut out blossom and stem ends. Do not pare or core. Cut in eighths. Combine apples with 3 cups of water. Simmer, covered, until soft. Line a colander with 3 thicknesses of cheesecloth; set over a large bowl. Turn apples into colander; let drain 4 hours or overnight. Do not press apples. You should have 4 cups of juice. Sterilize 4 (8 oz) jelly glasses. In large kettle combine apple juice, sugar and mint leaves. Stir to dissolve sugar and bring to a boil. Boil, uncovered, without stirring, about 1 hour to the jellying point. Skim off foam. Strain jelly to remove mint leaves. Add a few drops of green food color to make a delicate color. Pour in jelly glasses and seal.

ASPIC JELLY

Take 1 tablespoon of good extract of meat and 2 quarts of water, a small onion chopped fine, a clove of garlic, a pinch of celery seed, a sprig of thyme, a carrot chopped fine, the rind of a lemon and a few drops of tarragon vinegar. Cook until vegetables are done. When done add 2 large tablespoon of unflavored gelatin which has been mixed with enough cold water to dissolve, the juice of 1 lemon and the slightly beaten whites of 2 eggs. Let come to a boil and simmer 15 minutes. Strain; pour into a mold and refrigerate. Use to garnish meat dishes.

CIDER SAGE JELLY

1/2 c boiling water
3 tablespoon dried sage, or 6 tablespoon fresh sage
1 1/2 c cider
3 3/4 c sugar
1/2 c liquid pectin
yellow food coloring

Pour boiling water over sage. Cover and let stand 15 minutes. Strain. Add more water if needed to make one-half cup. Add cider and sugar. Heat to boiling. Add few drops of coloring. Add pectin, stirring constantly. Boil hard for one minute. Skim and pour into hot sterilized jars. Seal. Makes 4, 1/2 pints.

PEPPER JELLY

6 c chopped sweet peppers
2 c chopped hot peppers
2 large jars chopped pimentos
4 c white vinegar
21 c sugar
2 teaspoon red or green food coloring
4 bottles fruit pectin

Boil peppers, pimentos and vinegar 15 minutes. Add sugar and boil 15 minutes. Add food coloring and pectin, boil and stir 7 minutes. Pour into hot jars and seal. Makes about 11 pints.

JALAPENO JELLY

2 c cider vinegar
1 lb jalapeno peppers, seeded
6 c sugar
1/2 teaspoon butter or vegetable oil
3 oz liquid pectin
10 drops green food coloring

In food processor or blender, blend peppers and half the vinegar until smooth. Combine pepper mixture and remaining vinegar; add sugar and butter or oil. Bring mixture to a hard boil, stirring constantly. Boil for 5 minutes, stirring constantly. Stir in pectin, return to full boil and boil for 1 minute, stirring constantly. Remove from heat. Stir in food coloring. Immediately fill jars. Seal. Process in boiling water bath for 5 minutes. Makes 7 half pints jars.

MARJORAM JELLY

1 c boiling water
2 tablespoon dried marjoram
1/3 c lemon juice
3 c sugar
1/2 c bottled fruit pectin
2 or 3 drops red food coloring

Pour boiling water over marjoram and let stand 20 minutes. Strain through cheesecloth. Add enough water to make 1 cup. Strain lemon juice through cheesecloth. Put both liquids in saucepan and add sugar. Stir well and bring to a boil. Add pectin, while stirring; add coloring and continue to stir until liquid reaches full rolling boil. Boil hard for 30 seconds. Remove from heat, skim off foam and pour into sterilized jars or jelly glasses. Seal. Makes 4 medium glasses.

Note: This is a jelly that is served as a relish with cold cuts or a roast. To make Sage Jelly follow above recipe, substituting 2 tablespoon dried sage leaves for the marjoram and green food coloring for the red.

HOT PINEAPPLE JELLY

1 can (1 pint 2 oz) pineapple juice
3/4 c cider vinegar
5 1/2 c sugar
1 teaspoon dried crushed hot red peppers
1 bottle liquid fruit pectin
green food coloring

Put all ingredients, except pectin and food coloring in pot and mix well. Bring to a boil, stirring. Add pectin and bring to a full rolling boil; boil hard 1 minute, stirring. Remove from heat and skim off foam. Stir in few drops food coloring. Pour into jelly jars or glasses. Makes 8 medium glasses.

Acknowledgements

Thanks to all of the people who have tasted the hot sauce, stuffed peppers and other foods for us.

Greenup Christian Church Tasters: Ruth Cordell and grandson David Cordell, Eunice Eastham, Faye Johnson, Love Conley, Bonnie Gillum, Martha Collins, Clara Baker, Ruby Petry, Patty, Gibson, Ethel McBrayer, Kathryn Reed, Frances Spaulding, Sharon and Heather Nicholas, and Donald, Judy, Andrew and Todd Liles.

Little Sandy Tasters: Delbert and Carolyn Collins, Jim and Lorraine Kirk, Pattie, C.B. and Smokey Kitts, Jimmy and Lori Grizzle, Zip Fiffe, Julie Cordle, Ora Jean Hill, Debbie Thomas, Walt and Lucy Cooper, Norman Archy, Ed Glockner, Joe and Pam Gordon, Sophie Craft, Bob and Sissy Davis, Kenny and Linda Douglas, Ray Stephens, Oleta Slone, Joe Baer, Jimmy Bradford, Ruth Jenkins, George Scott, Willard and Kathy Grubb, Frank and Doris Cooper, Jim and Lorraine Kirk, Jim Qualls, Charlie Ray Worthington, Monty Webb, Bill Braden and Anne Adams.